GARLAND STUDIES IN

# THE HISTORY OF AMERICAN LABOR

*edited by*

**STUART BRUCHEY**
ALLAN NEVINS PROFESSOR EMERITUS
COLUMBIA UNIVERSITY

T0347271

# TRADE UNIONS AND THE BETRAYAL OF THE UNEMPLOYED

## LABOR CONFLICTS DURING THE 1990s

---

IMMANUEL NESS

Routledge
Taylor & Francis Group

LONDON AND NEW YORK

First published 1998 by Garland Publishing

Published 2018 by Routledge
2 Park Square, Milton Park, Abingdon, Oxon, OX14 4RN
52 Vanderbilt Avenue, New York, NY 10017

First issued in paperback 2018

*Routledge is an imprint of the Taylor & Francis Group, an informa business*

Library of Congress Cataloging-in-Publication Data

Ness, Immanuel.
    Trade unions and the betrayal of the unemployed : labor conflicts during the 1990s.
        p.    cm. — (Garland studies in the history of American labor)
    Includes bibliographical references and index.
    ISBN 0-8153-3179-7 (alk. paper)
    1. Trade-unions—New York (State)—New York—History—20th century. 2. Unemployment—New York (State)—New York—History—20th century. 3. Labor disputes—New York (State)—New York—History—20th century. I. Title. II. Series.
HD6519.N4N48 1998
331.89'09747'09049—dc21
                                                                98-18640

ISBN 13: 978-1-138-99375-4 (pbk)
ISBN 13: 978-0-8153-3179-7 (hbk)

# Contents

# Tables and Figures

# Preface

While trade unions have an interest in mobilizing the unemployed politically, they almost never do. The primary argument of this book is that trade unions need to minimize unemployment to expand their power against management and government. It is through mobilizing the jobless for the expansion of unemployment insurance that unions can lessen the threat of lower wages, reduced union density, and accompanying weaker bargaining positions. The mobilization and the formation of alliances with the unorganized unemployed would also reduce divisions within the trade union movement between skilled and unskilled workers. It is the argument of this book that despite these advantages, trade unions have rarely organized the unemployed, because they represent a potential threat to organizational control, leadership, and legitimacy. Moreover, the interests of the unemployed conflict with those of the securely employed trade unionists. This book examines the problematic relationship between unions and the unemployed in New York City during the early 1990s.

This book identifies three arenas of union responses to unemployment: (1) autonomous trade union action; (2) joint trade union action through established labor bodies; and (3) responses to unemployment through ad hoc coalitions of trade unions and outside activist organizations. It is hoped that the case studies examined in this book will help expand and modify understanding of the role of the relationships between trade unions and the unemployed by recognizing the influence of organizing strategies. My research of unions in four diverse labor markets in New York City suggests that hiring hall unions produce exclusive organizing strategies that have deeper accountability to their members but organizing objectives that are limited to serving the narrow interests of core members. Conversely, workplace-based unions typically engender class-oriented unions with narrow accountability to members but deeper organizing objectives that extend beyond immediate members.

Although I am solely responsible for the research and writing of all the contents of this book, I would like to thank all those who helped me in this endeavor. In particular I would like to thank the organizers, trade union leaders, and jobless participants in the struggle to advance the conditions of unemployed people in the seemingly hostile political environment of the early 1990s. This struggle, which appeared to come from nowhere contributed to a reexamination of the conditions of unemployed men and women who are often left to bear the burden of joblessness on their own. The political pressure of activists on national, state, and municipal government levels contributed to a reevaluation of federal policy on unemployment culminating in the creation of new policies to improve the conditions of the long-term jobless in November 1991. The jobless activists' remarkable success in helping to shape national political opinion that influenced federal unemployment policy is a stark reminder of the enduring potential of organization and mobilization in bringing about social change. Conversely, the success of the mobilization of relatively few workers also exposed the failure of the leaders of the organized labor movement to mobilize members and non-members to defend and improve the conditions of working people. In part, this recognition of the moribund state of the labor movement helped to spur the changes in AFL-CIO leadership that came in the mid-1990s. This book's objective is to analyze and identify the individual, organizational, and structural causes that foster and prevent union efforts to organize marginal workers.

One of my enduring regrets is that the heat of organizing is often accompanied by disagreement, conflict, and misunderstanding. I encountered personal and philosophical differences in my participation in organizing efforts among the unemployed in New York City. Nonetheless, I am forever grateful to colleagues and organizers who I worked with to mobilize jobless workers in the early 1990s. In particular, I would like to recognize Keith Brooks for his persistence and dedication to organizing and defending the rights of the unemployed. Keith set an example for countless labor and community organizers who have known him by demonstrating the possibility of winning organizing campaigns even against long odds.

I would like to thank my intellectual mentor, Frances Fox Piven, for her patient advice, and assistance in this project. Through her own record of scholarly work and activism, Dr. Piven demonstrates the genuine possibility of joining the all too often bifurcated worlds of academia and social action. She serves as an inspiration for my past and current work. I would also like to thank John Bowman, Robert Engler, Joseph Murphy, and Stanley Aronowitz for helping me to frame the theoretical and empirical arguments in this study. I would like to thank my colleagues at the American Politics Dissertation Seminar: especially Lori Minnite, Thomas Kriger, and Mike McCullough. Critical advice and support was provided by a number of friends: Chris Agee, David Smith, Ron Hayduk, and Vinny Tirelli. Invaluable research and archival assistance were provided by the staff of Tamiment Labor Archives at New York University and the New York regional office of the U.S. Bureau of Labor Statistics.

In the process of transforming a dissertation into a book I received valuable assistance, encouragement, and support from Steve London, Joe Wilson, and Morton Berkowitz at Brooklyn College. I would also like to thank Evelyn Fazio for reading and suggesting valuable revisions in the final manuscript. I eagerly look forward to working with her in the future. I am thankful to Deane Tucker and Chuck Bartelt of Garland Publishing for their valuable assistance and support. Lastly, I would like to thank Jeanette Zelhof and Clare Newman for tolerating me through writing the manuscript and encouraging me to go on to new work. Naturally, I take full responsibility for any errors, omissions, and oversights of the manuscript.

Immanuel Ness

# Introduction

## TRADE UNIONS AND THE UNEMPLOYED: CLASS DIVISIONS AND UNION POLITICAL POWER

The national economic recession that began in the autumn of 1990 hit the New York labor market hard, more than doubling unemployment in less than four years, from under 6 percent to over 13 percent by early 1993 (Ehrenhalt 1991, 1992, 1993; Lafer 1992). The recession had a devastating effect on unionized workers in New York. Declining employment in the textile and printing industries was followed by a decline of service and financial sector jobs. The resulting drop in city and state revenues increased unemployment in the highly unionized public sector. This book is a study of how unions in the City responded to the crisis and why they responded as they did.

Unemployment has always represented a threat to the power of labor unions by reducing the number of employed workers who are members of unions, and by intensifying labor market competition for jobs. The relation between unemployment and declining labor market power is illustrated by the Phillips Curve, which demonstrates that a scarcity of jobs tends to drive down the price of labor by producing competition for jobs between the unemployed and the employed (Piven and Cloward 1982).[1] This difficulty is intensified by a weak system of unemployment insurance benefits. Unemployment insurance and other labor market safeguards such as minimum wages reduce the pressure on the working population by providing a supplemental source of income to the unemployed. As these safeguards have clashed with the requirements of postindustrial capitalism for labor market flexibility, they have been increasingly challenged by organized capital (Sabel and Piore 1984).

These problems have been aggravated by the increasing numbers of workers who have lost union memberships upon becoming unemployed, or who have never had the opportunity to join unions. In the absence of organized union protection, these workers have had extremely limited means to defend their unemployment benefits, while their claims have been contested with increasing frequency by employers (Burtless 1991; Levitan and Shapiro 1987). As a result, the reduction of jobless benefits from the 1980s to the 1990s reversed the trend from 1937 to 1977 toward longer maximum potential duration of benefits (Vroman 1990; Brecher and Costello 1992; Brooks and Ness 1991).

In addition to the dramatic drop in the number of weeks of available benefits, there was a decrease in the percentage of the unemployed collecting benefits, from more than 70 percent in 1975 to about 33 percent in 1990. This decline resulted from tighter federal and state standards, which caused more benefit denials and disqualifications and hindered the ability of the system to care for the long-term unemployed, who are counted among the jobless but do not receive benefits (U.S. Department of Labor 1991, 1992).

Thus, the unemployment that accompanied the 1990s recession was particularly crippling for unions, since fewer benefits for the unemployed meant lower wages and diminished bargaining power for the employed—even those in unions. Although pressure from organized labor and independent unemployed organizations in the early 1990s increased public attention to growing unemployment, the federal government only partially restored unemployment insurance benefits that had been cut in the late 1970s and early 1980s. In New York, as in other cities, deterioration of the unemployment system was, in short, devastating for organized labor (Goldfield 1989).

In response to these external challenges to trade union power in the early 1990s recession, labor unions and organizations of the unemployed initiated independent and collective political efforts to reinstate unemployment benefits that were cut in the 1980s. Some unions contemplated organizing and/or forming alliances with the unemployed to fight for the extension of government unemployment benefits.

In the winter of 1991, a coalition of some 25 New York unions formed in response to rising unemployment. During the summer and fall of 1991, the coalition, which became known as the New York Labor Campaign on Unemployment, held formal meetings and collaborative sessions to consider various collective labor union strategies. These proposals ranged from building a national movement for the extension of unemployment insurance to organizing the unemployed, both within unions and at state unemployment centers. Some unions organized unemployed former members for political action. Some formed coalitions to develop proposals to generate public- and private-sector jobs in New York City.[2] Most, however, did not participate or even support collective or independent mobilization activities of the unemployed, despite the significant threat to their power posed by high levels of unemployment and a weak unemployment benefit system. At best, these labor union efforts can be characterized as mixed. This book examines the inconsistencies between union interests and union actions—the problem that, though union leaders often voice support for efforts to respond to rising unemployment, they tend nevertheless to oppose efforts to mobilize jobless workers independently through their unions or in association with union coalitions.

## OUTLINE OF THE BOOK

This book investigates three arenas of union responses to unemployment. First, it examines union policies and activities in response to unemployment. Unions were selected from each of four distinct sectors of the economy that feature a variety of policies, from the most inclusive to the most exclusive with regard to membership. All of these unions are noteworthy for the actions they have taken in response to high unemployment. Their policies are examined during tranquil periods of stable employment and in crisis periods of joblessness.

Second, this study examines the policies of established building trades unions in response to high and rising unemployment in their organizations through the formation of coalitions to directly assist their own unemployed members. Finally, a study is made of the efforts of an ad hoc coalition of labor unions and community groups that formed in early 1991 to assist the unemployed. One campaign promoted the extension of federal and state unemployment insurance benefits and another labor campaign advocated a regional industrial development policy to create new jobs for New Yorkers.

Generalizing from the case studies of trade unions in New York City, this book argues that trade union officials representing organized labor in New York are not devoted to defending the broader economic interests of their marginal members, their jobless former members, and the unorganized working class. These marginal workers are predominantly newcomers to the labor market—women, minorities, and immigrants. Based on the investigation of the responses of unions in New York to rising joblessness in the early 1990s, race, ethnicity, and gender stratification seem to reinforce the proclivity of unions to neglect unemployed workers. The interests of these workers sometimes conflict with those of union leaders and core members. The case studies suggest that trade union leaders are reluctant to pursue long-term policies that advance their interests because of a desire to avoid internecine conflicts. Such conflicts are threatening to union leaders because they seem likely to undermine traditional union hierarchies. Further, union officials fear that mobilization of unemployed and marginal workers to advance their interests could threaten their leadership positions within the shrinking unions and labor markets in which they so securely operate.

It should be noted, however, that even with regard to the interests of entrenched union leadership, the tendency to subordinate the interests of marginal and unorganized workers could be self-destructive to the labor movement. Labor union leadership has been losing its historical connection with a majority of workers who, in the past, represented an important part of its power base.[3] Today's trade union leaders are becoming ever more aware of the diminished power that results from the declining share of union members in the labor market.[4]

During the 1990s recession, New York City union officials did endeavor to portray themselves as leaders of the organized and unorganized working class, voicing support for extensions of unemployment benefits and jobs creation programs. Yet, on the whole, they were unwilling to take the actions necessary to effect these goals or to expand working-class power. In fact, in many cases, they actively discouraged efforts to mobilize the unemployed, and within the unions themselves, they restricted participation of the rank-and-file membership in important decisions.[5]

These observations are corroborated by trade union officials interviewed for this book who either tacitly or explicitly recognize that their dominant concern is leadership continuity, often at the expense of union power. While some may empathize with the unemployed, they are unable and/or unwilling to assimilate these groups into their organizations. Trade unions are responsible for sustaining and often aggravating social and economic fault lines. Undeniably, rising unemployment creates threatening divisions in unions between working and non-working members. Wherever possible, trade unions that faced growing unemployment in the early 1990s refrained from integrating disgruntled unemployed workers into their organizations through associate membership or unemployed councils.[6] To do so might have disturbed the fragile balance of power among members of their organizations. However, some building trades unions in New York City were compelled by their members to respond to unemployment in their organizations. This tendency to respond vigorously to unemployment raised an interesting question about the influence of distinct labor markets in determining union actions. Why are longshoremen, construction, and other unions that recruit their members through hiring halls unions willing to mobilize their members to combat unemployment while industrial unions tend to shirk involvement with the unemployed, even in periods of high unemployment?

Yet hiring hall unions, as will be shown, have their own methods of excluding or ignoring marginal and underemployed members of the larger workforce. As a result of a widespread reluctance to mobilize rank-and-file membership and enlarge participation, trade unions currently function on economic, social, and political fault lines that can be expected to split if the interests of unemployed workers and the unorganized masses are not advanced by union leaders. In New York City, these divisions tend to reflect the structure of labor markets in which labor unions operate, and therefore seem to divide workers on the basis of skill, craft, professional status, race, and ethnicity. Instead of providing the organizational support that might help empower the broader working class, the unions studied here tend to reinforce the boundary lines of intraclass conflict, stymieing advancement of labor power by restricting membership, and whenever expedient in a narrowly political sense, abandoning marginal members and the unemployed.

Unions that organize workers through hiring halls appear to have deeper accountability to their members but organizing objectives that are limited to serving the narrow interests of core members.

Conversely, unions that organize members through workplaces typically engender class-oriented unions that have organizing strategies with narrow accountability to members but with deeper and more far-reaching organizing objectives that extend beyond their immediate members. The paradox of these labor market-organizing strategies is that exclusive craft-oriented unions that organize unions through hiring halls often represent high-wage workers are more responsive to unemployment than inclusive class-oriented unions representing lower-paid workers.

In declining industries that have inclusive, class-oriented organizing strategies, restrictions on participation by non-members as well as members in union affairs limit responsiveness to unemployment because mobilizing workers requires broad participation, along with inclusion of new members who may be at odds with union policy. Yet in order to maintain control over their organizations, union leaders have shown themselves quite willing to limit participation and membership. In shrinking industries such as manufacturing, however, where unions are able to maintain a consistent share of the declining labor market, union leaders are often reluctant to mobilize workers once they become unemployed, since jobless workers are not expected to return to the labor market as competitors. When faced with a choice between shoring up their personal power and pursuing the long-term interests of the unions by addressing the unemployment problem, leaders of inclusive workplace-based unions unfortunately tend to choose the former.

On the other hand, the membership structure among hiring hall unions influences union officials to respond decisively to unemployment. As will be demonstrated, however, the unwillingness of building trades unions to mobilize and incorporate African American, Latino, and Asian construction workers who are not members of their unions is motivated by an organizational strategy to maintain economic control over a shrinking yet lucrative sector of the construction industry.

## TRADE UNION MEMBERSHIP POLICY AND UNEMPLOYMENT

The unions chosen for this study are representative of a diversity of industrial sectors of the economy and membership models. These case studies suggest that the organizing strategies of unions are responsible for their varying policies regarding political mobilizations. While all unions shun unemployed and marginal workers if they can, unions that organize through hiring halls are more responsive to laid-off members than those in manufacturing or service unions that organize their members through workplaces. The exigencies of unemployment on labor market organizing strategies also tend to induce inclusiveness or exclusiveness of unions with regard to membership. Entrance requirements among building trades unions often operate to exclude minorities, immigrants, and women. Such exclusionary unions tend to represent middle- and high-wage skilled, white male workers. These unions tend to be attentive to core members, but are on the whole indifferent to the needs and demands of unemployed workers outside their industrial labor markets. On the other hand, garment production unions typically include low-wage, unskilled and semi-skilled female workers of all races and ethnic groups. While these unions distribute unemployment more equally among their members, ironically, they take even less interest in the plight of the unemployed than do hiring hall unions. They are reluctant even to take action on behalf of unemployed persons who are part of their labor market.

There are a number of reasons for this. One is simply that hiring hall unions (longshoremen, building trades, printing, musician, and arts unions) allow members to maintain their membership even after they are laid off. Exclusive unions in which the rank-and-file members remain attached to their unions are thus likely to experience more immediate pressure to respond to unemployment in their industries than class-based unions in which members leave the union when they are laid off from their jobs. That unemployed workers remain members of craft unions does not prevent management from laying them off, but it does force union leaders to contend seriously with joblessness in the industry.[7] On the other hand, inclusive industrial and service unions that organize members through the workplace with few membership conditions often restrict member participation in union action and can thus resist pressure from members to fight unemployment or support social policies that might alleviate its effects on former members.[8] Since workers who lose their jobs are terminated almost immediately as members of inclusive unions, union leaders are not obligated to respond to their grievances.

As a rule, the inclusive unions in this study have taken an interest in forming ad hoc coalitions with other unions and external community organizations of the unemployed. These unions tend to support social policies that benefit low-income workers, such as minimum wage laws, unemployment insurance benefits, and government financed health insurance. They are more likely than exclusive unions to participate in labor and community-based ad hoc coalitions on unemployment, which in turn push unions beyond the traditional bureaucratic machinery of the established labor movement (see chapter 5). However, they are less willing to organize the ranks of disgruntled unemployed workers. Conversely, the exclusive unions in this study tend to prefer alliances with established labor, business, and political organizations and tend to prefer programs that directly benefit their members to the exclusion of workers in other industries.

This study of trade unions and the unemployed in New York will contribute to an improved understanding of the factors that lead trade unions to organize the unemployed and the factors that lead them to avoid the unemployed. This will be accomplished by empirically qualifying and extending some important theoretical speculation about trade unions and by incorporating an understanding of the influence of labor markets on union organizing strategies toward the unemployed. The review of the theoretical literature on union responses to unemployment that follows in Chapter 1 should help define the theoretical significance of this book.

## NOTES

1. In labor markets with a shortage of employment, competition for jobs drives down labor costs for those who are employed. As Piven and Cloward (1982) point out:

> When unemployment falls, wages rise; when unemployment rises, wages fall. The Phillips curve was thus consistent with Marx's thesis regarding the industrial reserve army of labor, for it is suggested that high levels of unemployment weaken the bargaining power of workers. However, economists did not define the trade-off between unemployment and wages as a reflection of conflicts over the distribution of wealth; they tended instead to see it as an unavoidable fact of nature. (26)

2. The most prominent of these groups was the "Labor Coalition to Rebuild New York," formed in 1990 by the more progressive labor unions,

many of whom were hurt by unemployment stemming from layoffs and plant closures.

3. The argument that labor unions have lost their previous social function as representative of large segments of the working class is made by Giovanni Arrighi, "Marxist Century—American Century: The Making and Remaking of the World Labor Market," in Samir Amin, Giovanni Arrighi, Andre Gunder Frank, Immanuel Wallerstein, eds. *Transforming the Revolution: Social Movements and the World-System* (New York: Monthly Review Press 1990). Arrighi argues that organized labor is unable to prevent the spread of poverty among women, ethnic and racial minorities, and immigrant workers in advanced capitalist countries.

4. See Louis Uchitelle, "Labor Federation Expresses its Vulnerability in Hostile Times," *The New York Times*, February 26, 1995, for an analysis of the AFL-CIO's recognition of its declining political and economic clout resulting from a failure to mobilize members and the public around issues of concern to organized labor.

5. Labor union critics recognize trade union officials as engaging in a widespread effort to restrict membership participation in order to discourage challenges from insiders and outsiders in their organization. See Herman Benson, *Democratic Rights for Union Members: A Guide to Internal Union Democracy* (New York: Association for Union Democracy 1979).

6. The notion of including their former unemployed workers as associate members into their unions is considered incomprehensible by most trade union leaders, who scoff at these suggestions as absurd.

7. Benson has shown, for example, that where union members actively participate in union meetings, leaders are more likely to respond to membership concerns (Benson December 1994).

8. See *Union Democracy Review*, No. 100, December 1994. According to Paul Levy, a director of the Association of Union Democracy, ordinary union meetings in the U.S. are attended by perhaps 3 percent to 4 percent of a union's membership and usually nearly half of these are incumbent officials or staff members. Since many union constitutions require meeting attendance as a prerequisite to running for office, the Association for Union Democracy contends that only 2 percent of all membership is usually eligible for leadership positions.

# Trade Unions and the
# Betrayal of the Unemplyed

# CHAPTER 1

# Trade Union Mobilization: Worker Power and Organizational Strategy

The restrained response of organized labor in New York City to rising unemployment is consistent with much of what the theoretical literature tells us about the equivocal relationship of unions to the unemployed. It would have been surprising, in view of this literature, if trade unions had reacted vigorously to a loosening labor market and declining unemployment insurance benefits by mobilizing the unemployed or joining with them politically.

Social scientists have provided two general approaches to the dynamics of the relationship between trade unions and the unemployed. Some, including Marxists and other leftists, have argued that labor unions have an interest in organizing the unemployed to expand and defend labor's political and economic power. These theorists examine the impact of unemployment on trade unions and explain why the unemployed should be mobilized as a means of expanding and consolidating working-class power.[1] On the other hand, a substantial body of literature emphasizes the hindrances to alliances between labor unions and other marginal groups. Much of this literature characterizes the relationship of trade unions to the unemployed as fraught with uncertainty and fear, partly because the unemployed—while occasionally helpful to labor—can easily be exploited by management against unions. But this is not the only reason unions tend to be timid about forging relationships with the unemployed. While some social scientists recognize the potential

3

benefits to unions of mobilizing the unemployed, many agree that trade unions have actually shunned and excluded the unemployed in order to maintain leverage, organizational stability and continuity in leadership.[2]

## TRADE UNION INTEREST IN ORGANIZING THE UNEMPLOYED

The literature that emphasizes union interest in organizing the unemployed features three important points of view concerning trade union relations with marginal workers like the unemployed. The first treats unions as representations of working-class political power; the second emphasizes the importance to unions themselves of minimizing intraclass conflict; and the third tends to focus on structural economic challenges to union power.

### Expanding Working Class Political Power

The idea that labor unions must inevitably organize the unemployed is most commonly associated with the work of Karl Marx (1864), and has dominated classical approaches to trade unions and marginal workers. From this "classical" conflict perspective, it is crucial to understand labor unions not as mere bargaining agents for specific groups of workers but as the vanguard of the broad social interests of the working class. Unions are not merely representatives of union workers with jobs but also workers who are poor, unemployed, and without union membership.

According to Marx, trade union activity tends to progress from narrow economic bargaining to broader organizational and political action. In his address to the General Council of the First International, Marx asserts that trade unions have "not fully understood their power" and are "too exclusively bent upon local and immediate struggles with capital," so that they remain "aloof from general social and political movements." For Marx, then, the critical task for organized labor is to build coalitions to assist all working class movements. In particular, Marx believes that the interests of the unorganized (which includes the unemployed) and those working for the lowest wages should be supported by labor unions as a means of expanding working-class power. Marx concludes that trade unions must transcend their tendency to defend the narrow interests of narrow segments of workers and learn to act deliberately as organizing centres of the working class in the broad interest of its complete emancipation. They must aid every social and political movement tending in that direction. Considering themselves and acting as the champions and representatives of the whole working class, they cannot fail to enlist the non-society men into their ranks. They must look carefully after the interests of the worst paid trades, such as the agricultural labourers, rendered powerless by exceptional circumstances. They must conceive the world at large that their efforts, far from being narrow and selfish, aim at the emancipation of the downtrodden millions.[3]

This argument is parallel to contemporary views that the decline of the American labor movement stems from its failure to build coalitions between skilled and unskilled workers (Davis 1986; Moody 1988) and with new social movements (Aronowitz 1973; Brecher and Costello 1990; Winpisinger et al. 1984). Yet unlike these contemporary analysts, Marx is optimistic that labor unions can eventually develop a broad social consciousness. Marx's teleology of unrelenting labor activism does not anticipate the reversion of labor unions from a commitment to broad political action to a fixation on narrow economic bargaining.

Rosa Luxemburg (1906) also believes it is in the interest of unions to organize marginal workers, but is far more skeptical than Marx that trade union officials will advance beyond their "businesslike" direction and undertake a mass struggle drawing the "widest sections of the proletariat" into the fight. While Luxemburg is aware that unions are reluctant to organize the poor, she also argues that unions ultimately will fade into irrelevance as a consequence of their failure to build intraclass alliances. Unlike other Marxist analysts of the early twentieth century, Luxemburg is acutely aware of the bureaucratic tendencies of trade unions which temper support for the far more numerous unorganized and unemployed workers, and the failure of trade unions to mobilize their own members. Since trade union officials are incapable of recognizing the need to build a broad working-class movement, the "struggles of the masses will be fought out without them" (Luxemburg 1906, 207). The disregard of the unemployed and unorganized by trade unions has, according to Luxemburg, led to their growing insignificance in the labor movement.

Lenin (1920) shares Luxemburg's view that trade unions have become unprogressive organizations under the leadership of "reactionary leaders" who are "agents of the bourgeoisie." According to Lenin, trade unions "inevitably . . . reveal *certain* reactionary features, a certain craft narrow-mindedness, a certain tendency to be non-political." However, he considers it a mistake for leftists to completely stop participating in trade unions and to "create new and *artificial* forms of labor organization" (541). In short, Lenin and Luxemburg disagree on where the majority of workers are found. While Luxemburg considers the unemployed and the unorganized to embody the vast majority of workers, Lenin believes that "trade unions and the workers' cooperatives are the very organizations in which the masses are to be found."[4] The choice between participating in trade unions and transforming them into progressive organizations or organizing marginal and unemployed workers represents a recurrent debate among political analysts who seek to expand working-class power.

## Intraclass Conflict and Declining Union Power

There are more recent arguments that favor the organization of the unemployed by trade unions. One of these emphasizes the effect of internal strife within unions, and its link to declining union power (Arrighi 1991; Davis 1986; Goldfield 1989; Moody 1990; Pontusson 1991; Touraine 1986). This school of thought tends to portray the histories of labor unions as alternating between periods of "class conscious" action and routine bargaining with management.

The theorists highlighting intraclass strife in unions tend to regard workers as class-conscious actors but they are less optimistic that the labor unions representing them will function as working-class organizations. These writers are also more skeptical than Luxemburg that workers can mobilize outside of established organizations on a class-wide basis. For instance, Touraine (1986) asserts that, in the industrial stage of capitalism, the labor movement's political power has always resulted from a capacity to unite skilled workers and semi-skilled workers who would find it difficult to oppose industrial "scientific management" on their own. However, in the aftermath of these successful movements, he contends, the established unions have subordinated their capacity for social mobilization to consolidate their gains for skilled and professional workers through collective bargaining with management.[5] He depicts late twentieth-century unions as agents of professional and skilled workers who are indifferent to the concerns of the lower ranks of the working class. While organized unions still have political and economic power, their lack of class-consciousness and their limited scope of action with respect to the underprivileged have sharply curtailed that power. Labor's influence is further reduced by deindustrialization. Rising unemployment, moreover, diminishes labor's collective bargaining leverage with management by decreasing their market power. As a result of all these factors, trade unions no longer challenge the system of social and economic organization as they once did. If labor unions continue to neglect divisions within the working class, Touraine predicts their power could decline even further. This book will illustrate that this is precisely what is happening on the ground. Structural divisions in the labor force are crippling trade unions politically, particularly in their responses to unemployment and underemployment.

## The Structural Economic Challenge To Labor Power

The divisions within the working class were aggravated by the decline in the global economy that began in the early 1970s. Pontusson (1991) observes that the rise in low-paying jobs and mass unemployment in advanced capitalist countries has weakened labor's leverage vis-a-vis governments and employers.[6] Even more significantly, political and economic changes have inflamed intraclass conflicts within trade union organizations, often challenging the very legitimacy of their remaining organizational structures. Trade unions in advanced industrial countries are therefore under pressure to respond to these conflicts of interest over jobs, skills and occupational status, wages, and other benefits.

Arrighi (1991) contends that part of the labor movement's weakened condition comes from its inability to organize marginal economic groups that are at the greatest risk of economic dislocation, and yet are active participants in a "cost-cutting race for cheap labor." These groups undermine the previous gains of past struggles by competing with unionized workers for low-skill jobs. The failure of organized labor to organize such workers—minorities, women, immigrants, and other new proletarian groups—has eroded much of the unions' previous social function and social base.

The connection between unemployment and declining labor union power should give unions a good reason to organize the unemployed to build labor market power. While the theories described here offer compelling explanations of the importance of organizing the unemployed for unions, approaches that emphasize organization and leadership tell us some of the reasons why trade union leaders have not organized them.

## WHY TRADE UNIONS DON'T ORGANIZE THE UNEMPLOYED

Social scientists who focus on why trade unions have not organized the unemployed stress the influence of the internal structure of unions on leadership attitudes toward rank-and-file workers and outside groups like the unemployed (Davis 1986; Goldfield 1991; Lipset et al. 1968; Michels 1915; Miliband 1991; Mills 1971; Piven and Cloward 1979). To account for the waning influence of the labor movement, this literature accentuates organizational stability as the most significant consideration determining labor union actions.

### Organization and the "Iron Law of Oligarchy"

Labor's failure to become a progressive force is often ascribed to the ideological drift of union leadership, rather than internal organizational considerations that tend to promote accommodation with established authorities.[7] Michels (1915) takes a different approach to studying social organizations. In his study of the German Social Democratic Party, he observes that the internal policies of all such organizations are antithetical to revolutionary and socialist policy goals. As a consequence of the inevitable oligarchic nature of bureaucratic organizations like labor unions and political parties (identified by Michels as the "iron law of oligarchy"), radical movements are destined to contain their militancy and become conservative once they obtain power.[8] For Michels, democracy is little more than a struggle for power between an old minority and an ambitious minority intent on the conquest of power (Michels 1915, 342).

Michels argues that the political elite who assume the key positions in labor and political organizations cynically utilize what could be broadly beneficial revolutionary ideology as a means of gaining organizational and political power. Once in office, these officials' priority becomes the stabilization and reproduction of their own political power. As a result, established organizational leaders often downplay the very ideology that has brought them to power. Union leaders of working-class origin are less likely to defend the interests of their members once they assume power. These leaders are the most inclined to reconcile themselves to the existing order. As unions mature into bureaucratic organizations, union leaders who began as agitators must transform themselves into leaders who have "technical knowledge" in the administration of large and complex organizations that benefit from the wealth that trickles down from corporate profits (Michels, 280). In short, they are transformed from activist proletarians to good businessmen concerned with technological change in the manufacture of commodities, the sources and costs of raw materials, the state of the markets, and the wages and living standards of the workers in different regions of the industry (Michels, 281).[9]

While his analysis of oligarchic organizations is useful, Michels underestimates the possible effect of labor militancy on the expansion of unions' organizational power. Even as established trade unions resisted mobilization of new workers, the trade union movement experienced its greatest numerical growth during the upsurge of militant trade union organizing during the 1930s and 1940s. Michels's static analysis of organizational expansion does not take into account social change because it focuses almost exclusively on periods of social tranquility. This focus lends to the misperception that organizations expand their influence only through conservative policies that do not threaten stable relations with management, the state, and established social institutions.

It is true that union officials are often unresponsive to their own members' interests. The case studies herein will demonstrate this empirically. But Michels's does not provide a credible explanation for this phenomenon beyond his belief that trade union leaders lack moral and ethical standards of behavior. His moralistic perspective is evident in his depiction of American labor leaders of working-class background:

> According to the testimony of the well-informed, the American working class has hitherto produced few leaders of whom it has any reason to be proud. Many of them shamelessly and unscrupulously exploit for personal ends the posts which they have secured through

the confidence of their fellow-workmen. Taken as a whole, the American labor leaders have been described as "stupid and cupid." (288)

There is no denying that labor leaders have often exhibited the degenerate behavior described by Michels. However, this behavior is not more common among trade union leaders than among leaders of other organizations, including corporations, political parties, organized crime syndicates, even the Church. Michels's observation does not reveal much about what is unique about unions beyond the obvious fact that union leaders are interested in maintaining their power for personal advantage.

What is missing from the literature on trade unions and the unemployed is an examination of the different organizational strategies that serve to expand and reduce trade union power against management and the state. Trade unions are not entirely analogous to political parties or most other membership organizations. Unlike political parties, trade unions seek not to organize disparate voters but to organize workers in discrete labor markets. This study argues that union organizing strategies linked to these labor market differences have a pivotal influence on specific trade union policies toward the unemployed. In short, unions that organize workers individually tend to have greater accountability to their members when they become unemployed than unions that organize workplaces collectively. Ironically, unions that organize workplaces tend to represent poor and unskilled workers who usually have a greater need for protection.

### Leadership Threat as Grounds for Excluding the Unemployed

More recent accounts of labor organizations have incorporated Michels's view that bureaucracy is inevitable as organizations increase in size and complexity. Lipset, Trow, and Coleman (1956) argue that union bureaucracy reduces democratic participation as it increases the power of trade union leadership and also preserves stable relations with management. Trade union bureaucracy ensures the accountability' of unions in their relations with management. But union bureaucracy also reduces sources of organized opposition by strengthening the power of top officials over ordinary members.

To some extent, these studies seek to understand why union leaders view genuine democratic participation as antithetical to the expansion of union power. Whether unions are viewed as conciliatory or militant actors, argue Lipset, Trow, and Coleman, they must minimize internal dissent that results in conflicts exploitable by management. And whatever its principles, internal opposition often serve the interests of management while reducing the unity of the union. Indeed, according to Lipset, Trow, and Coleman, democratic conditions and greater membership control can be effective only in small associations or units (14).[10]

In an argument that parallels that of Lipset, Trow, and Coleman's analysis that opposition reduces unity, Miliband (1991) argues that opposition to trade union leadership often arises from union activists who "are more radical and militant than their leaders." Union activists "have always formed the major radical ingredient" in their unions and are the "main opposition to their moderate leaders" (57). Miliband views Michels's iron law of oligarchy not as a division between unions and their members but as a division between leaders and left activists. The intermittent attempt by trade union leaders to suppress the power of militant opponents within their unions is viewed by Miliband as a means of expanding their capacity to pursue moderate policies (Miliband, 67).

Piven and Cloward (1979) observe that social circumstances inhibit the unemployed from taking action. Unlike employed workers who can protest by striking, the unemployed are not drawn together by their relations at the workplace. Trade unions could therefore serve an important function in channeling the anger and frustrations of the unemployed, but their conservative tendencies lead them to exclude the unemployed. They recognize that organizational imperatives shape union responses to their declining power and condition how they view and deal with unemployed workers as members and agents of social change. While the poor lack stable organizational resources, formal organizations are usually unable to represent the interests of the poor as a result of their "cautious and moderate character." (26). Conversely, since the poor are disgruntled and often volatile, they are unlikely to make stable and supportive members or allies of labor unions. Trade unions tend to lose touch with the unemployed and are not organizationally prepared or even willing to mobilize the jobless to control the effects of unemployment.

The threat that union leaders perceive as arising from internal opposition raises serious questions for unions in New York that seek to mobilize or form alliances with the unemployed. Stability in leadership may be jeopardized, and with it, the integrity of organizations themselves, both by the mobilization of former members and by joint political action with external groups like the unemployed.

## Labor Markets and Trade Union Organizational Strategies

The opportunities for trade union power and challenges to trade union control discussed in Lipset, Trow, and Coleman display the complex relationship of unions to the unemployed and other unorganized outside groups. Theorists who study the labor insurgencies of the 1930s and 1940s attest to the contradictory relationship between trade unions and the unemployed, but they do little to explain the differences that motivate unions to respond differently to unemployment. Studies of the labor market considerations of individual unions provide a partial explanation for the variations in union policies and strategies on unemployment. According to Marks (1989), for instance, the dissimilar organizational communities that are formed by different labor markets pivotally influence union organizational strategies within their individual labor markets (recruiting new workers, collective bargaining, worker participation) and within the larger labor market (industrial relations legislation, incomes policy, unemployment and industrial policy).

In his comparison of nineteenth and early twentieth century union political action in Britain, Germany, and the United States, Marks argues that individual trade unions are more active than working-class political parties in expressing the interests of workers in society (3). Marks contends that the reluctance of the American Federation of Labor to engage in national politics until the end of the nineteenth century contributed to the rise of autonomous union action in the United States. The early success of the A. F. of L. in recruiting new unions stemmed from a policy of pursuing "limited but common goals" that allowed individual unions and labor officials to continue to maintain their autonomy in the labor movement. This autonomy in political action persists among individual trade unions that continue to maintain their affiliation with the AFL-CIO while pursuing policies that conflict with the leadership of the labor federation.

According to Marks, union objectives are distinct from political parties that seek to create broad-based, national organizations. Unions reflect the structure of labor markets that both define their potential members and serve as the primary means of improving the living conditions of their members through bargaining with management over wages and work conditions. The decentralized structure of the labor movement in the United States promotes great diversity in individual union political orientation and action that is rooted in the diversity of labor organizations functioning in specific industries and occupations. Marks contends that it is therefore inappropriate to study union interests in aggregate and compare union movements across societies (5).

According to Marks, the social resources of workers in their occupational communities and their bargaining power in the labor market are intimately linked to their political strategies. Workers with ample social resources tend to be relatively successful in defending their economic and political power through the formation of stronger and more cohesive unions. Conversely, poor and unskilled workers who are likely to benefit most from social organization are unlikely to form unions for themselves (8-11) and receive a minimum of protection from established unions once they join. Strong unions in the labor market tend to pursue economic strategies through bargaining directly with their employers. Weak unions tend to pursue political strategies to improve wages, hours, and working conditions.

My research on trade union responses to unemployment in the early 1990s confirms Marks's theory that the organizational strategies of unions are structured by the distinct labor markets in which their members work. It also enhances this theory by demonstrating particular ways in which specific markets determine union strategies. This research shows that unions organized on the basis of individual skill categories effectively maintain their interests in closed labor markets, whereas unions representing members on the basis of workplaces are less successful in defending the common interests of their members due to the chronically fluid labor markets in which their members work. While all union leaders seek to retain power over their organizations, union officials who represent workers in exclusive closed labor markets tend to be under greater pressure to respond to unemployment and crises in their industries.

It is clear from the literature that many unions' exclusive focus on leadership continuity and organizational stability often conflicts with the defense and expansion of union power through coalition-building political mobilization of the unemployed. But this does not change the fact that unions must ultimately participate for their own good as well as the good of the working class, in political action involving the interests of external groups like the unemployed. As Marks admonishes, even if unions should be considered self-interested organizations, it is imperative that they appreciate the long-term value of assisting the unemployed as a means of organizational self-preservation.

The next chapter surveys the ambiguous relationship of unemployed workers to labor unions through an historical overview of organized labor's role in the unemployed movement in nineteenth and twentieth century America. The review will demonstrate how, on the one hand, the unemployed represented the organizing raw material for new trade union leadership, and how, on the other hand, they threatened the legitimacy and absolute power of trade union leadership over the labor movement.

## NOTES

1. Folsom (1991), for example, notes that the unemployed were critical to labor struggles during the 1930s depression. In 1934, the Unemployed League of Ohio helped organize a mass picket line of 6,000 workers in support of striking workers at the Auto-Lite factory in Toledo, forcing management to settle.

2. There are countless instances of desperate unemployed workers replacing striking workers. Explanations of the problematic association between the employed and unemployed abound in the theoretical literature. Some of this work argues that the unemployed and the unorganized threaten the organizational stability and leadership of trade unions. Some argue that trade union leaders fear the militant influence of jobless people on rank and file workers, which is at least as threatening as the possibility that the unemployed will replace strikers (Davis 1986 55-64).

3. Marx 1987, 36-37.

4. V.I. Lenin, "Left Wing" Communism—An Infantile Disorder (originally published June 12, 1920) in *V.I. Lenin: Selected Works*, (New York: International Publishers 1976, 542).

5. Touraine points to the decline of the core industrial working class under postindustrialism and the expanding gap between skilled and unskilled workers as the primary causes of the decline of a class-conscious labor movement. The growing disparity between professional and marginalized classes makes it "more difficult for the labor movement to elaborate a general economic social program" (Touraine 1986 168). Labor unions, then, have

become little more than narrow interest groups for more affluent professional and skilled workers.

6. The LO (Trade Union Confederation) of Sweden is acutely aware of this threat. In response to proposed reductions in government unemployment benefits in late 1992, the trade union leadership has suggested a general strike against the government (Svensson 1993).

7. Lenin, for example, focuses on the betrayal of Marxist ideals by the German Social Democratic movement rather than on the party's oligarchic structure to account for its lack of success (see Lipset, Trow, Coleman 1956, 6).

8. In his analysis of the oligarchic tendencies of organization, Michels argues that political organization inevitably leads to power, which is always conservative. This internal oligarchic tendency makes it impossible for democratic organizations to practice democratic policies. As organizations grow, their policy is governed by "prudence" and even "timidity." "The party, continually threatened by the state upon which its existence depends, carefully avoids everything which might irritate the state to excess." Organization, then, supersedes revolutionary fervor and democratic ideals as the "vital essence of the party." See Michels 1915, 333-341.

9. Michels' criticism of union leaders as corrupt and undemocratic is analogous to Marx's criticism that union leaders are "narrow and selfish." However, while Marx is optimistic that unions will transform into representatives of the working class, Michels believes that the oligarchic attributes of union leaders make this metamorphosis impossible.

10. In the view of Lipset, Trow, and Coleman, union democracy is most likely to become institutionalized in settings where members retain affiliation with the larger organization while also forming smaller subgroups that are autonomous from the larger organization (15).

# CHAPTER 2

# The Unemployed in Historical Perspective: Opportunities and Challenges to Trade Union Power in Nineteenth and Twentieth Century America

To understand the scope of the tension between unions and unemployed workers it is important to consider the history of their relationship in the United States. An analysis of the concerns and interests of unions before and after they are established provides a glimpse into why organizations formed in strife tend to avoid conflict after being recognized as legitimate and authoritative representatives of workers.

Four problematic themes run through the history of the relations of trade unions to unemployed and marginal workers: (1) ongoing tension between employed and unemployed workers; (2) unions' need to organize marginal workers; (3) the influence of oligarchy in the relationship of unions to the unemployed; and (4) union leadership competition as a factor in the mobilization of the unemployed.

By competing for jobs and driving down wages unemployed workers have repeatedly reduced the job security and bargaining power of employed workers. Trade unions have sometimes insulated a narrow group of core members by managing the hiring process and preventing outsiders from competing for jobs in their industries. Controlling the gateway to jobs has been even more important to unions representing workers employed in industries experiencing enduring waves of unemployment. For example, the well-documented success of longshoremen and construction unions reflected their unique abilities to control hiring halls in industries subject to recurrent waves of cyclical unemployment.[1] Their effectiveness depended on the capacity to restrict access to their respective labor markets by screening out marginal workers competing for jobs.

Although unemployed and marginal workers compete with employed workers in unions, they also present an opportunity for expanding organized labor's numerical and organizational power. Ordinarily, labor organizations, like business firms, seem to have an aversion to outsiders, particularly unemployed and unskilled workers. Yet the mobilization of marginal workers sometimes provides the basis for expanding the power of competing factions in and out of unions.

Marginal and unemployed workers were typically shunned by hiring hall unions seeking to maintain control over shifting and erratic labor markets. Unemployed workers also presented an ongoing threat to the wages and job security of unions that could not control the hiring process and insulate their members from the vicissitudes of the labor market.

On the other hand, during periods of high unemployment, jobless and marginal workers have frequently formed a foundation for expanding the labor movement. Unions have found it advantageous to mobilize these remote workers to expand bargaining power with management. Organized labor's growth in United States history occurred amid these periods of high unemployment when jobless workers without formal protection were receptive to radical organization and unions were willing to pursue militant strategies to gain their loyalty. The importance of mobilizing marginal workers to unions is appraised by Goldfield:

> To achieve certain broader goals, but even to defend their narrow economic interests in times of crisis, unions must reach out and ally themselves with other constituencies. Their success often depends on it. While their tendency to take up the interests of these other constituencies is neither natural nor inevitable, there is a certain logic to it. Their reliance on numerical strength for greater economic and political leverage suggests such a course (1987, 75).

The political influence of the Knights of Labor, Industrial Workers of the World (IWW), Trade Union Unity League (TUUL), and Congress of Industrial Organizations (CIO) mushroomed during these periods of economic uncertainty. Even the leverage of the cautious American Federation of Labor (AFL) expanded dramatically during the 1870s and 1930s depressions, when some renegade unions organized workers on an industry-wide basis.

Mobilization of discontented groups like the jobless has always posed opportunities and dangers to trade union leadership. Insurgents have periodically challenged established union leaderships for control over the labor movement. In an environment of high unemployment union officials were forced to organize the unemployed to gain allegiance of disgruntled members and prevent outside challengers from taking a leading role in the labor movement. When prosperity returned, labor insurgencies usually disappeared or reverted to narrower conservative oligarchic strategies. In turn, new waves of marginal workers often continued to threaten wage gains of union members. Those unions unable to control their industrial labor markets were continually exposed to these pressures. Because union officials often reverted to standard oligarchic patterns, concerns with organizational and leadership continuity tempered their passion toward the unemployed. And since the unemployed tended to deplete often-scarce union resources, most leaders considered them to be an unwanted nuisance. In theory, union leaders have supported the notion of unemployed organizing, but in practice, unions have historically shunned them whenever possible. Paradoxically, the rise of unions representing industrial and service workers through the workplace allowed union leaders to ignore their own unemployed members when they were laid off. However, unemployed members of hiring hall unions have been threatening to the organizational stability of trade unions. Where workers were organized into the union structure (as they often were among craft unions), unemployed workers and outsiders frequently disturbed stable relations among leaders, members, and employers.

Given the extensive job insecurity of the nineteenth century, a small number of unions have succeeded in controlling the hiring process and limiting competition within individual labor markets. However, these safeguards were usually available only to select white male workers. African-Americans, immigrants, women and other minority workers were often excluded. Typically, unions formed on the basis of craft or skill had little interest in building a broader working class movement among workers who were not members. Their activities were limited to bargaining over wages and benefits with private employers. They were far less interested in securing government benefits for the larger industrial working class. Industrial unions bargained on behalf of skilled workers while leaving unskilled and marginal workers out in the cold. However, in both the nineteenth and twentieth centuries, unionization rates remained low among industrial workers who were almost always exposed to shifting market pressures.

Ironically, sometimes the leadership of strong unions that could control access to labor markets faced challenges from members in times of economic decline when their unions could not provide expected jobs. Pressure from unemployed members was particularly acute in these unions representing cohesive occupational communities of workers who experience cyclical unemployment. Since some of these workers were organized individually, they came to expect referrals from their unions when they became unemployed. In these cases, union officials had to respond more forcefully to unemployment or risk internal dissension and challenges to their legitimacy.

Labor historians of the nineteenth and twentieth centuries have documented the impact of militant unemployed organizing on union control over the labor movement. In response to systemic unemployment in the period before 1930, fledgling unions, unemployed workers, socialists, anarchists, and liberal reformers periodically emerged to organize workers neglected by craft unions. These working-class organizations (Knights of Labor, IWW, TUUL, AFL, CIO) often called upon government to provide financial support for jobless workers and their families when the private economy could not generate employment. While their demands for jobs and public relief usually went unheeded by government leaders, they successfully conveyed the message that unemployment was not an individual fault, but a structural feature of the capitalist economy.

## UNIONS AND THE UNEMPLOYED IN THE NINETEENTH CENTURY

While unions have identified with the predicament of unemployed workers from their origins in the early nineteenth century, they have seldom regarded the jobless as a realistic base to strengthen the organized labor movement. Workers were tormented constantly by unemployment resulting from economic depressions. Rather than providing a source of support, the unemployed were usually seen by leaders as a drag on union resources. Periodic formation of trade unions protected individual craft workers from rising joblessness while neglecting the much larger numbers of marginal and unemployed workers. By regulating the flow of labor into slack labor markets, early nineteenth century unions could sometimes protect privileged members from chronic unemployment. But they did little to protect most workers who lost their jobs. Trade union power was highly contingent on business conditions, rising during upswings of economic growth and weakening in the trough of business cycles. Although declining business conditions undermined unions, union officials did almost nothing to minimize unemployment. The Mechanics Union of Trade Associations, the first central labor association in America, which formed in Philadelphia in 1827 to protect working members from unemployment, did nothing to assist those non-members who lost their jobs in the depression of 1829 (Folsom, 21).[2] Neglect for unemployed and marginal workers by established trade union leaders was a recurring feature of the early nineteenth century. This disregard would redound to organized labor's disadvantage by sustaining the reserve army of jobless workers, driving down wages, and contributing to layoffs among the ranks of working members. By the late 1830s, most U.S. trade unions had vanished as a result of "the double pressures of employers and unemployment, which ended their treasuries and their basis of organization" (Folsom, 53). While unions often rejuvenated when economic prosperity returned, they were again threatened during recurrent periods of economic decline and concomitant high unemployment.

The 1873 depression swelled the ranks of the unemployed to as much as three million. However, even as the new economic breakdown challenged those few craft unions that could defend their members from rising unemployment, most union officials continued to ignore industrial workers who lost their jobs. These established unions responded only after sustained challenges from insurgents mobilizing industrial workers from both inside and outside organized labor. Still, some union activists and unemployed organizations appealed to the government to fund public works projects for workers who could not find jobs. In New York, the Spring Street Central Labor Council and 20 independent unions joined to demand government support for jobless workers. Under Peter J. McGuire, the Tenth Ward Workingmen's Association organized jobless workers to demand local government jobs, money, or produce, and a six-month suspension of all evictions for the unemployed and their families (Folsom, 113). On December 13, 1874, McGuire, a leader of the Committee of Safety, a New York City unemployed organization, helped mobilize a demonstration of 15,000 unemployed workers in Tompkins Square Park to demand public employment from the mayor. The rally was crushed violently by 1,500 New York City police officers wielding clubs against protesters.[3] McGuire later became a founding member of the Brotherhood of Carpenters and Joiners, which drafted a call for the convention that led to the formation of the Federation of Organized Trades and Labor Unions in 1881. The organization consolidated with the more militant Knights of Labor to form the American Federation of Labor in 1886 (Galenson 1940).

Responding to the inactivity of craft unions on behalf of unemployed industrial workers, the Order of Knights of Labor gained prominence among industrial workers who became unemployed without economic recourse during the early 1870s. While the Knights of Labor initially restricted membership to employed workers, by 1878, these qualifications were relaxed to include unemployed workers and small business owners.[4] The Knights of Labor organized working and unemployed workers to defend wage scales, the eight-hour day, and public works programs. As unemployment escalated in the 1880s, the Knights of Labor skillfully united male skilled craft workers with unorganized unskilled workers, small business owners, women, and African Americans.[5] At its peak in 1886, estimates of Knights of Labor membership ranged from 700,000 to one million (Foner 1975). Some local branches of the Knights staged prominent strikes against industrialists, the most famous of which was the vast railroad strikes led by Joseph Buchanan against the Wabash, Missouri Pacific, and Union Pacific railroads (Folsom, 142).

As a leader in the AFL, McGuire promoted the organization of jobless workers against unemployment in the new depression of 1893. Radical AFL leaders agitated the jobless and demanded relief for the estimated 1 million to 4.5 million workers who became unemployed without a national program to address their survival needs (Folsom, 153-154). Some AFL local unions organized unemployed workers into federal trade unions. These efforts culminated in late August 1893, when national AFL trade union leaders sponsored a mass meeting to demand immediate government action in response to rising unemployment.[6] Trade union leaders and members of the Socialist Labor Party attending the meeting called upon government to fund public works and road construction and to enact legislation reducing the work day (Folsom 1991, 151; Foner 1975, 238-241). These events were followed in the fall of 1893 by a mass meeting of 10,000 workers in Chicago, addressed by Henry George and a reluctant Samuel Gompers (Folsom, 239).[7] Continued growth of the industrial workforce in the 1890s induced AFL leaders to support resolutions for jobs and relief for the unemployed at the national convention in Chicago during December 1893. At the meeting, AFL unions called upon city, state and federal government to provide adequate relief for the jobless and that all men be provided a job by government when the private sector could not or would not provide one.[8] Pressure from recently unemployed and marginal union members compelled union leaders to respond to rising joblessness. At a meeting of unemployed workers held on January 30, 1894 at Madison Square Garden in New York, Gompers admonished the government for allowing mass unemployment to continue: "{[I]n a country such as ours, rich as a nation could be . . . large masses of our citizens were forced to endure hunger because unemployed." Gompers went on to say:

> Let conflagration illuminate the outraged skies!
> Let red Nemesis burn the hellish clan
> And chaos end the slavery of man! (Foner 1975, 240)

Members of the Socialist Labor Party who attended the mass demonstration and derided him (Foner 1975, 240) probably provoked Gompers' fiery speech in defense of the unemployed.

## THE AMERICAN FEDERATION OF LABOR TURNS TO CONSERVATISM

By 1894, the AFL reasserted a position of craft exclusiveness and opposition to industrial unionism and by the turn of the century, craft unionism became the guiding philosophy. This sentiment was made clear by Gompers at the AFL convention in 1903:

> The attempts to force the trade unions into what has been termed the industrial organization is pervasive of the history of the labor

movement, runs counter to the best conceptions of the toilers' interests now, and is sure to lead to the confusion which precedes dissolution and disruption. (Galenson, 18)

The lack of job security and other protection for the majority of industrial workers allowed radical organizers to compete with indifferent leaders of craft unions who formed the largest part of the AFL. At the turn of the century, militant socialists formed the IWW to challenge the oligarchic leadership of the established union movement by organizing industrial and unemployed workers neglected by most AFL unions. From its origins in 1905, the IWW was intent on mobilizing disparate workers into a single organization capable of representing workers industry-wide. The IWW mobilized unemployed workers to reduce the threat the jobless posed to union members (Foner 1965).[9] The IWW manifesto of 1905 transcended the narrow craft mentality of AFL unions by speaking to the common fears of job insecurity experienced by craft and industrial workers:

New machines, ever replacing less productive ones, wipe out whole trades and plunge new bodies of workers into the ever-growing army of tradeless, hopeless unemployed. As human beings and human skill are displaced by mechanical progress, the capitalists need use the workers only during that brief period when muscles and nerves respond most intensely. The moment the laborer no longer yields the maximum of profits, he is thrown upon the scrap pile, to starve alongside the discarded machine. A *dead line* has been drawn and an age-limit established, to cross which, in this world of monopolized opportunities, means condemnation to industrial death. (Kornbluh, 7)

Rather than forming an autonomous organization, the IWW sought to build alliances among militants in different labor organizations to struggle for expanded rights and protection for industrial workers. The AFL continued to oppose any form of organization of the unemployed. While the national leadership of the AFL publicly sympathized with unemployed workers, it considered agitation and mass action to be ineffectual in ameliorating their position. Even as national unemployment swelled to 4 million during the 1914-1915 depression, Gompers asserted that political action was useless:

> If demonstration, as you propose, could meet the present situation
> and solve it there would be no hesitance on the part of the Executive
> Council of the American Federation of Labor to co-operate, but to
> follow the leadership of any one or any body of men when the matter
> presumed to us is for mere agitation purposes alone, without any
> practical results occurring, we must respectfully decline to permit
> our movement to be used for any such purpose. (Foner, 453)

While the AFL opposed any form of government relief or public jobs,
it supported the building of shelters and the provision of food rations
for homeless people during the winter months (Foner, 453). Despite
the inaction of the national AFL leadership, IWW activists continued
to organize unemployed workers to demand government jobs,
reduction of the workday, and relief measures. While the IWW
achieved notable victories in organizing unemployed workers in many
localities throughout the United States, its demands were largely
unheeded by U.S. President Woodrow Wilson and other government
officials, who even refused to collect statistics on the number of
workers who were unemployed. (Foner, 453-461)[10]

## THE PASSIVE RESPONSE OF UNIONS TO
## UNEMPLOYMENT IN THE 1930s

The upsurge in the labor unrest of the 1930s provides yet another
example of how militant unemployed organizing caused the AFL and
organized labor to lose control over the core of the labor movement
and spur the formation of a new, expanded labor movement
encompassing low-wage industrial workers.

The relentless and unmanageable rise in unemployment in the
early 1930s posed an unparalleled challenge to the power of organized
labor. From March 1930 to March 1931, conservative government
estimates of unemployment reveal that unemployment increased
tenfold, from 492,000 to 4,644,000. In the next year, unemployment
doubled to over 9 million before peaking in March 1933 at over 15
million (Bernstein 1970, 254-257; Rosenzweig 1976, 37; Piven and
Cloward 1979, 45-46).[11] Few industries were invulnerable to
unemployment. For example, the Ford Motor Company payroll
dropped from 138,142 in March 1929 to 37,000 in August 1931
(Rosenzweig 1976, 38). The vast majority of the poor who became
unemployed had no protection against homelessness and hunger.

Without government relief to alleviate their plight, many unemployed workers resorted to living in unauthorized shantytowns and squatter communities. Others engaged in mob looting, street marches, and rioting (Piven and Cloward 1979, 48-53). In the hostile environment of the Great Depression, several militant left-wing organizations began to organize these radicalized unemployed workers to fight for their survival needs. These groups initiated the struggle for the creation of a government unemployment insurance system. While the AFL was conspicuously absent from efforts to mobilize the unemployed, organizers and radical members of individual unions joined the fight to defend the unemployed. Even before the stock market collapse of October 1929, Communist leader William Z. Foster agitated for the rights of unemployed workers within the AFL through the Trade Union Education League (TUEL).

Goldfield (1991) contends that the American labor movement during this period should be characterized as broader than the movement to organize unions. He argues that conventional descriptions of the labor movement as conservative craft unions affiliated with the AFL neglect a substantial segment of the American labor movement. These excluded workers include the unemployed, African Americans, unorganized industrial workers, and other militant political organizations led by Communists, Socialists, and other leftist parties influential in the 1920s and 1930s. Goldfield (1991) claims that the often-volatile waves of unemployed and rank-and-file protest organized by Communists and other militants in the early 1930s challenged the control and legitimacy of the AFL within the labor movement (1276). The mass strikes of 1934 that united the unemployed and rank-and-file workers in Toledo, Minneapolis, and San Francisco (Folsom 1991) and the growing reputation of the CIO forced the old guard in the AFL to reassess their earlier staunch opposition to unemployment insurance and the welfare state (Yellowitz 1968). The threat posed by rival industrial union organizing efforts is conclusively evident in the AFL's August 1936 proclamation against any union forming alliances with the CIO:

> [T]he Executive Council orders and directs that each union affiliated with the so-called Committee for Industrial Organization withdraw from and sever relations with said Committee . . . Any union now affiliated with the Committee for Industrial Organization, not announcing its withdrawal therefrom on or before September 5,

1936, shall thereupon by this order stand suspended from the American Federation of Labor. (Galenson, 20)

While some Communist and Socialist organizers in AFL unions were concerned about industrial workers and the unemployed, most AFL leaders remained indifferent to these workers. Some leaders feared that if government were to provide unemployment insurance benefits the ability of unions to organize and represent members would erode significantly.[12] From the 1890s to 1934, the AFL was a steadfast advocate of the unrestrained free market and, under the leadership of Gompers and then William Green, staunchly opposed public relief for the unemployed, fearing that government programs would interfere with union efforts to bargain with private employers. As the 1930s depression wore on, the vast majority of American workers had no protection from unemployment. In 1928, only 34,700 workers were enrolled in trade union-administered unemployment insurance plans, and less than one percent of the national labor force was covered by voluntary unemployment plans (Folsom, 389). Hesitation to support creation of a government-administered unemployment insurance program left the AFL exposed to fierce criticism from both rank-and-file members and outside challengers. Soon the AFL was to be overshadowed by militant organizers inside and outside the established labor movement who were intent on building a larger labor movement based on broader principles of working-class solidarity. In early 1932, the AFL Committee for Unemployment Insurance and Social Security was formed in a conference in New York City by insurgent members of the AFL, many of whom were influenced by Communist organizers. AFL national leaders did not sanction the group. Under Louis Weinstock, an immigrant house painter, the Committee for Unemployment Insurance and Social Security pressed AFL leaders to support an expansive unemployment insurance program. This plan gained endorsement among a growing number of insurgent AFL locals throughout the country. In September 1932, Weinstock disrupted a national AFL convention in Cincinnati to appeal for delegate support of the principle of government unemployment insurance for jobless workers. His unauthorized speech embarrassed AFL leaders into calling a vote on government unemployment insurance for both recently and long-term jobless workers. Delegates at the convention voted 300 to 5 to support the measure. Weinstock later went on to testify before Congress in support of unemployment insurance on behalf of 800 AFL member locals. These competitive pressures from among militant organizers in the labor movement obliged the AFL national leadership to recognize and confront the problem of mass joblessness during the 1930s.

## UNIONS AND MOBILIZATION OF UNEMPLOYED WORKERS IN THE 1930s

A brief chronology of the 1930s unemployed movement, a period of economic uncertainty and trade union stagnation and decline, provides a context for understanding the ambiguous relationship between labor unions and the unemployed and the role of leadership competition as a factor in the mobilization of the unemployed. Three national unemployed groups were involved in unemployed organization: (1) the TUUL, which launched the Unemployment Councils of America, run on a national level by the Communist Party; (2) unemployment groups that emerged from the League for Industrial Democracy, an offshoot of the Socialist Party; (3) and the Conference on Progressive Labor Action (CPLA), under the leadership of labor educator A.J. Muste. Each of these organizations attempted to advance the immediate and long-term cause of the unemployed on the local and national levels. Independent labor unions and labor radicals played an important initial role in the formation of these groups.[13] The AFL and its affiliate unions were markedly absent in any major organizing efforts, even though its power had declined precipitously during the 1920s as a result of reduced membership and growing unemployment. It was only after these efforts became a threat to established trade union leadership that the AFL seriously began to support relief and jobs for the unemployed.

Initial organizing drives of the Communists were spearheaded and organized by militant trade union leaders. In 1921, underground party activists formed the Unemployed Council of Greater New York, with support from 34 local unions which included affiliates of the AFL, the IWW, and independent unions. Active efforts by the Communist Party to organize jobless workers during the 1920s failed to sustain local unemployed organizations (Leab 1968). Despite these early failings, the Communist Party considered organizing the unemployed a major plank in the formation of the TUUL labor confederation in August 1929.[14] While organizing the unemployed began on a shop and factory basis, these efforts were expanded to neighborhood organizing after the Crash of October 1929 increased joblessness on a mass scale. Much of this early organizing paid dividends for the party, which could mobilize the unemployed without competition. On March 6, 1930, the Communist Party-sponsored International Unemployment Day brought out hundreds of thousands of jobless workers in cities and towns across the country.

According to Rosenzweig, Socialist and Musteite organizers who entered the fray in the early 1930s overshadowed the Communist Party's early-undisputed advantage in the organized unemployed movement. These groups used less dogmatic approaches geared to local support and relief. In response, the party also shifted to individual and local level grievances for relief and other complaints.

Even as the Communist Party's ideological influence was waning, local Committees of Action were formed by the TUUL to represent the unemployed in grievances with relief agencies. These efforts continued after the introduction of the New Deal jobs programs, which gave local committees expanded power as bargaining agents for workers employed in the Works Progress Administration programs, and began to shift to trade union activities.

During the 1920s, the Socialist Party emphasized conferences for propaganda purposes rather than unemployed organizing. Unemployed workers were viewed as an unstable force, difficult to organize into the party (Rosenzweig 1979). Even after the start of the Depression, the Socialist Party emphasized ideological, abstract issues, such as "Socialism in Our Time" (Rosenzweig 1979). It was only after younger activist members entered the party following Norman Thomas's run for president in 1932 that active unemployed organizing began to take place. The League for Industrial Democracy started organizing unemployed workers by handling local grievances and organizing demonstrations in support of unemployment insurance in a manner similar to the early organizing efforts of the Communist Party.[15] This grassroots activism fostered development of trade union support among the unemployed. Rosenzweig (1979) explains that the Socialist committees:

> raised the political and social consciousness of its members by altering their views about government relief, by introducing them to principles of trade union organizing, by fostering interracial cooperation, and by reinforcing weakened bonds of community solidarity. (500)

In some instances, the unemployed supplied discernible support for organized labor. Most visible of these actions was the Milwaukee streetcar strike of 1934, in which the Socialist Party organized 13,000 unemployed demonstrators supporting the strikers.[16] In other parts of the country, similar labor struggles were supported by local Socialist unemployed organizations. For example, unemployed demonstrators advanced the cause of RCA and Campbell Soup workers in Camden, New Jersey (Rosenzweig 1979). Creation of federal jobs programs in the mid-1930s provided employment for about one-third of the 15 million unemployed workers. Some of these workers had developed close ties to Socialist Party and League for Industrial Democracy organizers. These same Socialist unemployed organizations became local bargaining agents for those employed by federal jobs programs. Many of these organizations' locals were recognized as bargaining agents for project locals. On a national level, Socialist unemployed organizations were subsumed into the Workers' Alliance, led by unions of WPA workers. But the prevalence of national relief programs and the organization of WPA workers diminished the significance of the unemployed to Alliance organizers, who united with the Communist Party and Musteite Unemployed Leagues under the Popular Front. The Popular Front strategy moderated the demands of the unemployed and culminated in fewer local struggles and reduced grassroots activity around unemployment (Rosenzweig 1979).

A.J. Muste and his labor organizer followers as a counterweight to the AFL, Communist Party, and Socialist Party formed the Conference on Progressive Labor Action in 1929. The Conference on Progressive Labor Action soon became a vehicle for launching a national independent unemployed movement in 1932. Musteites used the unemployed as a power base, downplaying ideology and emphasizing local grievances as a primary component in their organizing strategy (Rosenzweig 1975, 1976). Ultimately, the National Unemployed League came to be viewed as a way of uniting unemployed and employed workers. In small- and medium-sized towns where the radical ideologies and abstract objectives of the Communist Party and Socialist Party were suspect, Musteite-led National Unemployed League (NUL) organizers were successful in organizing the unemployed. In rural Pennsylvania and Ohio, the NUL was able to mobilize unemployed workers by resolving local demands and grievances and operating from an outwardly apolitical functional base. But by 1935, the movement evolved from its initial pragmatic approach to a more radical, Trotskyist-dominated ideology, in part contributing to the Musteites' decline in prominence.

In April and May of 1934, however, Musteite attempts to form alliances between unemployed and employed workers were realized in the strike by AFL Federal Local Union 18384 against Electric Auto-Lite Company of Toledo, Ohio (Bernstein 1969; Brecher 1973). The Lucas County League organized unemployed workers who banded together with their employed counterparts in mass pickets and demonstrations. A favorable settlement with the company was reached, but not before a violent confrontation with the National Guard. A mass picket of 10,000 striking and unemployed workers prevented 1,500 strikebreakers from leaving the factory in Toledo. The crowd responded to gas bombs, gunfire, and other attacks by local police deputies "with a seven-hour barrage of stones and bricks, which were deposited in piles in the streets and then heaved through the factory windows." A day later, the Ohio National Guard ordered nearly 25,000 men to the factory gates, including eight rifle companies, three machine gun companies, and a medical unit (Bernstein 1969, 221-229). The implications of the strike's use of jobless workers threatened both business and established union leaders by clearly demonstrating the positive role of the unemployed in furthering the needs of striking workers and their unions.

In 1935 and 1936, as more unemployed found work in government jobs, some NUL locals supported workers in strikes against the WPA and other government projects over wages and grievances.[17] When unemployment declined, Musteite organizers left the NUL to join efforts with the Steelworkers of America and other emerging industrial unions, and many of them eventually became union leaders (Rosenzweig 1975).

While the Musteites could not duplicate the Toledo Auto-Lite strike on a massive scale, the events demonstrated that solidarity between trade unionists and the unemployed was possible, and was of potential benefit to trade unions. Ultimately, the Musteites lost influence as unemployment declined in the late 1930s and as the NUL leadership became radicalized by the incorporation of the Trotskyist American Communist Party.

The unemployment movement of the 1930s demonstrates that alliances can be formed between trade unionists and the jobless for their mutual gain. However valuable these alliances were for building working-class power, union leadership rarely joined forces with unemployed workers to advance their common interests. When unemployed organizations joined forces with employed rank-and-file union members, trade union leadership frequently opposed them. According to Bernstein, it is unclear whether the Musteite Lucas County Unemployed League was invited by the local union representing striking Auto-Lite workers or they came on their own volition. But the AFL national union confederation certainly did not support alliances between the striking workers and the organized unemployed (Bernstein, 221-229). This suggests that, while these efforts contributed to activism within the labor movement during a period of high unemployment, they also posed a challenge to AFL and individual union leadership.

## POST NEW DEAL: ORGANIZED LABOR REVERTS TO CONSERVATISM

New Deal and government jobs programs established under the Roosevelt administration contributed to the growth of trade union activities once unemployed groups began to bargain collectively for their former members. Rosenzweig observes this accommodating tendency among the Socialist unemployed committees:

> The unemployed movement did not disappear, but did settle into a more orderly movement, which acted as a local bargaining agent for relief recipients and Works Progress Administration (WPA) workers, and a national lobby for higher relief appropriations. Large demonstrations or eviction resistance occasionally flared up, but more often the unemployed organizations quietly carried out trade union and lobbying functions. (1979, 500)

The 1930s unemployed movement demonstrated that solidarity and organization were potentially advantageous both to jobless, employed workers, and trade unions, setting the precedent for organization of workers once unemployment declined.

Mike Davis (1986) considers the rise of labor militancy in the 1930s a challenge to both the AFL trade union leadership and an opportunity for liberal-minded labor leaders who formed the Committee for Industrial Organization (CIO) to channel the radical energies of the broader labor movement into a national organization of industrial labor. Davis argues that the new industrial unionism of the

1930s emerged out of a highly uneven and discontinuous movement of organized workers that mobilized unskilled and minority industrial workers who were isolated from the organized labor movement (53). The escalation in unauthorized strike activity was not only a threat to the leadership of the AFL and union leaders over the labor movement, but also an opportunity for dissident trade union leaders with financial resources and liberal political support to unite these diverse workers' movements. The CIO successfully unified radical autonomous mass movements of industrial shop committees into a cohesive bureaucratic force. Communist and radical leaders who could not be easily controlled were eventually purged from the organization after the militant labor movements were integrated into the CIO.

The CIO's rise to prominence as a national labor movement of wage and salaried industrial workers in the early 1940s did not prevent it from assuming some of the bureaucratic characteristics of the AFL by the late 1940s. In his study of American labor leaders, C. Wright Mills (1971) concludes that, upon consolidating power in the 1940s, the CIO substantially ignored a large segment of unorganized low-wage workers (primarily in the U.S. South) as it advanced the interests of a new aristocracy of high-wage industrial workers.

While trade unions often tend to neglect workers outside their organizations, Mills asserts that leaders must remain attentive to the interests of working members because "on occasion rank-and-file leaders have upset the rule of the big shots of the union world" (106). Invariably, he maintains, union leaders will face latent opposition to their leadership from disgruntled members of their union whose interests are not served by them:

> Sometimes the images held by his own boys are so pleasant to behold that the labor leader, even as the other men, tries hard never to look beyond them. But everyone in the union is not his boy; and the opposition may rudely shove its contrasting images before him. It is hard to push such rude images away and still be seen in the mirror. To retain power means to deal successfully with these obtrusive views, for they may reflect something of the shifting ideas of the rank and file, and they may influence what this rank and file will come to believe. (13)

Trade union leaders often forget that their predecessors gained power in the 1930s and 1940s as militant activists who provided accessible alternatives to the distant and oligarchic leadership of the AFL for unorganized, unskilled, and immigrant workers:

> Many of the men who came into the union world out of the upheavals of the Thirties began as grass roots militants. Their images of what they were working for may not have been well thought out or very systematic but they were urgent about what they were doing. In all this, they reflected the mood and capacity of sections of the hard-pressed rank and file whom they organized.[18]

New generations of minority, immigrant, and women workers during the second half of the twentieth century found themselves without unions willing to defend their interests in an even more malevolent economic environment. Union leaders who choose to grapple with troubling issues like unemployment potentially unleashed forces of opposition within their unions, and so, as Lipset, Trow, and Coleman argue, they prefer to detach themselves from these annoyances.

According to Miliband (1991), opposition to trade union leadership often arises from union activists who "are more radical and militant than their leaders." Union activists "have always formed the major radical ingredient" in their unions and are the "main opposition to their moderate leaders" (Miliband, 57). Miliband views Michels' iron law of oligarchy not as a division between unions and their members but as a division between leaders and left activists. The intermittent attempt by trade union leaders to suppress the power of more militant opponents within their unions is viewed by Miliband as a means of expanding their capacity to pursue moderate policies (Miliband, 67).

In the struggle for the direction of the labor movement in the 1930s and 1940s, militant political action was often dampened by leadership demands for increased control and stability over their new organizations. This transformation led to fewer sit-ins, strikes, picket lines, and increased cooperation with authorities. Oppenheimer (1940) notes that the unemployed movement during the 1930s can be "characterized by a gradual evolution from the position of a purely conflict group to an organized and responsible relationship with authorities" (Rosenzweig 1976, 46). In the mid-1930s, the loss of vitality and spontaneity occurred simultaneously with unification of the leadership of fragmented unemployment movements into the Workers Alliance of America. As former activists in the unemployed movement developed close relations with New Deal authorities, they became "lifeless leaders in a lobbying organization for national relief and unemployment insurance" (Rosenzweig 1979).

## ORGANIZED LABOR'S SURRENDER TO SYSTEMIC UNEMPLOYMENT

Even as unionization has expanded the protection of workers during the twentieth century, unemployment has endured as a feature of the U.S. political economy, rising consistently since the end of the Second World War through the early 1990s. Since the 1940s, trade union leaders have intermittently supported both creation and expansion of legislative efforts to control and compensate for systemic unemployment through full employment programs and the extension of unemployment insurance benefits. These efforts have seldom been successful, in part because leaders of the AFL-CIO and international unions rarely considered unemployment a priority to their organizations and the trade union movement.

The Full Employment Bill of 1945, the first effort to establish full employment as a human right that was made part of the Democratic Party's 1944 platform by Franklin Roosevelt was never passed by Congress. The bill's supporters included the AFL, CIO, and other organizations representing people of color, women and youth. Dissension between the AFL and CIO and the death of Roosevelt contributed to the bill's failure to pass in Congress. In 1974, when the Humphrey-Hawkins Full Employment Bill was first introduced, unemployment was under 5.2 percent. In January 1979, following legislative enactment, unemployment was 5.8 percent, on its way up to 8.9 percent in 1982. The AFL-CIO did not support passage of the bill when it was first introduced, although it subsequently sponsored a watered-down version of the original bill introduced by the Congressional Black Caucus. Soon after Congress passed the bill into law, the mandate to reduce unemployment to 4 percent and to make the fight against unemployment a national priority had vanished.[19]

In the absence of strong union-mediated support of jobs and employment benefits, national jobless rates have increased regularly since 1944, when President Franklin Roosevelt declared employment a "human right."[20] Since the end of the Second World War unions have failed to provide a viable response to the accepted economic doctrine that a certain level of unemployment is necessary to keep inflation in check.[21] The economic trade-off between unemployment and inflation made during the 1970s and 1980s has been costly to workers, raising "natural rates" of joblessness in the U.S. to as high as seven percent. Unions can only safeguard their own membership and, increasingly, for a growing number of unions, preserving union jobs has been a formidable task as a result of the growing tenacity of their business opponents and an increasingly hostile political and legal environment against organized labor.

Until the late 1960s, when American industry was affected by expanded global competition, the AFL-CIO and its member unions were successful in providing a modicum of job security for membership. However, unions protected their members' jobs at the expense of workers at the margins of the labor force. And increased integration of the global economy in the second half of the twentieth century reduced the competitive advantage of American industrial workers vis-a-vis foreign workers. Growing competition from foreign producers has increased employer hostility towards unions and their members, and employers no longer guaranteed job security. For the first time since the end of World War II, unions have been faced with shop closures and mass layoffs.

Unions, then, have been unable to prevent systemic unemployment and subsequent rank-and-file layoffs. Instead, they have tried to influence the manner in which job loss and rehiring occurs among their own members. They have taken it upon themselves to generate routine procedures of allocating unemployment to members. "Although unable to prevent job loss itself from occurring," political scientist Miriam Golden argues "unions do influence the criteria according to which particular workers are selected for redundancy or layoffs. Unions thereby enact different principles of justice, playing a normative role in the workings of the market."[22] Golden suggests that such policies may be traced to the union officials' and union activists' priority of protecting their organizations— particularly the seniority systems that regulates employment security among union members.[23]

According to labor historian Alexander Keyssar, management favored the institutionalization of seniority systems after 1935 as a means of dividing workers and promoting labor peace. He argues that seniority systems were instituted, often with the complicity of union leaders, to "[enhance] the security of some workers while heightening the insecurity of others." While seniority systems have protected many workers from the uncertainty of unemployment, they have also "reinforced social divisions within the working class and within unions," limiting the potential of "unified working-class political action."[24] While unemployment rates have held relatively steady since the 1870s (with the exception of the 1930s), workers in the late-twentieth century were unemployed for longer spells than they have been in the past. Until the 1930s, unions did not yet institutionalize seniority protection in the workplace. Most sectors of the workforce were subject to frequent bouts of unemployment:

> Between 1870 and 1930, unemployment was a fairly egalitarian affliction among working people. Men and women had nearly identical unemployment frequencies, although women tended to be jobless slightly more often in occupations that had both male and female members. The difference between immigrant and native unemployment levels was also small. And age played only a minor role in determining a person's chances of working steadily: teenagers were unemployed more than adults, but the gap was modest, and among men between the ages of twenty-five and fifty-five, there was no difference at all. (Keyssar, 22)

Although unemployment rates have not changed considerably, Keyssar argues frequencies of unemployment have declined since the early twentieth century. Unemployment tends to occur most frequently among minority workers who have few skills. At the same time, he notes that the mean duration of unemployment seems to have increased (21-23), making the jobless more dependent on unemployment benefits. Thus, a smaller proportion of the labor force, one that is primarily comprised of racial minorities is shouldering the overall burden of unemployment. In 1982, one-third of all black workers experienced unemployment, compared to one-fifth of white workers.

American labor history is dominated by a pattern of neglect for marginal and unemployed workers. For much of this history, trade union officials have considered the unemployed a nuisance and have typically excluded them from membership in their organizations. Unions normally function as representative organizations exclusively for working members. Jobless workers were usually shunned by oligarchic union organizations because they were a drain on scarce resources and challenged the legitimacy of union officials. Only rarely did union objectives include mobilizing jobless workers. In times of economic decline these standard relations with the unemployed were thrown out of balance as jobless workers often bargained down wage rates and took jobs away from working members. Unions have also been threatened by insurgent leaders in and out of the established labor movement who sought to mobilize the disruptive energies of unemployed workers as a radical force for social change and organization building. The labor insurgencies of the 1870s, 1890s, and 1930s unified marginal and unemployed workers with jobless union members, while energizing the established union movement to support the organization of unemployed workers.

As the next chapter will show, trade unions in New York City continue to be tormented by the threat of unemployment in the 1990s. Trade unions have been unable to defend their members from the rise in unemployment in New York City that has accompanied the structural slowdown of the American economy in the early 1970s. The inability of trade unions to defend their members' job security in four key sectors of the New York economy will demonstrate union leaders' need to respond to the economic problem of unemployment in their organizations.

## NOTES

1. For an examination of U.S. waterfront longshoremen unions see Howard Kimeldorf, *Reds or Rackets? The Making of Radical and Conservative Unions on the Waterfront* (Berkeley: University of California Press, 1988) and Bruce Nelson, *Workers on the Waterfront: Seamen, Longshoremen, and Unionism in the 1930s*, (Urbana, Illinois: University of Illinois Press, 1988). For a survey of building trades unions, see Mark L. Silver, *Under Construction: Work and Alienation in the Building Trades* (Albany: State University of New York Press, 1986 and Mark Erlich, "Who Will Build the Future," *Labor Research Review*, 7(2) Fall 1988.

2. Folsom documents an account of the relation between unions and the unemployed in the late 1820s from Louis H. Arky, "The Mechanic's Union of Trade Associations and the Foundation of the Philadelphia Working Men's Movement," *Pennsylvania Magazine of History and Biography* 76, April, 1952.

3. Hundreds of protesters, including women and children, were injured by police officers during the Tompkins Square Park rally. Samuel Gompers, the first president of the American Federation of Labor, reported that police

officers attacked "wherever the police saw a group of poorly dressed persons standing or moving" (Folsom, 121-122).

4. Philip S. Foner notes that while non-working people were allowed to become members of the Knights of Labor in 1878, the organization deemed that three-quarters of all members had to remain employed at all times.

5. See Philip S. Foner, *History of the Labor Movement in the United States*. Vol. 2, *From the Founding of the A.F. of L. to the Emergence of American Imperialism*. 2nd ed. New York: International Publishers, 1975. (check this citation)

6. The AFL dispatched George McNeill of the national office on a tour of eastern and Midwest cities to speak at unemployed meetings in Albany, Buffalo, Toledo, Detroit, Owosso, Indianapolis, Cincinnati, and Columbus (Foner 1975, 238).

7. Following the meeting, a committee of trade unionists who were elected at the meeting assisted Chicago authorities in placing 3,400 unemployed workers in temporary jobs working in the Chicago drainage canal and street repairs (Foner 1975, 239).

8. The two resolutions proposed by Thomas J. Morgan, a member of the Machinists International Union, are documented by Folsom (152-153):

> *Resolved*, That while this convention applauds the human efforts of private individuals to relieve the terrible distress of the unemployed, at the same time we must respectfully, but emphatically insist that it is the province, duty and in the power of our city, state and national governments to give immediate and adequate relief. *Resolved*, That a system of society which denies to the willing man the opportunity to work, then treats him as an outcast, arrests him as a vagrant and punishes him as a felon, is by this convention condemned (153) as inhuman and destructive of the liberties of the human race, and *Resolved*, That the right to work is the right to life, that to deny the one is to destroy the other. That when the private employer cannot or will not give work the municipality, state or nation must.

It is noteworthy that almost a century later, during the recession of 1990-1991, the AFL-CIO declined to make unemployment insurance extensions one of its three legislative goals (see Chapter 6).

9. For a comprehensive chronology of the IWW see Philip S. Foner, *The History of the Labor Movement in the United States*, Volume 4, *The Industrial Workers of the World, 1905-1917* (New York: International Publishers, 1965).

10. The IWW was active in mobilizing unemployed workers New York, Portland, St. Louis, Sioux City, Des Moines, Salt Lake City, and Providence during the 1914-1915 depression.

11. These unemployment statistics are from Robert R. Nathan, "Estimates of Unemployment in the United States, 1929-1935," *International Labour Review*, 33, January 1936, 49-73.

12. Unlike European unions, American unions were never able to control the unemployment insurance funds of their members. See B. Stevens, "Labor Unions, Employee Benefits, and the Privatization of the American Welfare State," *Journal of Policy History*, 2, 3 (1990), 233-260.

13. See Daniel J. Leab, "'United We Eat': The Creation and Organization of the Unemployed Councils in 1930," *Labor History*, 1968. Leab documents that trade union representatives from 34 AFL and independent unions participated in the "Unemployment Conference for Greater New York," in March of 1921, later forming the Unemployed Council of Greater New York.

14. At a time when many trade unions excluded black workers and black workers were themselves suspicious of the motives of unions, the TUUL became a principal proponent of unity of black and white workers, and attempted to establish such multiracial unity in unions that it formed from 1929 to 1935. According to labor historian Philip Foner, when the TUUL federation dissolved in 1935, many of these unions "were transformed into nuclei for the CIO organizing drive." See Philip S. Foner, *Organized Labor and The Black Worker, 1619-1973*. New York: International Publishers, 1976.

15. The party was particularly successful in Chicago, where it organized 25,000 unemployed members into local Workers' Committees (Rosenzweig, 1979).

16. See Roy Rosenzweig, "Socialism in Our Time: The Socialist Party and the Unemployed, 1929-1936," 20(4), *Labor History*, Fall 1979. Rosenzweig documents the following July 1934 *New Republic* report on the Milwaukee streetcar strike: "The strike had apparently collapsed . . . By sundown, however, the Workers' Committee on Unemployment, an organization of 13,000 jobless, largely under Socialist control had thrown its members into the picket lines" (499-500).

17. The strike against the New Haven Premier Pajama Company is a notable example of a NUL-supported labor action. (Rosenzweig 1979)

18. C. Wright Mills. *The New Men of Power: America's Labor Leaders*, 2nd edition, (New York: Augustus M. Kelley Publishers, 1971) 165.

19. For an assessment of union efforts to fight full employment, see Helen Ginsberg, *Full Employment and Public Policy: The United States and Sweden* (Lexington, Massachusetts: Lexington Books, 1983).

20. Cyclical waves of recession and recovery economy have disguised a 40-year rise in unemployment in the U.S. economy. Since the 1970s, these economic cycles have tended to produce deeper troughs during recessions and weaker economic recoveries.

21. Economist Milton Friedman coined the term "natural rate" of unemployment, which holds that inflation tends to rise when the unemployment rate is low, and falls when the unemployment rate is high. Economists have modified the term "natural rate" to the less distasteful "nonaccelerating inflation rate of unemployment" (NAIRU). For an explication of the economic relationship between unemployment and inflation see Paul Krugman *The Age of Diminished Expectations: U.S. Economic Policy in the 1990s*, (Cambridge, Massachusetts: MIT Press, 1992), Chapter 3.

22. Employing a rational choice model in a comparative analysis of job reductions at British Leyland between 1979 and 1980 and the Italian Fiat works in 1980, Miriam Golden (411) contends that trade unions that are facing work-force reductions will acquiesce to these job losses where seniority is used and shop stewards are protected. When firms have discretion in selecting workers for job loss, unions may resist if the shop floor organizations are threatened. This analysis extends Golden's rational choice analysis of organizational control, where the legitimacy of trade union leadership may come under threat should firms have discretion in selecting workers for job loss and unions are excluded from participation. See Miriam Golden, "The Politics of Job Loss," *American Journal of Political Science*, Vol. 36, No.2, May 1992:408-430.

23. Golden (411) holds that an "ahistorical" rational choice explanation is more convincing than arguments that assert the importance of radical shops, powerful shops, union structure, management credibility and employee preferences in determining outcomes in labor struggles. Thus, where seniority systems exist, unions will permit job loss to occur, where no seniority system exists, Golden argues that unions will *"attempt to defend jobs, possibly with strike action."*

24. Alexander Keyssar. "History and the Problem of Unemployment," *Socialist Review*, Volume 19(4), 1989.

# CHAPTER 3

# Rising Unemployment and Declining Trade Union Power in Four New York City Labor Markets

The postindustrial transformation that began in the early 1950s and intensified in the 1970s has significantly compromised the economic power of trade unions in the United States. An important feature of the shift from manufacturing to services is the slowdown of the American economy since the early 1970s, and the concomitant rise in unemployment. From 1970 to the 1990, average national unemployment rates have increased from under 5 percent to more than 6 percent, climbing to more than 10 percent in the early 1980s and early 1990s recessions.[1] The shift from manufacturing to services has decimated the nucleus of organized labor's strength that is rooted among unskilled and semi-skilled male workers.[2] For manufacturing employment has consistently provided dependable and secure jobs for unskilled and semi-skilled workers who have failed to find comparable jobs in the service sector.[3] A corollary of the structural decline in manufacturing employment is the significantly diminished ability of unions to maintain wages for those workers who remain in the industry. The entry of large numbers of young, female, and minority workers in the U.S. labor force during the 1970s and 1980s has expanded competition for jobs and has coincided with the disappearance of jobs at adequate wages.

Competition for the stable medium-wage manufacturing jobs that were once broadly accessible to workers of all skill categories has deepened unemployment and weakened the ability of unions to maintain high wages. The rise in contingent labor—temporary, part-time, and contract work—has further reduced trade union power. Some economic analysts attribute the inability of unions to restrain rising unemployment and declining wages to their growing insignificance among low-income workers that formed the core of the organized labor movement earlier in the century.[4] This chapter examines the capacities of unions in New York City to sustain wage and income levels. Taking Marks's argument into account, this chapter considers the different effects of rising unemployment on the capacities of unions in four distinct sectors of the local labor market to defend the wages and jobs of workers.

## FROM MANUFACTURING TO SERVICES

From the 1960s to the 1990s the New York economy was transformed from one with a broad industrial base into an economy dominated by finance, insurance, real estate, and consumer services. The transformation is most evident in downtown Manhattan and on the Brooklyn waterfront, where large office buildings and high-rise luxury apartments have replaced sweatshops, warehouses, industrial buildings, and tenements that were the trademarks of the urban landscape for most of the century.[5]

The economic power represented by the spectacle of modern high-rises has not enhanced employment opportunities for the millions of unskilled workers who are entering the labor force. As the New York and U.S. economies rebounded from the steep economic recession of the early-1990s, government and business continued to eliminate jobs to control costs and increase profitability.[6] Unlike previous generations of urban workers, the new urban poor do not have access to the manufacturing jobs that were available before the economic transformation of New York. The new urban poor in New York City face an oppressive economy characterized by expansion without job growth.

Expansion of finance and business services (which tends to generate capital without providing many new jobs for the working poor) has not replaced the one-million jobs lost in manufacturing from the 1950s through the 1990s.[7] The precipitous decline in manufacturing has led to high unemployment even during periods of economic expansion.[8] Recessions, of course, have proved devastating in the absence of manufacturing employment. Over 275,000 manufacturing jobs disappeared during the 1970s, and another 150,000 manufacturing jobs were permanently lost in the 1980s.[9] City employment contracted from a high of 3.8 million in 1969 to 3.1 million during the 1977 fiscal crisis and to 3.2 million in the 1993 recession in the absence of a strong manufacturing base. Even during the expansion years of the 1980s, New York City's employment never recovered to the 3.8 million-level reached in 1969.

This chapter will examine how trade union and worker power is compromised by this rising unemployment, as well as by comprehensive shifts in the labor market. It will also investigate employment patterns in four primary occupational sectors from 1950 to 1990: manufacturing, construction, services, and government, focusing on how workers in different racial, ethnic, and skill categories groups are affected by industrial restructuring. A central question of this review is how these shifts are allocated among both union and nonunion workers, and how these labor market changes affect trade union power in different sectors of the economy.

## SECULAR DECLINE IN MANUFACTURING JOBS

Although manufacturing never dominated the New York economy exclusively in the way that automobiles dominated Detroit or steel ruled Pittsburgh, the industry has historically provided the most important source of employment for the city's working poor.[10] The New York manufacturing sector is primarily comprised of small- and medium-sized producers dispersed in industrial zones throughout Manhattan and the outlying boroughs.[11]

While large producers never controlled manufacturing in New York, small-scale and dispersed production has proliferated throughout the city. New York has provided advantageous economies of scale, for instance, to the apparel industry. These benefits include proximity to the fashion industry, abundant low-cost labor, a large local market, and access to national and international markets. New York's position as an international design and fashion center means a constant demand for textile and apparel fabricators and finishers.

Local labor, however, is prevented from taking full advantage of these benefits. Labor costs continue to be moderated by a large immigrant population flowing into the city and working in illegal sweatshops that pay workers a fraction of the minimum wage. Even in sectors of the industry still organized by independent trade unions, wage competition from nonunion undocumented workers in the informal economy continues to dampen wages. Indeed, immigrant labor in the New York apparel industry has swelled in the last 20 years. In the early 1970s, there were less than 200 sweatshops in New York City. By the 1980s, the International Ladies Garment Workers Union estimated there was 3,000 sweatshops employing over 60,000 sweatshop workers and homeworkers.[12] By the early 1990s there were as many undocumented workers in apparel sweatshops in New York City as there were unionized apparel workers in New York State.[13]

This problem has been compounded by the fact that the concentration of production in midtown Manhattan has been eroding since the early 1960s, when commercial and residential rezoning began to push production industries away to the outer boroughs and beyond the city limits. Moreover, the dispersion of manufacturing has eroded the potential political and economic strength of manufacturing workers and the unions that represent them. The absence of large-scale industrial facilities makes organizing workers difficult for trade unions because there are so many employers to target. In a study of the decline of New York City's manufacturing industry, sociologist Robert Fitch shows that in the 1950s the Rockefeller family planned to "transform the entire area from 59th Street to the Battery into one giant [central business district]" that would displace small apparel and textile manufacturers from the area.[14] The realization of the Rockefeller zoning scheme to maximize finance, insurance and real estate development has led to property speculation that has closed down most of the remaining apparel and print industries on Manhattan's west side. Manufacturing employment in Manhattan fell 32.5 percent from 276,000 to 186,600 in the 1980s. Destruction of the manufacturing zone on Manhattan's West Side is a notable example of deindustrialization. But even in the outer boroughs of Brooklyn and the Bronx, services and government employment have displaced manufacturing as primary sources of employment for unskilled low-income residents.[15] Many workers eke out a living in the informal economy of illegal sweatshops, car services, and underground trade. The biggest industry in the poorest neighborhoods of Brooklyn and the Bronx is religion. But while the soup kitchens, street fairs, and used clothing giveaways sponsored by Pentecostal and evangelical sects may provide the bare necessities and swell the ranks of the faithful, they do not create jobs.

The dominance of finance and business services is a recent development in the New York City economy. Early in the 1950s, the City's economy could be divided into five major industrial sectors. Its diversity was buttressed by a large and sprawling manufacturing base, which provided jobs for the unskilled workers most vulnerable to labor market changes. As a result, New York City has had lower rates of unemployment than most urban centers during national economic recessions. However, the decline in manufacturing has not been accompanied by the expansion of corporate service jobs for many of these semiskilled and unskilled workers pushed out of production jobs. Indeed, as the manufacturing industry was hemorrhaging jobs, other sources of employment were also leaving New York. From 1965 to 1988 the number of Fortune 500 headquarters in New York declined from 128 to 48.[16]

From the mid-nineteenth century to the 1960s manufacturing was a reliable source of jobs for the New York economy. In 1950, over 1.1 million New Yorkers were employed in the city's expansive manufacturing sector. Employment held steady throughout most of the 1950s, never dipping below 900,000. During the 1960s, however, manufacturing employment declined noticeably, dropping from 931,000 jobs at the beginning of the decade to 831,000 jobs in December 1969. Again, the number of manufacturing workers in New York plummeted from 782,000 in January 1970 to 505,000 in December 1979. Nor did the collapse in manufacturing employment cease during the local economic recovery of the late 1970s through mid-1980s. Even as the New York economy recovered after the mid-1970s fiscal crisis, manufacturing employment continued a steep decline to 349,000 at the decade's end, only to slip further during the 1990s as employment hit a nadir of 276,000 in January 1993.[17]

The scale of job loss in New York's manufacturing industries is far greater than the national average. Table 3.1 compares the decline in manufacturing employment in New York City to national employment trends. While manufacturing employment has held steady nationally through much of the period 1950-1993, it has declined dramatically over the long term in New York City.

**Table 3.1: Manufacturing Employment (000's) in New York City Compared to National Manufacturing Employment 1955-1993[18]**

| Year | United States | % Change | New York City | % Change |
|------|------|------|------|------|
| 1955 | 18,882 | 23.9 | 1,019.3 | -1.9 |
| 1960 | 16,796 | -11.0 | 946.8 | -7.1 |
| 1965 | 18,062 | 7.5 | 865.1 | -8.6 |
| 1970 | 19,367 | 7.2 | 766.0 | -11.5 |
| 1975 | 18,323 | -5.4 | 536.9 | -29.9 |
| 1980 | 20,285 | 10.7 | 495.7 | -7.7 |
| 1985 | 19,260 | -5.1 | 407.7 | -17.8 |
| 1990 | 19,110 | -0.8 | 337.5 | -17.2 |
| Nov. 1993 | 17,709 | -7.3 | 298.0 | -11.7 |
| % Change 1955-93 | | -6.2 | | -70.8 |

## Shortage of Manufacturing Jobs for Unskilled Workers

Racial and ethnic segmentation and fragmentation also characterize manufacturing in New York. Historically, manufacturing has provided few opportunities for black workers. A primary cause of today's occupational segregation is that the industry began to decline in the 1950s, about the same time black workers entered the regional labor force in large numbers.

Bailey and Waldinger suggest that the decline in manufacturing as a route for unskilled labor into the labor market has reduced the ability of black and Hispanic workers in New York to find employment:

> What was true in New York as of the late 1950s rapidly changed. As manufacturing declined, the city lost its historic function as a staging ground for unskilled newcomers. Whereas manufacturing jobs had long permitted 'immigrants access in to the mainstream economy (albeit to the bottom rungs of the socioeconomic ladder),' the growth of employment in services—whether consisting of high-level jobs or low-skilled jobs in traditionally female occupations—had negative implications, especially for black males.[19]

Stafford finds that black workers continued to have lower labor participation rates in manufacturing than Hispanic and white workers in the mid-1980s. In 1982, 18 percent of black males and 9 percent of black females were employed in manufacturing; proportions substantially lower than for blacks in manufacturing jobs nationwide.[20] Black manufacturing workers in New York tend to be segmented into a small number of low-paying industries—including production of electronic equipment, household appliances, children's outerwear, motor vehicles and equipment.[21]

Conversely, manufacturing is a growth sector for Hispanic workers concentrated in low-wage jobs of the industry. Hispanic workers have higher representation in manufacturing than either white or black workers. While they comprised just 16 percent of the labor force in 1982, they accounted for 26 percent of all workers employed in manufacturing in that year. White workers have tended to find jobs in the production of durable goods, while Hispanics have overwhelmingly found employment in production of nondurable goods. While 10.6 percent of the New York City labor force is employed in manufacturing, 17.4 percent of Hispanics are employed in manufacturing, and larger numbers are employed in the low-paying manufacturing of nondurable goods. Hispanic workers have found work in the large number of small manufacturers of apparel and food processing industries that have declined at a slower pace than the higher paying durable manufacturing jobs.[22] Immigrant Hispanics in particular have been over represented in such jobs. In 1980, 35 percent of all Hispanic immigrants were employed in these positions, while only 9 percent were employed in professional services, compared to 15 percent of all New Yorkers.[23]

New York's thirty-year shift from a differentiated industrial economy to a postindustrial economy, then, has become more evident as the city's population has become more racially and ethnically heterogeneous. The disappearance of manufacturing has tended to produce a shortage of employment for black and Hispanic workers entering the labor market. And services and government have not generated a sufficient number of jobs to replace those lost in manufacturing, which provided a reliable source of income for unskilled workers in New York City for most of the century. From 1970 to 1980, native-born black workers were concentrated in public sector employment (a labor market that weathered austere cuts during the early-1990s) and underrepresented in industrial employment.

Between 1980 and 1987, the growth in service jobs for native-born black workers (23.9%) more than offset the continued decline in manufacturing employment (23.6%), but many of these newly service sector jobs paid considerably lower wages than manufacturing and were more vulnerable to public sector budget cuts.[24]

The result of such trends, both in New York and throughout the country, has been higher levels of unemployment among black and Hispanic workers than among white workers. The seasonally adjusted national average rate of unemployment for the fourth quarter of 1992 was 7.3 percent; the unemployment rate was 6.4 percent among white workers, 14.2 percent among black workers, and 11.6 percent among Hispanic workers.[25] While official unemployment averaged 10 percent among all workers in the New York region, during 1992 the average unemployment rate was 9.0 percent among whites, 14 percent among blacks, and 15.1 percent among Hispanics.[26] A recent survey by the Community Service Society of New York demonstrates that even these figures understate the high rates of unemployment and low labor force participation among black and Hispanic men and women.[27]

Urban economist Walter Stafford confirms that high rate of unemployment among black and Hispanic workers to long-term exclusion from core sectors of the New York City economy.[28] As white workers have entered core sectors of the economy, he notes black and Hispanic workers have been ensnared in low paying declining economic sectors. Exclusion from nonsupervisory jobs in growth sectors of the economy is considered to be a primary obstacle to black and Hispanic employment mobility.[29] Black and Hispanic workers have also been virtually excluded from 130 of 193 rapidly growing private sector industries in the urban economy, which account for nearly 60 percent of private sector employment.[30]

Some of the unemployment problems described here may well derive from deliberate manipulations of the local labor market by employers. According to Lafer, private employers have contained labor costs by constructing a segmented labor market, separating primary and secondary sectors to restrict certain workers from higher paying jobs. Labor market segmentation allows employers to offer raises and promotions to a limited number of typically union employees without providing similar benefits to increasing majorities of nonunion workers. The result is "a situation much like that of multinational corporations in Third World countries," where there is a strong incentive to create secondary jobs for nonwhite workers at poverty wages.[31] Low-wage jobs that are made available by public and private employers to nonwhite workers in New York tend to consist of temporary, seasonal, part-time, and contract work without benefits.[32] Relegation of large numbers of entry-level black and Hispanic workers to the contingent backwater of the labor market increases pressure on trade unions struggling to protect unskilled and semi-skilled workers; it is difficult to organize workers competing fiercely for the same low-wage jobs.[33] Moreover, as labor markets slackened in the 1980s and early 1990s, even these jobs began to disappear, and private and public employers in New York City were unable to generate enough jobs to reduce the resulting structural unemployment among black and Hispanic workers.[34]

### Declining Leverage of Trade Unions and Low-Income Workers

The broad decline of manufacturing has diminished trade union power in New York City. Mass industrial layoffs and plant closings threatened the survival of trade unions during the 1970s and 1980s, seriously reducing their membership and revenues. Loss of membership has weakened the capacity of trade unions to maintain their pensions, health insurance plans and other member services.[35] Subcontracting production to low-cost producers who employ part-time, temporary, and contract workers has also diminished trade union economic strength. To combat these trends, unions have sometimes merged with other local unions to strengthen their membership base and remain financially viable.[36]

However, trade union density has remained high even as manufacturing has declined. Although manufacturing in New York City declined by over 70 percent from 1955 through 1993, unions continue to dominate what remains of the industry. For example, union membership in apparel manufacturing remained in the range of 65 percent to 70 percent through much of the decline. In 1970, unions representing apparel manufacturers negotiated settlements for 70.2 percent of the 249,000 workers employed in the industry. By 1994, the apparel manufacturing industry contracted to under 99,000 workers, but unions still represented nearly 65 percent of workers in the industry.[37] But the maintenance of union density does not compensate for the shrinking of the membership base and the increased competition for jobs, which tend to curtail unions' leverage in contract negotiations. Trade unions that represent apparel and publishing workers are particularly weakened by the rise in nonunion undocumented immigrant workers who are paid below the minimum wage.[38] The disappearance of apparel and printing jobs from the early-1950s to mid-1990s has significantly weakened trade union political clout and bargaining power with employers.[39] Table 3.2 compares changes in union density in the United States by labor market and Table 3.3 compares changes in union density in New York State and the United States.

**Table 3.2: United States Trade Union Density by Industrial Labor Market**

| Year | Manufac-turing | Construc-tion | Service | Govern-ment | Total |
|------|------|------|------|------|------|
| 1991 | 20.3 | 21.1 | 5.7 | 36.9 | 16.1 |
| 1983 | 27.8 | 27.5 | 7.7 | 34.3 | 20.7 |
| 1975 | 36.0 | 35.4 | 13.9 | 39.5 | 28.9 |
| 1970 | 38.7 | 39.2 | 7.8 | 31.9 | 29.9 |
| 1966 | 37.4 | 41.4 | n/a | 26.0 | 29.6 |
| 1953 | 42.4 | 83.8 | 9.5 | 11.6 | 32.5 |
| 1947 | 40.5 | 87.1 | 9.0 | 12.0 | 32.1 |
| 1939 | 22.8 | 65.4 | 6.0 | 10.8 | 21.2 |
| 1935 | 16.4 | 54.4 | 2.6 | 9.0 | 13.5 |
| 1930 | 7.8 | 64.5 | 2.3 | 8.5 | 12.7 |

Sources: Derived from Troy, Leo and Neil Sheflin, *U.S. Union Sourcebook*, Table 3.63, 3-15, 1985; and Employment and Earnings, Vol. 39, No. 1, 228-231, Bureau of Labor Statistics, U.S. Department of Labor (January 1992).

**Table 3.3: Percent Organized in New York State and U.S.**

| Year | New York State | United States |
|------|------|------|
| 1939 | 24.7 | 21.2 |
| 1953 | 35.6 | 32.5 |
| 1960 | 31.9 | 28.6 |
| 1975 | 43.2 | 29.9 |
| 1980 | 36.5 | 23.2 |
| 1994 | 26.3 | 16.1 |

Source: Derived from U.S. Union Sourcebook and New York State Department of Labor Statistics.[40]

For the most part, however, trade unions have not altered traditional forms of labor management relations in response to these events. They have instead continued to collaborate with employers to improve productivity, to secure federal and state government aid, and to support legislation that protects American industries from foreign imports.[41] Part of the reason for this can be found in the history of American labor unionism. Industrial trade unions organized in the early twentieth century with the narrow goal of employer recognition, workplace contractualism, and collective bargaining are legally constrained from confronting deindustrialization with political action through the strike and other forms of worker mobilization.[42] As long as workers remained indispensable to industrial production, the strike remained a compelling threat against management. But the trade union threat of labor action was undermined by postindustrial restructuring from manufacturing to services that began to accelerate in the late 1960s as the share of black, Hispanic, and immigrant workers began to expand.[43]

When trade unions invoke the strike threat, they have great difficulty achieving their goals. Trade unions electing to confront management by engaging in strikes or walkouts are faced with three primary obstacles that undermine their power. First, high and rising unemployment provides a surplus of replacement workers available for management to counter the strike threat. Second, the employer threat to close plants and lay off workers is far more intimidating than the strike threat that can be deployed by labor unions. The strike threat is only effective in industries where unions possess strong control over the market for labor. But these industries are declining in number as a result of technological development, which produces a small number of highly skilled jobs and a large number of unskilled jobs. Finally, management's ability to abandon industrial facilities and relocate to other states and abroad, where more advantageous economies of scale are available, tends to make labor action weak.

Labor's reduced power is also certainly related to trade union reluctance to engage in aggressive action in conflicts with industrial management. In New York City, trade unions are made particularly vulnerable by the dispersed nature of manufacturing production, which compounds the difficulty of winning a strike at a small and isolated plant.

## CYCLICAL BOOMS AND BUSTS IN THE CONSTRUCTION INDUSTRY

Patterns of employment and joblessness in the building trades differ somewhat from those in manufacturing. While the construction industry employs far fewer workers than the manufacturing industry, it has maintained a consistent number of workers over the past four decades. In January 1950, 110,000 workers were employed in construction, one-tenth as many as the more than one million workers in manufacturing. As manufacturing employment disappeared over the next four decades, the one-to-ten disparity in employment closed substantially to a ratio of one-to-three. Table 3.4 illustrates the cyclical pattern of construction employment—in sharp contrast to the secular decline in manufacturing employment. Whereas manufacturing employment declined by over 70 percent from 1950 to 1990, construction employment increased by 33 percent. There were an average of 112,600 workers employed in New York City construction jobs in January 1990, 2,600 more than in January 1950.

**Table 3.4: Highest and Lowest Monthly levels of Employment in Construction and Manufacturing in New York City: 1950-1993**

|        | Construction | | Manufacturing | |
|--------|------|------|------|------|
| Year   | High | Low  | High   | Low   |
| 1950   | 131.4 | 105.2 | 1115.5 | 990.2 |
| 1955   | 111.8 | 95.0  | 1065.7 | 972.1 |
| 1960   | 135.2 | 118.6 | 970.8  | 912.4 |
| 1965   | 114.6 | 103.1 | 889.8  | 832.2 |
| 1970   | 110.3 | 99.7  | 796.7  | 730.1 |
| 1975   | 85.7  | 72.2  | 555.4  | 519.9 |
| 1980   | 80.8  | 70.5  | 508.9  | 483.5 |
| 1985   | 114.1 | 95.0  | 416.1  | 398.7 |
| 1990   | 117.2 | 112.4 | 344.3  | 323.1 |
| 1993   | 87.9  | 78.7  | 296.9  | 275.9 |

Source: Derived from U.S. Department of Labor (unpublished data)

Yet, as a result of the expansion of commercial building activity that began in the early 1970s, expansionary and recessionary employment cycles in construction are more conspicuous than in previous boom and bust cycles. As the construction industry has become dependent on private development, recessions have tended to produce higher levels of unemployment because of lack of public development projects that once helped to maintain the construction industry during economic recessions. From July 1971 to February 1978 more than half of all construction workers lost their jobs as employment dropped from 118,000 to a low of 57,500. From January 1976 to August 1978 construction employment remained below 70,000. Construction employment recovered during the 1980s building boom, reaching a record high of nearly 126,000 in September 1989, one month before the October stock market crash.

The emphasis on luxury residential construction at the expense of public housing development has also contributed to the higher levels of unemployment in the industry. As the New York economy declined in the late 1980s and early 1990s, reduced demand for luxury apartments and private offices pushed up unemployment in the construction industry. Construction employment bottomed out again in the early 1990s, reaching a low of 78,700 in February 1993, the lowest level of employment in the industry since the fiscal crisis 12 years earlier. New York City's comparatively high-wage construction sector now generates less employment than in all but one of the ten largest cities in the nation.[44]

In some ways, surprisingly, the cyclical patterns of employment of construction workers have a more devastating impact on labor than does the steady decline in manufacturing jobs. While construction workers usually remain tied to their industry during recessions, plant closures in manufacturing permanently displace workers. Unemployed manufacturing workers rarely find jobs in their industry. Most find jobs in other semiskilled and unskilled industries or relocate to new areas in search of employment. As a consequence of adjustments to the gradual but steady decline in manufacturing employment, unemployment rates among manufacturing workers are generally lower than among construction workers. Even though manufacturing employment fell by over 750,000 between 1950 and 1990, unemployment was considerably higher in construction than manufacturing. The 1992 annual average unemployment rate stood at 27.3 percent among New York's construction workers, almost double the 14.4 percent unemployment among New York's manufacturing workers.[45] Workers employed in manufacturing must confront unpredictable closures at small and medium-sized plants in disparate locations, but construction workers frequently lose jobs in huge waves. Even during good times, the construction industry is plagued with seasonal waves of unemployment associated with the ordinary short-term nature of employment contracts, and weather and climate factors that interrupt work. These discontinuities in employment compound the problem of maintaining full-time year-round work.[46] In the building boom year of 1988, construction employment fluctuated from a low of 113,100 to a high of 125,900 employed workers, a change of 10.2 percent.[47]

## Building Trades Union Power in New York City

The building trades industry is organized on the basis of local craft unions that maintain control over entry into the trade and refer members to jobs with building contractors. Local craft unions operate their affairs autonomously and represent workers in specific construction trades. The organization of unions on the basis of craft places barriers on collective action in the face of severe fluctuations in employment and unemployment that characterize the industry.

The primary function of building trade unions is to maintain control over the labor market for construction workers and provide employment security for members. Fragmentation of construction craft unions narrows the ability of trade unions to control the labor market. And high and persistent levels of unemployment both weaken the organizational power of trade unions in collective bargaining and endanger the legitimacy of union leadership, who are expected to maintain job security in the industry. A recent study of construction union leadership by Mark Silver demonstrates their most important concern to be keeping members employed on a consistent basis.[48]

> [M]ost [union leaders] see their ability to stay in elected office as largely contingent on their success in placing members on jobs, distributing employment opportunities and keeping overall unemployment at an acceptable level (or at least giving the impression of doing everything possible to do so). In other words, the primary focus of union activity is the reduction of unemployment.

Yet, although employment security is one of their primary objectives, construction unions find it difficult to control unemployment during economic recessions. Building trade jurisdiction and laws that prohibit trade unions in different crafts from coordinating their activities restricts the capacity of local unions to protect their membership and reduce industry unemployment through joint action.[49]

### Employment Discrimination in the Building Trades

A primary feature of the New York construction industry is exclusion of nonwhite workers. Even with the implementation of civil rights legislation in the 1960s to alleviate employment discrimination, black and Hispanic workers have been excluded from the industry. Indeed, black employment in construction has actually declined in New York since the 1960s.[50] Bailey and Waldinger argue that the inability of black workers to penetrate construction in New York City results from institutional barriers that restrict black and other minorities access to the industry. These barriers are often connected to the unions themselves. Trade union control over the informal relationships governing entry into the construction trade limits job opportunities for black workers. And as Silver argues, discrimination against minority workers is aggravated by perpetually unstable conditions of employment in construction.[51] Building trade unions' attempt to exercise market control and reduce unemployment for their working membership leads to the exclusion of minorities who are trying to break in to the industry.

### SERVICE SECTOR: ABUNDANT JOBS AT LOW PAY

The growth in New York City's service economy from the 1950s through the 1990s has more or less coincided with the rapid decline in manufacturing employment. Service sector employment increased in New York City from over 500,000 jobs in 1950 to over 1.15 million jobs in 1993, a gain of 56.5 percent. The trend in New York, in fact, has been more extreme than in other major U.S. cities. As Bailey and Waldinger explain, "in New York the rise of services took place earlier, and the shift away from goods production was more far-reaching than elsewhere in the country."[52]

While service jobs have replaced a large share of the jobs lost in manufacturing during the 1970s and 1980s, service sector workers have not maintained comparable wage levels. An analysis of service employment in New York demands sketching the differences in compensation between public and private sector service jobs. Private sector employment is dominated by clerical labor, where compensation and benefits are significantly lower than in jobs in health, education, and social services. In addition, employment security is no longer a certainty in the private sector. There is evidence that the severe job losses experienced during the 1980s in manufacturing are being replicated in the 1990s in service occupations as firms seek to cut redundant white-collar workers.[53]

Employment stratification is an important feature of the service sector. A substantial share of the growth in white-collar service jobs has occurred in the higher skilled and better paid occupations that tend to be nonunionized. Between 1970 and 1980 managerial employment in New York increased by 27.7 percent to nearly 275,000 workers, and employment among professionals increased by 16.6 percent to over 457,000.

Yet while service employment has increased as a whole by a modest 5.8 percent to 329,000, clerical employment has actually declined during the 1970s by 6.2 percent to 566,000. Despite the received wisdom that the service sector is a source of jobs, there is evidence that entry level and subordinate jobs in white collar sales and clerical occupations that employ large numbers of women and minorities has grown much more slowly than jobs in finance or business services.[54] Contrary to the popular myth of rapid job growth among white-collar workers, service sector jobs are not a bastion of employment growth for new, lower-skilled workers entering the labor force as was manufacturing employment until the 1960s.

### Service Sector: Numerous Workers—Scarce Unions

With the exception of some workers employed in proprietary hospitals, private universities, and non-profit institutions, private industry service sector workers are typically not represented by trade unions. Less than 15 percent of New York State's service workers, in fact, are unionized. These few are represented by the local trade union affiliates of the autoworkers, teamsters, hotel and restaurant workers, and hospital workers. The nonunion jobs of the other 85 percent or so tend to pay relatively low wages and benefits and do not provide the job security that is available in public sector service jobs and unionized manufacturing employment.

As a result, what worker organizations there are in the service sector are notoriously weak. Rigid employer opposition to trade unions is a significant obstacle to service sector organizing, which tends to be limited to nonprofit sectors—hospitals, universities, voluntary organizations, and cultural institutions. Drives to unionize in the expanding for-profit service sector (which includes restaurants, cafeterias, hotels, private clubs, and supermarkets) have met with firm employer resistance and evasive tactics, like the subcontracting of services, which makes it difficult for unions to target employers.[55] Moreover, low density of trade union membership in the services, both public and private, weakens bargaining power with management and contributes to organized labor's shortcomings in accelerating wage growth. The dearth of bargaining power in the service trades translates into substantial employer opposition and intensified labor conflict during collective bargaining with management.[56]

## GOVERNMENT JOBS: GOOD JOBS AT RISK

Public sector jobs have been threatened frequently during economic recessions, when city and state revenue shortfalls have destabilized the city's finances. Employment in the public sector tends to follow patterns of expansion and contraction in the regional economy showing a trend similar to that of employment in construction and service industries.

Uninterrupted municipal job growth from the end of the Second World War came to an abrupt end in the 1975 fiscal crisis. In the aftermath, trade unions representing public sector workers agreed to wage restraint in exchange for job security for their working members, and local government restraints were initiated in both wage and job growth.[57] As a result, there are fewer labor market protections for unemployed public sector workers. As financial and real estate speculation fueled the New York City economic recovery during the 1980s, tax revenues increased and public sector employment recovered. After declining 21.5 percent from 1975 through 1983, municipal employment increased 22.5 percent to 238,000 between 1983 and 1989.[58] With the stabilization of government employment in the 1980s (interrupted occasionally by intermittent recessions) the size of the municipal government budget had expanded significantly. In constant 1982 dollars, New York City spent over $21 billion in 1990, compared to under $8.6 billion in 1961. City expenditures declined from $21.1 billion in 1975 to $16.5 billion in 1983, before rising back to spending levels approaching the period prior to the mid-1970s fiscal crisis.[59] Public sector job security was again imperiled in the 1990s in the wake of the deep regional recession that followed the October 1987 stock market crash. As a consequence, public sector service jobs that once offered greater job security than private sector service jobs have been threatened. Cyclical downturns in the private economy have depressed New York City's revenue base, producing layoffs and hiring freezes in municipal government.[60]

These changes in public sector occupational stability have had dire consequences for black workers who have relied on government jobs more than most groups. Employment segmentation and job discrimination in private industry have restricted entry into growing industries of the core economy, forcing many black workers to rely on government and public jobs as a primary source of employment. Black workers excluded from well paying service jobs have tended to rely on government employment. Twenty-eight percent of black workers, in fact, are employed in government services, which employ only 18 percent of the work force as a whole.

Although a larger proportion of black workers are employed in government jobs than in other sectors of the economy, many of these workers have formed a disproportionate share of unskilled and low-wage employees with less job security in the public sector itself. Black and Hispanic workers accounted for 42 percent of workers employed in New York City agencies in 1982, while they comprised 80 percent of city workers earning below $20,000 a year.[61] The wage disparity among black, Hispanic and white city employees is built on a system of racial and ethnic segmentation of employment within municipal city agencies. White workers tend to be employed in uniformed services (police, fire, and sanitation) and black and Hispanic workers in low-wage civilian agencies (social services, transportation, parks and recreation, health, education, and general services).[62] Secular decline in manufacturing and frequent cyclical swings in public sector employment have made minority, immigrant, and female workers prone to high levels of unemployment during economic recessions in New York City. Municipal job cutbacks have disproportionate effects on black workers, who tend to be employed in civilian services more vulnerable to layoffs than uniformed services.[63] These labor market obstacles for unskilled and minority workers present serious political and economic problems for public sector trade unions.

**Recessions, City Budgets, and Declining Trade Union Power**

Despite the chronic underrepresentation by unions of service workers in general, the public sector (dominated by service workers) was the primary source of trade union growth in New York City from the 1950s to the 1970s. And even as unionization in other sectors of the economy declined, public sector union growth continued unabated through the mid-1970s. The bulk of trade union growth can be attributed to increasing numbers of semiskilled and unskilled low-income service workers in public hospitals, social services providers, and recreation agencies who were seeking improved working conditions and higher wages through their unions. In just over 15 years public sector trade union membership in the United States swelled from slightly over 1 million in 1960 to over 3 million in 1976, accounting for over 80 percent of all trade union growth in the nation during the 1960s and 1970s.[64] Even these national trends do not match those in New York, where public sector union growth has been still greater. Trade union density among New York City government workers is now far greater than any sector of the economy. About 94 percent of the 326,000 persons employed by New York City on a full-time basis are represented by a union—a figure far higher than the 57 percent density rate among government workers in New York State and the 37 percent government sector density rate in the U.S. Civilian workers represent 81 percent (about 265,000) of all full-time public sector employees. District Council 37 of the American Federation of State, County and Municipal Workers (DC 37) and the United Federation of Teachers represents about 77 percent, or 204,000 of all civilian employees in New York City. DC 37, the largest municipal union in New York, represents about 130,000 workers.

Municipal trade unions, however, have considerably weakened in response to government austerity from the mid-1970s to the mid-1990s. Their activism in the 1960s and 1970s was followed by a period of conciliation, particularly in the aftermath of the New York City fiscal crisis. Leaderships once willing to organize the rank and file into demonstrations, petition drives and strikes, became increasingly moderate and accommodating to city government officials after city authorities officially recognized them. Maier argues that New York City government officials favored collective bargaining with experienced bureaucrats from large trade unions to bargaining with militant local union leaders or dealing directly with municipal workers. City officials considered these bureaucrats to be more capable of moderating the demands of trade union membership than local leaders.[65] In addition, Maier points out that the city recognized trade unions that were the largest and least democratic. City officials who supervised labor relations agreed on citywide contracts with large trade union organizations that had weaker connections to rank-and-file membership rather than negotiate with independent locals under democratic control.[66]

Since the 1960s, the relatively amicable negotiation of citywide contracts has been facilitated by the expansion of larger unions like American Federation of State County and Municipal Employees District Council 37 (DC 37) that represent large numbers of municipal workers and tend to be relatively indifferent to local union affairs. While many of the local unions affiliated with DC 37 conduct open forums with active participation by large numbers of members, important decisions and collective bargaining strategies that affect citywide contracts are decided by the parent union's executive director and staff. Union structure in DC 37 is antithetical to democratic rank-and-file participation and local control, so the process of collective bargaining is expedited through citywide negotiations (See chapter 3).

## CONCLUSION

This examination of the New York economy has shown how labor markets bear on worker and union power. On the whole, manufacturing production has deteriorated markedly, and construction has undergone bouts of growth and decline associated with seasonal and cyclical trends. While the service sector has expanded, it is fragmented into skilled and unskilled jobs and therefore has not replaced the high wage unskilled jobs lost in manufacturing. The government sector does not provide a dependable reservoir of decent jobs for minority workers, who form the largest segment of the working poor in New York City, and who can no longer rely on the manufacturing industry as they did in the 1950s and 1960s.

These problems in the labor market have tended to preserve the segregation of the labor market on the basis of race. The proportion of white workers in New York City to that of black and Hispanics in the two decades since 1970 has declined. But since black and Hispanic workers are concentrated in low-wage occupations and industries, they have not reaped advantages from the population shift. Labor market discrimination confines black and Hispanic workers to low-paying jobs in declining sectors of the economy, and these sectors offer few opportunities for advancement. Black workers have gravitated to the public sector where they have found low-wage employment niches in the civilian services that have little job security. Hispanic workers have disproportionately depended on work in low-paying jobs in nondurable manufacturing and services.

These changes in the local economy have tested the political and economic power of trade unions. Disappearance of manufacturing in New York City has virtually eliminated a primary source of union jobs for the unskilled working poor. Construction jobs remain dependent on the capricious nature of the local economy and the maintenance of union arrangements that dispense jobs to a core of favored white male workers. Concentration on luxury building at the expense of middle-income development has intensified job competition and increased minority unemployment in the building trades. The shift to a service-oriented economy has produced large numbers of high-paying professional jobs and even larger numbers of unstable part-time and temporary jobs, representing significant impediments on trade union organization. Government employment has provided a route to secure and dependable trade union jobs for the working poor, but recurrent state and municipal revenue deficits since the 1970s have exposed the limits of job growth in the public sector.

As will become obvious, unions confront the resulting explosion of unemployment in a number of ways. The abandonment of New York City by manufacturing firms has forced many unions in this sector to cut off all ties to their unemployed. Trade unions representing manufacturing workers have increasingly participated in efforts at industrial retention as a means of safeguarding jobs. It is true that textile workers who experience periodic seasonal unemployment continue to maintain association with their unions. But when apparel and textile manufacturers close or move their facilities, unions permanently sever ties to these workers. Conversely, building trades unions are compelled to maintain relations with their rank-and-file membership over longer duration's of economic recession, since the unstable nature of the industry forces unions to maintain hiring halls for their unemployed construction members seeking these high-wage jobs. But such unions often try to minimize unemployment by restricting the size of the labor market. Thus as the demand for construction workers contracts, building trades unions have recruited fewer apprentices and trainees, blocking entry of minority workers into the industry.

Such strategies can claim, at best, limited and temporary success in shoring up their bargaining power. There is no escaping the fact that high and rising unemployment resulting from labor market changes in manufacturing, construction, services, and government has undermined unions in collective bargaining and organizing. High and rising unemployment has further crippled the ability of unions representing workers with few skills to maintain and expand their positions. Indeed unions in all sectors of the economy now find themselves negotiating primarily over job security.[67] Such problems suggests the need to focus attention on how individual unions respond to unemployment, both in tranquil and chaotic times, and how and in what forms unions attempt to join together in coalitions to expand their power, the subject of the chapters that follow.

For trade unions, then, confronting the reality of industrial mobility, technological development, and rapid economic changes in the local and national economy means, in large measure, confronting the problem of unemployment. How do trade unions manage dissension that arises from layoffs and plant closures? What are the methods that trade unions use in confronting seasonal, cyclical, and long-term unemployment? What efforts, if any, are used by labor unions to minimize the impact of unemployment in their industries when joblessness reaches crisis levels? How do union officials' efforts to minimize differences by mobilizing marginal workers lead to internal conflict? And how should labor unions maintain their labor market power in a rapidly shifting economy? These are the complex questions that unions face in today's labor market. They require a specific understanding of the trade union actors in labor markets in various sectors of the economy. What follows in chapter 4, therefore, is an examination and critique on a case by case basis of the procedures with which trade unions representing each of the four economic sectors examined here respond to the problem of unemployment.

**NOTES**

1. See Peter Krugman, *The Age of Diminished Expectations: U.S. Economic Policy in the 1990s*, Cambridge, Massachusetts: The MIT Press, 1992, 27-34.

2. For an analysis of declining wages and employment among less-skilled male workers and its impact on trade unions, see Gary Burtless (ed.) *A Future of Lousy Jobs* Washington, D.C., The Brookings Institution, 1990, 4-12.

3. For analyses of the structural transformation of the American economy and its effect on employment, unemployment, and productivity see Barry Bluestone and Bennett Harrison, *The Deindustrialization of America: Plant Closings, Community Abandonment, and the Dismantling of Basic Industry* (New York: Basic Books, 1982); Sar Levitan and Isaac Shapiro, *Working But Poor: America's Contradiction* (Baltimore: Johns Hopkins Press, 1987); Bennett Harrison and Barry Bluestone, *The Great U-Turn: Corporate Restructuring and the Polarizing of America*, (New York: Basic Books, 1990); and Robert Reich, *The Work of Nations*, (New York: Vintage, 1991).

4. Burtless, 12.

5. There are a number of recent accounts that ascribe the dismantling of New York's manufacturing base to city planners, political officials, and speculators who were determined to transform the diversified economy to one dominated by finance and real estate. Drawing on Rockefeller family archives, Robert Fitch contends that the dismantling of the city's manufacturing industries was orchestrated by a financial and real estate elite whose goals were to increase land values by replacing low-rent housing and factories with high-rent professional and office buildings. See *The Assassination of New York*, New York: Verso, 1993.

6. Uchitelle, Louis, "Job Extinction Evolving Into a Fact of Life in U.S." *The New York Times*, March 22, 1994.

7. From 1950 to 1970, employment in New York City lingered in the range of 3.6 million workers, reaching a high of 3.8 million in June 1969. In the early 1970s, hundreds of thousands of manufacturing jobs in the city were permanently lost in mass layoffs and plant closures.

8. Gordon Lafer, "Minority Unemployment, Labor Market Segmentation, and the Failure of Job-Training Policy in New York City, *Urban Affairs Quarterly*, Vol., 28, No. 2, December 1992. Lafer, an urban economist, estimates there were roughly 67,000 annual job openings for 1.5 million New York job seekers in 1989.

9. U.S. Department of Labor, Bureau of Labor Statistics, Middle Atlantic Regional Office, unpublished data, 1994.

10. Though its industry was comprised of small and medium-sized shops, the New York manufacturing industry dominated the U.S. economy. In the early twentieth century, New York's manufacturing workers comprised

about 15 percent of all production workers in the nation. Most of these workers were employed in apparel shops that usually had fewer than 10 employees. See Melvyn Dubofsky. *When Workers Organize* (Amherst, Massachusetts: University of Massachusetts Press, 1968).

11. United States Department of Labor, Bureau of Labor Statistics, *Employment and Earnings, States and Areas*, (Washington, D.C., 1993). Durable goods production is concentrated in apparel, electronics, furniture and fixtures, footwear, chemicals, newspapers, publishing, printing and communications equipment. Food processing, beverages, bakery products, preserved fruit and vegetables, and dairy products dominate nondurable goods production.

12. Sassen, Saskia, "The Informal Economy," Mollenkopf, John and Manuel Castells, eds., *Dual City: Restructuring New York* (New York: Russell Sage Foundation, 1991).

13. Derived from Sassen, and *New York State 1991-1992 County Profiles*, Albany, N.Y.: New York State Bureau of Economic and Demographic Information, 1993.

14. Fitch, Robert *The Assassination of New York*. (New York: Verso, 1993), 28.

15. New York State Department of Economic Development. *New York State 1991-92 County Profiles*, (Albany, N.Y.: Bureau of Economic and Demographic Information, 1993). During the 1980s, manufacturing employment declined by 35 percent in Brooklyn and the Bronx, and by 25 percent in Queens. Also see Richard Harris, "The Geography of Employment and Residence in New York Since, 1950," in Mollenkopf, John and Manuel Castells, *Dual City: Restructuring New York*, (New York: Russell Sage Foundation, 1991), 132.

16. Drennan, Matthew P., "Local Economy and Local Revenues," in Brecher, Charles, and Raymond D. Horton, eds.,. *Setting Municipal Priorities*, 1988 (New York: New York University Press, 1987).

17. Bureau of Labor Statistics, Northeast Regional Office, New York, 1994.

18. Derived from U.S. Department of Labor, *Handbook of Labor Statistics* (Washington, DC: Bureau of Labor Statistics, August 1989), 290-291; U.S. Department of Labor, Employment and Earnings (Washington, DC: Bureau of Labor Statistics, November 1993); U.S. Department of Labor, unpublished data, (New York: Bureau of Labor Statistics, March 1994.

19. Bailey and Waldinger, in Mollenkopf, John and Manuel Castells. *Dual City: Restructuring New York*, New York: The Sage Foundation, 1993.

20. Stafford 1985, 58.

21. Stafford 1985, 68

22. Over 100,000 of 350,000 nondurable manufacturing jobs were lost in New York City during the 1980s, a decline of 28.8 percent while 57,013 of 144,629 durable manufacturing jobs disappeared, representing a steeper 39.4 percent decline during the decade. Bureau of Economic and Demographic Information. One of the few remaining large nondurable-manufacturing facilities is a Domino Sugar plant located on the Brooklyn waterfront. Domino is a subsidiary of the British Tate and Lyle Conglomerate.

23. See Bailey and Waldinger, in Mollenkopf, John and Manuel Castells 1993, 43-78. Stafford, 1985, demonstrates that black and Hispanic workers are concentrated in the lower skill and income categories of their occupations.

24. A Bureau of Labor Statistics showed that, in May 1994, most of the newly created service sector jobs created in the postindustrial economy for unskilled and semiskilled workers (clerical, nursing assistants, security guards, and material handling laborers, truck drivers) paid considerably lower wages than manufacturing and professional workers. See U.S. Department of Labor, Bureau of Labor Statistics. *Occupational Compensation Survey: Pay Only, New York, New York Metropolitan Area. May 1994*, Bulletin 3075-16, November, 1994.

25. U.S. Department of Labor, Bureau of Labor Statistics, *Employment and Earnings*, January 1994.

26. U.S. Department of Labor, Bureau of Labor Statistics, *Geographic Profile of Employment and Unemployment, 1992*, Bulletin 2428, July 1993. The average annual unemployment rate in New York City was 9.8 percent among white males, 16.8 percent among black males and 16.5 percent among Hispanic males. Unemployment averaged 8.0 percent among white women, 11.1 percent among black women and 13.2 percent among Hispanic women. The official rate of unemployment does not account for discouraged workers who have dropped out of the labor market and part-time and contingent workers who are employed on a seasonal basis. Black and Hispanic workers experience lower levels of civilian labor force participation than white workers, in addition to their consistently higher rates of unemployment.

27. Terry J. Rosenberg, *Poverty in New York City, 1993: An Update*, New York: Community Service Society of New York, 1994. The report finds that the rise in poverty results from declining labor force participation among all racial categories. In March 1993, Hispanic women had the lowest labor force participation among all groups and Hispanic men and women had the highest unemployment rates among all groups in the labor force. The report also found that New York City's population living below the poverty line

increased from 20.2 percent (1.39 million) in 1979 to 23.9 percent (1.65 million) in 1992. In 1992, the poverty rate was 12.3 percent among Non-Hispanic whites; 32.7 percent among Non-Hispanic blacks; and 39.9 percent among Hispanics.

28. Walter Stafford, *Closed Labor Markets: Underrepresentation of Blacks, Hispanics and Women in New York's Core Industries and Jobs*, (New York: Community Service Society of New York, 1985).

29. In the 20 industries that generated the largest number of jobs between 1978 and 1982, Stafford found that whites were 61 percent of the nonsupervisory workers, blacks 24 percent, and Hispanics 12 percent. Moreover, the study found that nonsupervisory jobs held by blacks and Hispanics in the private sector declined from 72 percent to 69 percent of the labor market from 1978 to 1982, reducing employment opportunities to workers entering the labor market. See Stafford 1985, vii-viii.

30. Stafford 1985, ix

31. Lafer, 221.

32. For a recent examination of the growth of the contingent labor force, see Virginia L. duRivage, ed. *New Policies for the Part-Time and Contingent Workforce.* (Armonk, NY: M.E. Sharpe/Economic Policy Institute, 1992).

33. See Sherri Grasmuck, "Immigration, Ethnic Stratification, and Native Working Class Discipline: Comparisons of Documented and Undocumented Dominicans," *International Migration Review*, Vol. 18(3), Fall 1984. According to Grasmuck, one of the primary functions served by undocumented workers from the Dominican Republic in New York is to insure the greater controllability by employers in the secondary labor market.

34. Lafer contends, moreover, that the scarcity of skilled and unskilled jobs limits the feasibility of most public policy proposals for worker education and retraining.

35. District Council 65 of the United Auto Workers was forced into insolvency in the early 1990s as a result of the default of its health insurance plan.

36. See Strauss, George and Daniel G. Gallagher, and Jack Fiorito. *The State of the Unions.* (Madison, Wisconsin: Industrial Relations Research Association, 1991). In New York City, rumors abound about possible mergers that would unite manufacturing unions battered by industrial closures and mass layoffs.

37. Derived from New York State Department of Labor, Division of Research and Statistics, 1970-1994.

38. It is true that, while unionized mass production in those areas has virtually disappeared in New York, specialty shops and production facilities

serving the fashion and publishing industries remain. But workers employed in these specialty industries typically have higher skill levels than workers employed in larger manufacturing facilities.

39. See Chapter 4 for an analysis of the responses of The Amalgamated Clothing and Textile Workers Union to unemployment in the apparel and textile industry.

40. *Employment and Earnings*, Volume 39, No. 1, 228-231, Bureau of Labor Statistics, U.S. Department of Labor (January 1992). National union membership data is for 1991.

41. See for example New York Joint Board activities in *Report of General Executive Board, ACTWU*, Sixth Constitutional Convention, Las Vegas, Nevada, June 7-10, 1993, describing efforts to assist in the modernization of shops to help them remain competitive. ACTWU reports that the union seeks to help employers obtain grants from the state and federal government to upgrade their plants.

42. The 1935 National Labor Relations Act that granted recognition to trade unions as representatives of workers legally circumscribed the ability of unions to engage in strike action. David Brody describes the operation of the system of workplace rights collective bargaining, grievances, and arbitration as the regime of *workplace contractualism*, which lasted from the late-1940s to the late 1960s. Brody contends that the system of workplace contractualism was determined by the nature of mass production industries and the legal system, which sought to establish order in labor-management relations. The Wagner Act forced trade unions to agree to abide by the terms of the contract in exchange for recognition by management. The no-lockout and no-strike clauses of contracts binds management and trade unions to accept the grievance and arbitration process as a means to settle labor disputes. See "Workplace Contractualism: A Historical/ Comparative Analysis," in Brody, *In Labor's Cause* (New York, Oxford University Press, 1993), 221-250.

43. The limitations placed on trade unions to engage in strikes and other forms of collective action during the 1930s and 1940s now also compromise their ability to confront management. In cities like New York, where the shift from manufacturing has ravaged the market power of labor, trade union action is particularly constrained.

44. Fitch, 261-263 and Appendix 14. Depending on the industry and seasonal unemployment, full time construction workers can expect to earn from $30,000 to $150,000 a year.

45. Geographic Profile of Employment and Unemployment, 1992, Bureau of Labor Statistics, July 1993, 125.

46. Bailey and Waldinger 1991.

47. Unpublished data, U.S. Department of Labor, Bureau of Labor Statistics, 1994.

48. Silver, Mark L. *Under Construction: Work and Alienation in the Building Trades.* (Albany, N.Y.: State University of New York Press, 1986).

49. Silver, 35.

50. Waldinger, Roger and Thomas Bailey. "The Continuing Significance of Race: Racial Conflict and Racial Discrimination in Construction," *Politics & Society*, 19, no. 3, September 1991.

51. Silver 1986.

52. Bailey and Waldinger 1993, 43.

53. Uchitelle, *New York Times*, March 22, 1994, D5

54. Bailey and Waldinger, in Mollenkopf, John and Manuel Castells, ed., *Dual City: Restructuring New York*, 1992, 52.

55. For example, there is frequent resistance to organizing in the food service, and lodging industries. In addition, even in union shops, employers frequently try to restrain wage gains in collective bargaining with trade unions. The Hotel and Restaurant Workers Local 6 strike against the Harvard Club in New York City that began in 1994 and 1995 is an example of management trying to increase work responsibility, reduce employee benefits, and job security for semiskilled and unskilled food service workers.

56. Examples of the weak labor market position of unionized service sector workers can be seen in the recent contract negotiations between unions and private universities, wherein trade unions have often resorted to the strike threat in order to exact concessions from management. During the early-1990s unions representing university clerical employees (Columbia University and New York University) have failed to make significant wage and benefit gains. Interview, Joel Lefebvre, Teamsters Local 840, a union that represents clerical workers, July 1991. In New York City's public and private hospitals, unions have had limited success in their efforts to trade off job security for income and benefit gains. See Gale Scott, "Hospital Unions Plan to Sue Over Layoffs, *New York Newsday*, October 27, 1994.

57. CETA (Comprehensive Employment and Training Act), produced federal jobs programs that provided a buffer for municipal government layoffs in the 1970s. President Reagan replaced CETA in the early 1980s with private sector employment programs under JTPA (Jobs Training Partnership Act), which had minimal impact on the labor market.

58. Brecher and Horton 36.

59. Brecher and Horton, The growth in the municipal budget accompanied the stabilization and modest growth of labor costs. In 1982 constant dollars, average city employee wages declined 1.5 percent from

$27,448 in 1975 to $27,035 in 1983 before rising 12.4 percent to $30,374 in 1989, See 17-45.

60. Bill Schleicher "Severance Pay Agreement," *Public Employee Press*, April 8, 1994. Mayor Giuliani's plan to lay off city workers resulted in municipal unions agreeing to a voluntary severance payment plan that would cut the city payroll by 9,500 workers in March 1994. In September 1994, the New York City Health and Hospitals Corporation announced plans to lay off 3,000 employees, severely diminishing wage growth in the industry, see Melinda Henneberger, "Lessons from Health and Hospitals' Unions," *New York Times*, September 26, 1994.

61. Stafford 1985.

62. Even as black and Hispanic workers have had greater access to city jobs that they have failed to make significant gains in salary between 1975 and 1986. Stafford concludes that the inequity in salary results from exclusion of blacks and Hispanics from skilled craft jobs, which pay significantly higher wages. See Stafford, 1989, 33-41.

63. Mark Maier. *City Unions: Managing Discontent in New York*, (New Brunswick, NJ: Rutgers University Press, 1987). See chapter 11 on union responses to the New York fiscal crisis.

64. Maier, 8-9

65. Collective bargaining in New York City has followed a protocol of pattern bargaining, under which civilian employees receive wage increases that are usually slightly lower than that received by uniformed employees. Since the fiscal crisis of the 1970s civilian and uniformed unions tended to bargain jointly through a system of coalition bargaining. Starting in 1988, the pattern of coalition bargaining broke down. For a discussion of municipal wage policy see chapter 12 of Brecher and Horton 1993.

66. The introduction of citywide collective bargaining law in 1968 forced the Social Services Employees Union (SSEU), to reaffiliate with Local 371 of DC 37. The new collective bargaining scheme introduced by the New York City Office of Collective Bargaining made it considerably more difficult for more militant unions like SSEU to negotiate independent contracts governing citywide issues. For a discussion of social service workers in New York see Maier chapter 5 (57-76).

67. Melinda Henneberger, "Lessons from Health of Hospital's Unions," *New York Times*, September 26, 1994. Facing threats to lay off workers, Denis Rivera, president of Local 1199, which represents workers employed in private hospitals, has traded wage increases for job security guarantees.

# CHAPTER 4

# Trade Unions and the Unemployed: From Formal Responses to Crisis Management

This chapter will compare and analyze unemployment policies of four unions who function in four different occupational sectors in New York City. Established union policy will be reviewed for each union, both toward normal levels of unemployment and responses to crisis situations. All unions chosen for study were active in organizing the unemployed and/or developing strategies in response to the growth of unemployment in the early 1990s.

A comparative analysis of trade union responses to unemployment in both ordinary and crisis periods shows how union actions vary as economic and political factors affect their organizational stability in various occupational labor markets. Understanding the different methods unions use in the face of normal unemployment levels will help account for responses during crisis periods by clarifying the often conflicting interests of unions and the workers they seek to protect, including those with the least seniority who are most threatened by layoffs. In crisis situations, such as the economic downturn in New York City in the early 1990s, unemployment escalates beyond anticipated ranges and normal safeguards for job retention are besieged.

The differences in union policies toward the unemployed tell us about how leaders' balance the cross pressures of the need to mobilize members to promote union power and the need to maintain organizational stability. On the one hand, workers who retain membership in unions after they are laid off continue to exert pressure on union officials to defend their interests during periods of unemployment. This tends to occur in exclusive unions that represent skilled workers. On the other hand, where members lose their union affiliation upon losing their jobs, union officials have no incentive to risk responding to unemployment. Inclusive unions that disregard the interests of the unemployed tend to represent poorer, less-skilled, minority, immigrant, and women workers. These unions do not respond to unemployment by membership mobilization unless their leaders' credibility is challenged by memberships responding to the pressures of distinct occupational labor markets.

Union policies studied here are from four unions representing four industrial sectors of the economy: service, manufacturing, government, and construction. These unions are the Local 259 of the United Auto Workers (UAW) representing mechanics and auto service workers at midsize and small dealerships in the New York metropolitan area; the Amalgamated Clothing and Textile Workers Union (ACTWU), representing chiefly unskilled labor in the New York City clothing and textile trade, often immigrants, women and people of color who work in relatively small shops for low wages; Local 420 of the Health Care Workers Union (also affiliated with the American Federation of State, County and Municipal Employees (AFSCME) representing hospital workers whose job security depends on municipal budgets; and the International Brotherhood of Electrical Workers, IBEW, Local 3, a trade union in the construction industry representing skilled, well-paid workers whose employment is often seasonal.

Workers represented by these four unions face different unemployment concerns. Seasonal and cyclical unemployment plague both the well-paid members of IBEW and the working poor represented by ACTWU; the deficits in city revenues, which reflect the overall business climate, jeopardize hospital workers jobs and wages, despite increasing demands on individual workers due to increased use of city health services. UAW workers face a permanent unemployment crisis because their industry is disappearing from the local economy in some instances. This is also true of garment workers whose shops are being relocated to areas with fewer restrictions or replaced by illegal sweatshops where employers pay undocumented workers a fraction of the living wages negotiated by ACTWU.

In this study, union responses to three forms of anticipated and unforeseen unemployment will be examined: (1) temporary cyclical and seasonal unemployment within the industry represented by the union; (2) permanent job loss among union members; and (3) permanent job loss among unemployed workers who are not union members. The analyses are based primarily on participation in union efforts to coordinate policies toward the unemployed and interviews conducted with union leaders, labor activists, and trade union observers from 1991 to 1994. In these interviews union and activist leaders were asked to explain action or inaction in connection with unemployment, specific to their unions and within the New York labor market in general. This study begins with an overview of standard responses to unemployment and the situations that arise in the unions from crisis level joblessness.

## STANDARD AND CRISIS RESPONSES TO UNEMPLOYMENT

When unemployment and job loss are at crisis levels, however, seniority referral systems and other union-implemented safeguards designed to minimize the effects of being without work are overwhelmed, and membership demand action by their union leaders. These situations are caused by myriad factors, most of which are beyond the scope of union influence. Unemployment crises, however, do pose a threat to union survival both economically and politically by contributing to in-house skirmishes. Unusually high levels of unemployment, therefore, could compel union leaders to form new policies not only to serve the needs of their membership, but also to maintain their own job security. Crisis responses result when unions can no longer regulate the incidence of unemployment. Facility closures and mass layoffs, for example, usually do not allow unions to designate the members who will lose jobs. Golden argues that unions customarily regulate unemployment by determining which workers will be protected from layoffs. But closings of entire shops obviate this function by depriving unions of the power to choose those members who will keep their jobs.[1] In the building trades industry and other craft unions, where workers have a close attachment to their unions, unemployed workers may pose a significant threat to union leadership, particularly if the unions operate as hiring halls by maintaining an employer referral list.[2] Friction between unions and their members may also result when mass layoffs occur in communities where workers live, as is the case of workers employed in municipal hospitals. In New York's public sector unions, where bonds between unions and their members are nebulous, conflict may be obscured because the rank and file depend less directly on union locals for defending jobs. For example, the far-reaching role of District Council 37 in the collective bargaining and grievance process with the City of New York tends to render union locals representing municipal employees less influential with rank-and-file members.

A comparative examination of four unions in New York City during relatively normal and crisis periods of unemployment will illustrate a variety of union responses to different categories of unemployed workers in and out of their organizations. The case studies empirically show the various ways in which trade unions in different sectors of the regional labor market defend their core members from job loss at the expense of neglecting marginal members and unemployed workers. This examination of four distinct unions in a time of high unemployment refines Golden's hypothesis by qualifying the labor market and organizational differences among them.

## SERVICE SECTOR: LOCAL 259 OF THE UNITED AUTO WORKERS

Local 259 is a small diversified union that predominately represents auto repair workers at dealerships throughout the New York metropolitan region. The union also represents a declining number of industrial workers employed at firms manufacturing components for aircraft, trucks, and automobiles in the same area. For most of its sixty-year history, the union has withstood plant closures and mass layoffs in manufacturing shops by maintaining a strong presence in the primary base of the auto dealerships. Even in the 1970s and 1980s, when the American auto industry declined, Local 259 survived by maintaining a concentrated presence in New York area auto dealerships. Although the U.S. auto industry was battered by declining sales as New York consumers continued to replace American cars with imported vehicles, older American cars were still on the road, requiring repair work. This left UAW member auto mechanics in demand.

In the early 1990s, however, domestic and foreign auto sales declined as the New York economy soured. Dealerships came under pressure to reduce costs and turned to layoffs. Some firms closed or went out of business, and in the process thousands of Local 259 auto mechanics became unemployed. The economic stability of the union was, and continues to be, threatened. From 1990 to 1994 membership declined by 50 percent from about 4,600 to about 2,000. This decline together with declining dues has had a calamitous affect on the union's economic viability and has contributed to cutbacks in union activities. In response to the decrease in funds, the union reduced operating expenses and, in the process, made its own contribution to unemployment with staff cuts through layoffs and attrition.[3] In response to these events, Local 259 has worked alone and with other labor organizations to form strategies for coping with and preventing pervasive unemployment.

Local 259 traces its origins to the industrial labor struggles of the 1930s and openly portrays itself as "militant from the start."[4] The union was organized as a New York local of the United Auto Workers in 1937, a year after major sit-down strikes and picketing by auto workers in Detroit. It originally represented truck and collision shop workers in New York City. Since the late-1930s, Local 259 has attempted to organize low-income auto workers and mechanics concentrated at larger auto dealerships in the region. Even as it began to do so during and after World War II, a substantial share of its largest auto manufacturing shops were converted into military parts factories.

During the 1980s, the union continued to advance a tradition of militancy and social support as key elements in winning organizing drives and contracts negotiation with management. Local 259 maintains that militancy is effective in obtaining settlements from employers, asserting that its past willingness to strike against management has contributed to its success in negotiating contracts beneficial to members, even amid management demands for worker concessions during the national economic recession of the early 1980s.[5] The union contends that this strategy of confrontation with management was successful in negotiating major contracts with auto dealerships and manufacturing firms in the early 1980s.

In fact, Local 259 members used the unemployment insurance system to win a strike against Consolidated Diesel (Con Dec), a military contractor with operations in Greenwich, Connecticut and Schenectady, New York. When Con Dec demanded concessions from the union in February 1982, 300 members of Local 259 went on strike at both plants. The union maintains that a critical moment in the 15-week strike came when strikers in New York State agreed to share their unemployment insurance benefits with strikers in Connecticut, where unemployment insurance is not granted to workers on strike. According to Local 259's account of the labor dispute, striking members at the Schenectady plant voted to send $40 each week from their New York State unemployment benefits to Con Dec strikers in Greenwich. The strike turned the tide against management and helping workers at both plants win a contract substantially superior to the one first offered. Local 259 maintains that the Con Dec victory set the tone for a successful round of negotiations and settlements with their primary employers—the Auto Dealers Association of New York, Cadillac Dealers, and regional manufacturers.[6] Following the Con Dec agreement, the union won a settlement that increased wages 30 percent and doubled welfare benefits at All-O-Matic (an automobile parts manufacturer in Queens), and successfully rebuffed a demand for give-backs by the Auto Dealers Association. Unlike other agreements, Local 259's contract did not establish a two-tier wage system among newer and older workers.

## Standard Responses to Unemployment

Although Local 259 leadership was creative in its use of the unemployment insurance system to challenge management in collective bargaining disputes, layoffs and shop closures continued to be a severe problem in the union's shops. Jobless benefits provide a valuable cushion for unemployed union workers during cyclical layoffs in the auto industry and permanent shop closures. While the union has been unwavering in its support for government jobs programs, worker retraining, and expansion of unemployment insurance, it did little to mobilize the unemployed in support of these social programs prior to the early 1990s, aside from signing on to public appeals and endorsing the expansion of government programs.[7]

Local 259 responds differently to the two typical forms of unemployment encountered by the union: secular layoffs, which result from permanent shop closings, and cyclical unemployment from auto dealerships, which results from recessions in the auto industry. Rank-and-file members who become unemployed due to industrial shop closings routinely lose affiliation with the union, as occurred when manufacturing jobs in New York City disappeared from the 1950s through the early 1990s. However, workers employed at auto dealerships tend to lose their jobs according to seniority lists and skill categories whenever the regional economy goes into recession. Since the union serves as a hiring hall for organized auto dealerships and repair shops, these workers maintain their ties to the union and are usually referred to other dealerships when there are openings for mechanics or parts workers.[8] The Local 259 unemployment referral system is intended to refer those who have been unemployed longest to jobs at auto dealerships first. However, unemployed workers with more advanced technical skills are often most likely to find referrals and jobs.[9] The union's assistance program for unemployed membership is best described as an employment agency where workers call or come in search of work.

The primary mechanism protecting workers is seniority. But when repair shops close permanently, as they did in the most recent recession, workers with differing seniority levels become jobless at the same time and must compete with one another for openings at existing dealerships. In these circumstances, political action in the form of coalition building and demonstration to shore up government supports and directly address the changing economy become necessary. Prior to the recession of the early 1990s, such action was not part of the union's agenda, since union leaders and most members did not see the need for it. That changed during the recession, when extremely high unemployment resulting in a 50 percent reduction in union membership jeopardized the financial stability and viability of the union, along with its bargaining clout with management.

## Unemployed Support Efforts in the Early 1990s

For more than 35 years since he assumed the presidency of Local 259, Sam Meyers has voiced his belief that unemployment in minority, poor, and working-class communities is damaging to the prosperity of the union and its members. Under Meyers' leadership, the union actively participates in trade union and community groups, devising strategies to combat unemployment and its attendant consequences. Meyers participated in national and regional efforts within the United Auto Workers and among progressive unions, and forged alliances with community-based organizations.[10]

During Meyers' tenure as president of Local 259, the union became racially integrated as large numbers of African American and other minority workers replaced white workers who retired. Because the union did not have a legacy of racial discrimination, no opposition emerged, as was the case in some disproportionately white building trade unions. The union represented semi-skilled auto workers in relatively well-paying and secure jobs, so no significant opposition was mounted either in or out of the union.

Meyers says that rising unemployment is continually a source of concern for his union. On a number of occasions, he has said that he approved the notion of organizing the unemployed to support creation and expansion of national and local jobs programs and supported bills to expand government labor market programs protecting the unemployed. "Our unions find it absolutely necessary to bring unemployed people together to see what we can do."[11] In an interview for this book, Meyers said that since his workers are employed at a variety of locations throughout the metropolitan area, it was more difficult to mobilize his members and the unemployed. Although Meyers said his union did not have "one central location," that could draw workers together, he saw the importance of "being a social union" that encourages workers to "help one another."[12] Meyers' said he was "committed to the UAW tradition of social unionism," indicating a concern that extends beyond collective bargaining to job security and the fate of working class communities. He also said that he recognized a responsibility to the rank-and-file membership to protect jobs. Meyers has affirmed these ideas in various public forums. At the United Auto Workers International Convention, for instance, he remarked:

> Brothers and sisters, one of the things that we need to understand is that in this day and age, I remember we used to comment if somebody got laid off in the plant and they left, the first thing they did is blame the union. 'Stinking union, what did it do for me?' We have to come together. . . . [W]e were taught, since I became a member of the UAW's great union 52 years ago, that some of the things we enjoy is by virtue of what we negotiate in contracts. But unless we get together and fight for the proper laws, for the proper kind of representation outside, we'll go down the drain together. Why? Because, brothers and sisters, GM, everybody, they consider us and who we are expendable. I don't see any white coats from the GM bosses. All we hear is that people are going to get knocked out of their jobs. Screw them as I said at the last convention. They should take some of our people, they'll show them how to run a

plant a hell of a lot better than these bastards that are running it now.[13]

At the same convention, Meyers' said that the United Auto Workers should make full employment a primary demand:

> When we say we call upon this and that . . . we should make demands on anybody who seeks to rule us, to say that we want a full employment environment. Who the hell makes these guys, the one percent, better than us? We are entitled to make a living for ourselves and our family and not be expendable, my dear brothers and sisters. We have got to demand . . . Whether it is Clinton—I don't care who it is. When you go through the streets of this country, our people have lost their bargaining power.[14]

Local 259's response to rising unemployment deviated from Meyers' rhetoric about the danger of unemployment to his members. In hopes of beginning to restore this power, Local 259 set in motion several efforts, during the late 1980s and early 1990s, to assist both unionized and nonunionized unemployed. They supported independent organizing efforts to extend federal and state unemployment benefits and create government jobs. A considerable share of this activity was directed by Miriam Thompson, education and political director for the union, who was the union's liaison with other unions and locally based organizations devoted to various kinds of social change.[15] One of her primary interests was developing organizing models to support government jobs programs and unemployment insurance extensions. At a meeting of dissident union officials and unemployed organizers in Philadelphia in December 1990, Thompson enthusiastically supported the idea of forming unemployed action groups modeled on Communist, Socialist, and Musteite organizations of the 1920s and 1930s.

The surge in local and national unemployment during the early 1990s put the notion of unemployed councils on the front burner for Thompson, who believed that making ties with local community groups would be central in developing an effective organizing campaign.[16] As a union official, she knew that Local 259 needed to respond to higher unemployment in the auto industry and at union repair shops. To build coalitions, Thompson allowed participation of other unemployed persons in Local 259-sponsored political events. She helped the New York Unemployed Committee (NYUC) in its own organizing efforts. In 1991 the union lent office space at its union hall in Manhattan to NYUC for telephone outreach when organizing demonstrations of unemployed workers recruited chiefly from unemployment offices. The main goal of the NYUC at this time was to promote and support legislation extending federal unemployment insurance benefits.

Local 259 also extended an invitation to unemployed workers recruited by NYUC to join union members at the Solidarity Day II AFL-CIO rally in Washington, D.C. on August 31, 1991. Jobless workers organized from unemployment offices in Brooklyn by the NYUC were given one of the three buses sent by the union to the Washington, D.C. rally. On the trip to Washington and back to New York, NYUC organizers spoke and distributed information to both Local 259 members and the unemployed recruited from jobless centers.

Continued unemployment in the winter of 1991 prompted Local 259 to discuss forming an independent union-based unemployed organization. Meetings and consultations were held on forming an internal unemployed organization with Sam Meyers, Miriam Thompson, Roberta Shlosko, a social worker and consultant to the union, and the two coordinators of the New York Unemployed Committee. Meyers wanted to demonstrate union support and commitment for unemployed Local 259 members by forming an unemployed organization.

Keith Brooks and I, coordinators of the New York Unemployed Committee from 1990 to 1992, worked with Miriam Thompson and Sam Meyers on a number of coalitions efforts.[17] The NYUC was interested in using Local 259 as a model of union-based unemployed organizing and as a base to recruit members. The first meeting was explorative and concentrated on "how to reach out to Local 259's unemployed."[18] Meyers said he was interested in forming self-help unemployed support groups within the union in what he called a "service model" for assisting the unemployed individually: "You need to look at the individual problems of the unemployed rather than the collective problems."[19] Accordingly, individual worker's problems took priority in the union's attempts to confront the unemployment crisis over the next three years. Undoubtedly, this initial policy was based on a practical understanding of the limited possibilities of collective action. Most likely it was also influenced by fears about cultivating an adversarial force of unemployed members within the union. While Meyers said that "I want to show our members that I care about their unemployment,"[20] the unemployed committees that were formed by the union were rendered largely ineffective as a means of restraining any real or imagined opposition that Meyers believed might emerge from them.

## Local 259's First Round of Unemployed Organizing

The first meeting of Local 259's unemployed workers was held on May 8, 1992, and included only union members laid off from auto dealerships. No distinct effort was made by the union to organize unemployed workers from the union's industrial shops whose jobless were usually permanent.[21] The primary focus of the May 8 meeting was to provide information on individual concerns, including: "retraining and job counseling, as well as survival needs such as unemployment insurance, and mortgage and rent deferments."[22]

This first meeting was attended by some forty unemployed workers, many of whom had lost jobs as a result of shop closures and mass layoffs. Union leaders and NYUC unemployed organizers led the meeting and gave presentations on how to gain access to assistance and service programs and the need for political action. In an address to the unemployed members, Meyers reiterated the union's concern for them, and the willingness of the union to help. Brooks's presentation to the gathering focused on the need for political action to support legislation to extend unemployment benefits.

While some participants expressed appreciation for the union's concern about their joblessness, the union reported that many came to the meeting with the expectation that the union would help them get jobs.[23] Other unemployed auto workers wanted the union to provide services, mainly health insurance and worker retraining, demands the union could not meet on financial reasons. Some meeting attendees questioned the union on its inability to defend their jobs, and other participants expressed grievances about being unfairly laid off. Clearly, individual complaints about unfair dismissals were concerns for the union to address directly with employers, and not functions of an unemployment council composed of activists and social workers.

The union's effort on behalf of the unemployed was limited not only by financial constraints but also by a potential conflict of interest with employers. At the first meeting of the unemployed in May 1991, unemployed workers and NYUC members suggested that the union establish an auto repair shop for the unemployed. A majority of the unemployed workers at the meeting expressed enthusiastic support for the initiative, with some members even offering to assist in the creation of the union-run shop. Meyers, however, rejected the idea because the union shop had the potential to interfere with friendly and cordial relations between union representatives and management, which according to Meyers facilitated collective bargaining. In follow-up meetings of the unemployed organizing team, Meyers warned that employers might object to the union's competing for business with a shop of its own. Many of the participants became angry and raucous and demanded a more focused union response to mass layoffs and long-term unemployment. But the union seemed to tell unemployed workers what they already knew: "unemployment was a serious problem for workers and the union." No union-based action was established other than plans for additional meetings addressing service-oriented topics for unemployed members. The union then planned more focused meetings on designated topics such as job training, resume writing, strategies for job searching, unemployed survival needs, and personal and family counseling.

Unemployed rank and file who came to the meetings quickly realized the union had little to offer other than sympathetic support.[24] One jobless worker from New Jersey who was invited to the union's first meeting angrily derided the union's leaders for failing to maintain his health benefits at a time when his wife was hospitalized with a serious illness. Many other workers communicated their disenchantment with the failure of the union to defend their jobs and wondered out loud how they would support their families when their unemployment insurance benefits ran out. Participation by unemployed union members at subsequent union unemployed meetings dropped steadily from forty to twenty to less than ten. The smaller meetings brought into focus ever-more intensive criticism from unemployed participants, who continued to rail about the union's inability to defend their jobs against management. Some attendees argued that the union needed to take more militant action against employers who unfairly laid them off; two members suggested the union file grievances against an employer—long after they had lost their jobs. The unemployed counselors and organizers running these meetings found that they could not satisfy the participants with Meyers' service approach to organizing the unemployed and became disheartened by the low turnout at the meetings.[25] Even as meeting attendance fell to few participants, the union continued to employ this approach until the meetings were discontinued while the union designed a new strategy.

## Local 259's Second Round of Unemployed Organizing

Prior to the formation of the second unemployed organizing effort, the union surveyed the needs of their unemployed former membership through a questionnaire sent out to more than 100 former union members in early 1993. The results of the survey indicated concern with obtaining jobs and maintaining income support during the search for new work. The union's unemployed members were less interested in information, counseling, and other service oriented programs proposed by the union.[26]

Despite the workers' interest in participating in an unemployed organization that delivered jobs, a second round of unemployed organizing, initiated in early 1993, was based exclusively on a service model of self-help mutual aid. The new organizing drive had more modest goals of demonstrating union concern and, whenever resources allowed, personally assisting the unemployed. This effort was directed by two Local 259 staff members, Roberson and Perry, under the direction of Shlosko and Ness.[27] By August 1993 the new union organizing effort became known as the "Local 259 Unemployed Council."

Helping jobless former members of Local 259 obtain unemployment insurance, welfare benefits, health care, and housing were the primary goals of the Unemployed Council. Council leaders intended to conduct regular meetings of long-term and recently unemployed members, and an "unemployed hotline" was established. One meeting was conducted by the union and attended by about 15 unemployed workers. Few unemployed members called the hotline for help and, with no financial resources allocated by the union for staff and other expenses, the local's unemployed council had difficulty providing even these few support services.[28] Enthusiasm died, meetings of the unemployed council's leadership dwindled in the winter of 1993, and the second unemployed organizing effort of Local 259 was disbanded in March 1994.

## Local 259 Unemployment Policy—What Went Wrong?

Events at Local 259 illustrate an attempt to address high levels of unemployment at an organizational level. They highlight the constraints on response at a union local with limited commitment of financial and organizational resources. They also reflect some confusion on the part of union leadership over what the goals of an unemployed organizational group should be. While Thompson was enthusiastic about directly supporting organization of the unemployed for political action, Meyers seemed motivated by a belief that the union should help its own unemployed workers individually, rather than organizing in such broad action. Leaders seriously considered mobilizing the unemployed but did not develop a practical method of doing so. In short, the union leadership failed to address the problem of unemployment as a whole, choosing instead to pursue a narrower approach by offering a few social services to their own members. Nor did the union mobilize unemployed members to pursue a political agenda that concerned the most vulnerable workers, such as unemployment insurance extensions or a jobs program. As a result the unemployed participants either secured new jobs at auto dealerships (with or without the help of the union) or severed their association with the union.

Thus, while the union displayed a semblance of concern about unemployment and job issues in the early 1990s, much of this concern was expressed through old rhetoric supporting the rights of workers to a job or a source of income. The prospect of absorbing active and angry laid off workers into the union's unemployed organization became a source of concern for Meyers, and was quickly tamed in 1992. While leadership communicated disappointment for the low turnout at meetings, no issue-based organizing drive was promoted that would have expanded participation nor was one discussed seriously, or implemented by the union. While there were no organized adversaries to Meyers's leadership, members of the unemployed committee said that participation was discouraged because of a fear that the unemployed would become a political base for leaders inside and outside of the union.[29]

Organizing unemployed workers for political action was seen as a threat by the entrenched worker-management hierarchy of Local 259, the kind of hierarchy that predominates in industrial unions, particularly, but not exclusively in UAW organizations. While Meyers was abstractly committed to the rhetoric of the old social unionism of the United Auto Workers union during the 1930s, he in fact allocated few resources to its renewal. The possibility of organizing potentially aroused jobless workers was at the very least an irritant to Meyers, but might well have emerged into an effective means for adversaries in the union to challenge his indecisive response to rampant unemployment and declining union power. Consequently, the union emphasized services to individuals rather than collective action on behalf of all workers. Authentic efforts to help unemployed former members in the form of service groups and information regarding access to direct services were further constrained by a limited capacity to implement these programs without financial or staff support. Local 259 may have gone further than most New York unions in supporting its unemployed workers, but its action was confined to displays of support, mobilization without goals, and meetings planned without tangible action. As a result, it remains a union with an uncertain future, jeopardized by a rapidly declining membership.

## MANUFACTURING: AMALGAMATED CLOTHING AND TEXTILE WORKERS UNION

The origins of the Amalgamated Clothing and Textile Workers Union (ACTWU) New York Joint Board can be traced to 1914, when New York City was the production center of the American garment industry.[30] Although garment manufacturing overshadowed other manufacturing industries in New York, textile production consisted primarily of small firms dispersed throughout the city. Such decentralization distinguished industrial development in New York from its counterpart in other major cities, which developed around centralized industrial complexes. According to labor historian Melvyn Dubofsky:

> Nationally, manufacturing firms combined and concentrated their productive facilities and management structures with an accompanying growth in the scale and size of their operations. In New York, the reverse occurred: the number of businesses increased and their size dwindled. In the age of Standard Oil, American Tobacco, and United States Steel, small firms with minimal capital investments carrying on limited production, characterized New York's industrial structure.[31]

Partly as a result of the small scale of manufacturing in New York, firms were unable to withstand economic recessions, leaving workers exposed to frequent layoffs and permanent shop closings. While textile and apparel manufacturing once provided an indispensable source of jobs for New Yorkers with limited skills, these jobs were often intermittent, and job security has been a problem for workers in this field since the turn of the century. Seasonal employment trends in the industry have produced frequent swings from full employment to massive unemployment. Data from 1907 reveals both the commanding position of garment manufacturing in New York and the serious condition of job insecurity produced by the industry. In 1907 unemployment in New York City ranged from 10 percent at the end of June to 34.2 percent at the end of December. In 1913, unemployment reached a high of 46.4 percent at the end of December, averaging 40 percent in the clothing industry.

High and unstable levels of unemployment provoked the garment worker unions to help maintain workers and their families through long periods of joblessness. In 1914, ACTWU introduced the first union-based unemployment insurance program in America that provided benefits to idle workers. ACTWU claims that their union-based jobless benefits program became a model that the federal unemployment insurance system developed two decades later during the Great Depression. "The union developed unemployment insurance as a service to union members and as a model to the country as a whole," according to Nick Unger, ACTWU's political action and education director. Unger suggests that the union's "consciously socialist reformist ideas" were replicated by other unions and later embodied in New Deal legislation.[32] More likely, ACTWU's model social programs reflected the daily economic needs of rank-and-file garment workers afflicted by seasonal patterns of joblessness. When the federal unemployment insurance system was introduced in 1935, the union benefit program was discontinued.[33]

The New York Joint Board of ACTWU continues to represent workers mainly employed in men's clothing production. The majority of union members manufacture men's suits and tuxedos, leather jackets, shirts, ties, and shoes. Other members fit and tailor garments in clothing stores serving primarily wealthy and upscale consumers. The union also represents workers employed in offices and warehouses, and workers who make photo albums and ship Xerox machines.

Globalization of textile production in the post World War II era has exacted a heavy toll on garment workers in the New York City area. Thousands of union organized garment shops have been closed since the early 1950s, and hundreds of thousands of workers have been permanently put out of work throughout the New York region. Job competition has intensified, and the union's ability to control the local labor market for garment workers has been impaired. Unlike most other trades, the garment industry has experienced unremitting unemployment for a 40-year period from 1950 through the early 1990s.

The New York textile industry is a microcosm of the deteriorating state of textile production in the U.S. In New York City, textile mill jobs declined by 67.8 percent from 38,500 to 12,400 workers between 1950 and 1993. Over the same 43-year period, the number of workers employed in apparel and other textile jobs declined by 75.3 percent from 340,700 to 84,000.[34] Nationwide, employment in ACTWU-organized industries declined 12 percent to 1.043 thousand workers from 1980 to 1990. The union anticipates that future employment will drop still further over the next 15-year period. Depending on projections of high, moderate, and low economic growth, ACTWU expected union membership to decline from 17 percent to 36 percent between 1990 and the year 2005.[35] The projected decline reflects an overall expected contraction of the industry, the growth of non-union competition, rising numbers of undocumented workers, and illegal sweatshops.[36]

If unemployment has always been a problem for ACTWU then, it is worse now than in previous generations, when workers lost jobs on a seasonal basis and were then rehired as production demands picked up.[37] Today, unemployment permanently dissociates rank-and-file membership from the union. When garment shops close down they typically never reopen. Although government unemployment insurance still functions as a safeguard for garment workers who become seasonally unemployed, unemployment benefits also temporarily maintain income support for workers rendered permanently unemployed as a result of mass layoffs and shop closures. According to Unger, when a garment factory goes out of business, very few people are reabsorbed into unionized firms, while some go to work in the non-union part of the trade. Very few workers go to work in the underground sweatshop part of the industry, which pays wages and benefits substantially less than the minimum wage.[38]

**ACTWU's Standard Responses to Unemployment**

In response to the bleak secular employment trends in the New York textile industry and the resulting decline in union membership, saving garment plants and union shops is a priority for the union. To prevent garment shops from leaving New York, the union underscores the importance of (1) organizing, (2) industrial retention, and (3) political action as long-term job retention strategies.

The extended pattern of plant closures in the garment industry has made organizing new shops a key element in the union's future viability. Another element in current efforts to organize new workers is the union's use of volunteers drawn from the membership. Volunteers take leaves of absence from their jobs and join organizing campaigns. ACTWU has expanded organizing outside the textile industry into other manufacturing and service industries, and according to the union, some of these campaigns have led to recognition and collective bargaining agreements in the New York area. Along with organizing efforts, the union also stresses the importance of industrial retention of remaining shops, working with employers to maintain competitiveness with non-union shops and non-regional competitors. The union helps employers modernize facilities by securing state and federal grants, and has monitored companies for indications of plant closings or relocations.

Because of ACTWU's weakening labor market position, the union's capacity to challenge management has substantially eroded. However, both organizing and industrial retention policies help management as well as the union. Garment firms whose workers are represented by ACTWU have an interest in the union's organizing new non-union shops, which improve competitiveness. Union support for industrial retention in the garment industry helps encourage New York State economic development authorities to direct resources for plant modernization. According to Unger, the garment industry is short sighted in pursuing short-term profits without interest in the long-term viability of the industry: "Left to their own devices [the garment industry] will behave like laboratory rats. Are we capable of lifting the industry into the real world? They have proven time and time again that they cannot."[39] A third component of the union's strategy to save and expand union jobs in the garment industry is political action through lobbying and campaigning for more favorable conditions for workers. The union lobbies on the local, state, and federal levels to advance economic interests of the textile industry.[40] ACTWU also vigorously supports efforts to advance the broad agenda of organized labor, including universal health care,[41] opposition to the North American Free Trade Agreement, and federal and state investments to create jobs. According to Unger, the union participates in as many as 15 campaigns at a time, strategically calculating the value of each organizing campaign to its members.

The deep economic recession in New York City in the early 1990s encouraged a new round of political action by the union in favor of unemployment benefits. Normally, federal unemployment benefits have been viewed with some ambivalence by the union. While government unemployment insurance benefits cushion ACTWU garment workers during seasonal unemployment, Unger argues that federal unemployment insurance benefits can also be a subsidy for an industry that permits firms to continue to pay their workers substandard wages and provide limited job security. He argues that unemployment insurance benefits inefficient employers at least as much as workers: "Unemployment insurance is a form of welfare for the industry. Workers can get [several] thousand a year from the unemployment insurance system . . . keeping [employers] from paying decent wages. Unemployment insurance is a form of subminimum wage."[42] Despite these criticisms of the industry's misapplication of the unemployment insurance system, the union actively supported extension of government unemployment benefits during the early 1990s recession.

On June 24, 1991, Clayola Brown, a vice president of the international union testified at a field hearing on unemployment insurance chaired by Senator Moynihan of New York.[43] Since many ACTWU members had exhausted their 26 weeks of unemployment benefits when their shops closed down, Brown used the opportunity to stress the importance of extending government benefits beyond 26 weeks.[44] In an appeal to Senator Moynihan, Brown said she "[didn't] have an answer for the operator at Dino Clothing, or the worker at Best Metropolitan Laundry, or the presser at Manhattan Coats. Maybe you should visit them and tell them why their benefits have run out so soon." Despite the overall decline of the garment industry, the recession in New York contributed to larger numbers of unemployed garment workers asking their unions about their unemployment insurance benefits. "Let me share with you a question that all union officials are getting every week these days," said Brown. "'What do I do when my unemployment benefits run out?' This is a new question for most of us."[45]

While Brown viewed the recession as an opportunity to "fix up the unemployment system before more of our members and other people have to suffer," she also stressed the importance of retaining industrial jobs in New York. Extending the length of unemployment insurance benefits was viewed as a means of ameliorating the problem of cyclical job loss to its members, not a formula to shore up the union's power by discouraging unorganized unemployed workers from bargaining down wage rates.

Building coalitions with like-minded progressive unions and community groups is the main form of political action for ACTWU. In the early 1990s the union joined coalitions in support of jobs and unemployment benefits. Under Unger's direction, ACTWU actively participated in the formation and direction of the New York Labor Campaign on Unemployment, an informal *ad hoc* labor-based organization created in spring 1991 (See chapter 6). The New York Labor Campaign on Unemployment demanded an extension of unemployment benefits for workers who had been without jobs beyond the 26-week allotment provided by the federal unemployment benefits system. Unger was a key player in developing political support among progressive unions for the New York campaign. Before the group formed, Unger negotiated the goals and limits of the new labor coalition.[46] In retrospect, he contends that the New York Labor Campaign on Unemployment had its political limits for the union:

> We believe that political action around where we live and work is a decisive effort for any strategy. So when something arises we look at it and ask if this is worth doing—fighting for jobs is our main goal. . . . How much you get involved in a fight over unemployment insurance—which is less a fight for us. Fighting is legitimate but it requires a broader vision.

Although Unger is sympathetic toward the unemployed (as a former unemployed organizer in the 1970s) he believes that organizing the unemployed is not part of ACTWU's strategy of building a strong union. Maintaining direct ties with unemployed former members is:

> highly unrealistic for us [because] we are trying to deal with the question of the fight over jobs inside the workplace. Unions are

trying to deal with the fact that they are losing membership. To maintain ties to unemployed folks? [We] have to consider the goals. Cadre training for what? Organizing the unorganized has been the strategy since the beginning but unions have to think of their goals.[47]

Unger speculates that any serious trade union effort to organize unemployed workers must also have the long-term goal of building a cadre of trade union activists as the Communist Party did in the 1930s. Once the unemployed return to work they would become organizers of the unorganized rank and file:

> So if you look at the models of the 30's, the Musteite direct action model leads to nothing and the Stalinist unemployed council model leads to training organizers for the CIO drives. Because when folks go back to work, these folks go back to work as guerrilla killers. They have honed their skills in the crucible of the street-community unemployed battles and learned a little class relations, political economy, whatever. This is the CP model.[48]

Putting unemployed people back to work was not a realistic goal for trade unions struggling to save jobs in the 1980s and 1990s. While ACTWU considered organizing the unemployed a worthy approach for other organizations, Unger said the union was more interested in defending surviving workers and advocating public sector economic revitalization to create new jobs.

Although support for longer unemployment insurance benefits continued through the early 1990s, the union mainly championed programs designed to retain and increase the number of textile jobs in New York. Again, the primary vehicle for advancing this jobs creation program was through coalition-building with like-minded organizations. The union played a leading role in organizing the Labor Coalition to Rebuild New York, based on a 15-point plan to stimulate manufacturing in the city and region through public investments. A result of the emphasis on job creation was that benefit extension, as protection for the unemployed, became a lower priority to the union.

**Political Action Without Workers**

ACTWU's limited policies toward unemployment demonstrate the difficulty of responding to the problem without membership participation. ACTWU is a leader and active participant in labor-based political action campaigns that are independent of the established labor movement. These *ad hoc* campaigns routinely go beyond the more circumscribed efforts of the New York Central Labor Council, the local affiliate of the AFL-CIO. Union leadership exercises central control over decisions to participate in these independent labor-based campaigns, often requiring approval on the international level and leaving little local autonomy. While the union often takes an independent course in the labor movement, the internal decision-making process is centralized and rank-and-file participation in union decision-making is discouraged. Political action is orchestrated by the union's leadership, which tends to favor lobbying and coalition-building to member and community involvement. The reluctance of the union to include members and unemployed former members in political action significantly limits the far-reaching objectives of creating greater opportunity and equality for workers.

Like UAW Local 259, ACTWU is a union that does not restrict membership to skilled white male workers. However, the union has no policy of resisting layoffs and shop closings through mobilizing rank-and-file members. Nor does it have a policy of formally organizing its unemployed former members. Workers who lose their jobs permanently tend to break off their association with the union. The union continues to maintain a relationship with unemployed seasonal workers but has not encouraged their formal participation in political demonstrations and rallies organized by the New York Unemployed Committee or other activist organizations.

The chronic nature of unemployment in the garment industry, moreover, precluded sudden discontent with ACTWU leadership as a result of the local recession of the early 1990s. There was no movement on the part of leadership to organize laid-off workers into jobs clubs or unemployed councils, as was the case of UAW Local 259. While seasonal garment workers may pose challenges to the union because they can exhaust their benefits before they are rehired—creating an opposing force in the union—this internal threat is minimized since the union does not organize its unemployed membership.

The union has a long history of representing immigrant and minority workers, dating back to the beginning of the century when a large portion of its membership was comprised of Eastern European immigrants. No formal ethnic or racial color barriers to membership exist in the union and ACTWU continues to represent large numbers of recent immigrants and female workers, though its leadership remains mainly white and male. There is no opposition movement to union leadership of the kind that sometimes develops in other unions, since race, ethnicity, and gender do not seem to impede employment. While the industry is rapidly constricting, the prevailing low wages and demanding work in the garment industry restricts the fierce competition for jobs that occurs in other industries. In fact, ACTWU and other garment unions are something of a menace to firms that organize company-dominated unions that discriminate against minority and immigrant workers.[49]

## PUBLIC SECTOR: LOCAL 420 OF DISTRICT COUNCIL 37

Local 420, a municipal union affiliated with District Council 37 of the American Federation of State County and Municipal Employees (AFSCME), represents nonprofessional support staff in New York City public hospitals. The union's members work in nursing support, custodial services, building maintenance, and transportation in public hospitals that serve primarily low-income residents. Typically, members are employed in occupations requiring minimal levels of specialization and education. While hospital support workers who are members of Local 420 earn comparatively higher wages than most semi-skilled and unskilled employees in New York City, their wages are substantially lower than those of doctors, nurses, technicians and other skilled public hospital workers.

Public hospital workers were the last large municipal employee group to be represented by a union in collective bargaining with the City of New York. The low regard hospital administrators had for their support staff is noted by James Farmer, former Director of the Congress of Racial Equality and one of the first organizers for Local 420: "They hadn't worked long. Many had come up from the South fairly recently—looking for any kind of job. They were expected to have a poor attendance record and everything else. They were looked upon as dirt—literally."[50] The drive to organize public hospital support staff was led by both AFSCME District Council 37 and

Teamsters Local 237. The two unions competed for members from the early 1950s through the mid-1960s. In November 1954, AFSCME District Council 37 consolidated separate locals that it had formed individually at public hospitals into Local 420, initiating a ten-year drive to gain recognition with municipal officials as a bargaining representative for hospital support staff. The initial goal of the union was to bring dignity to hospital workers who were granted few rights by city hospitals. In the early years, " . . . the major issue in 420 was dignity—human dignity: to be addressed as a human being, to be called Mister or Miss. This was the key thing."[51] Before the union organized hospital employees of the Health and Hospitals Corporation, the public agency managing New York City's hospitals, they were sporadically paid, penalized for taking leaves of absence, and dismissed for union activity. Local 420 played an important role in saving jobs through political action.

The New York City public hospital system grew dramatically from the 1950s through the mid-1970s, so that Local 420 became a major force (the third largest unit) within the District Council 37 union hierarchy, representing approximately 15,000 members working in New York City public hospitals. Even before receiving formal recognition from City Hall, the local was responding energetically against efforts by the city to close public hospitals. When the Health and Hospitals Corporation revealed its intention to close Fordham Hospital in the Bronx in May 1961, Local 420 organizers and representatives helped form the "Citizens Committee to Save Fordham Hospital," a coalition of workers and residents. This group then mobilized leaflet distribution, a letter-writing campaign to the mayor, picket lines and mass meetings.[52] The well-organized political campaign to save Fordham swayed HHC leaders to reverse the decision to close the hospital. Since the Fordham Hospital episode, Local 420 has used political action and mass mobilization in the fight to keep municipal hospitals open. The New York City fiscal crisis of the mid-1970s brought a new era of renewed municipal austerity, continuously subjecting the hospital system to budget cuts and threatening the jobs of Local 420 members.

During the economic downturn of the late 1980s and early 1990s, Local 420 members and other hospital workers became susceptible to municipal budget cuts yet again. The simultaneous loss of job security created a paradoxical situation in which demand for public health services was on the rise, yet the mandate for municipal solvency was jeopardizing the jobs that supplied those very services. City leaders continued to see laying-off public workers in municipal hospitals as an appropriate means of stemming budgetary deficits.[53] In collective bargaining with DC 37, HHC officials periodically threaten to balance the agency's budget by closing city hospitals and laying off the entire hospital support staff. In April of 1990, for instance, HHC officials proposed closing Harlem Hospital to decrease the agency's budget by $100 million. And in October 1990, Mayor Dinkins, who received considerable political support from most public unions and was viewed as a supporter of organized labor, said it was necessary to lay off 15,000 city workers to close an anticipated budget gap. According to the *New York Times* report, there was speculation that the warning of layoffs was intended to put pressure on unions during contract negotiations to reduce demands for wage and benefit increases.[54] Yet despite attempts by city leaders to reduce public expenditures through service cuts and hospital shut-downs, Local 420 has thus far resisted these efforts and averted layoffs.[55] Its task, however, is becoming ever more difficult. Mayor Giuliani's budget included deep spending cuts in the Health and Hospitals Corporation. The mayor's proposal to privatize public hospitals further endangered the job security of public hospital workers by consolidating parallel services and closing public hospitals.[56] The affect of the Mayor's proposed service cuts on public hospital workers was intensified by New York State's Governor George Pataki's budget proposals to significantly cut Medicaid expenditures.[57]

In response to such challenges, Local 420 has cultivated an independent reputation going far beyond the policies of DC 37 to protect its members from municipal job cuts. To prevent layoffs at public hospitals, the union mobilizes members for demonstrations supporting local and community interests, the most important of which are defending the services supplied by public hospitals and safeguarding the jobs of hospital workers. The local union also frequently takes part in demonstrations supporting civil rights issues, labor-community organizations and organizations of the unemployed. Local 420 president Butler maintains that the primary objective of the union in collective action is to protect the jobs of hospital workers. But the union also shows concern for the low-income communities where Local 420 members tend to work and live by mobilizing rank-and-file members and residents against public service cuts and private industry shop closings.

Butler claims, moreover, to put great emphasis on educating Local 420 members about the dangers of unemployment to their own job security:

> [Members] have to understand what this is all about—surviving without a job, seeking unemployment, having their dignity taken from them without a job. [Organizing] is like a medication to the workers so they don't feel 'I'm secure—nobody is going to touch hospitals—people are going to always be sick.' Let them know that the storm could come their way so they can get involved.[58]

By showing its members that they have common interests with the unemployed, the leadership has been able to justify its relatively unusual efforts to support jobs programs and unemployment benefit extensions through political action. The willingness of Local 420 to organize and participate in various forms of collective action defending the jobs of its own members and expanding protections to the working poor and unemployed is a unique example of a union moving beyond the common actions of most labor organizations. While most unions have no more than a passing interest in the economic security of the unorganized unemployed, Local 420 has often embraced the jobless and participates in marches and demonstrations as a standard response to job loss and unemployment.

**Building Community Coalitions**

Some of the motivations of Local 420 union leadership in protecting jobs and defending the rights of unemployed workers come from recognizing that the interests of community and the union are often one and the same. Accordingly, an important component of Butler's coalition-building strategy is connecting union-based struggles with the community's need to maintain essential hospital and health care services. Attempts by city officials to decrease hospital support staff or close hospitals outright are linked to the deterioration of basic services in the very working-class communities in which hospital workers live. As Butler explains:

> Everybody has to have a job to earn a living. So their job is working in the hospital. But after work they're in the community, they want to see safety, sanitation, better sanitation, better housing. So it's the

same as the community person who works for the transit, public library or Board of Education. I get sick and tired of hearing 'oh that's just the union,' but that's just the community.[59]

In the early 1990s, Local 420 directed attention to maintaining public hospital services in the community. Public demonstrations included union members, and their families, and community residents resisting service cuts in public hospitals.[60]

Another component of Local 420's coalition building is the union's activity on behalf of the non-union unemployed. While the union did not actively participate in labor-community coalition meetings on unemployment and job creation in the early 1990s, Local 420 was the only local union participating in demonstrations to support extending unemployment benefits. On two occasions in 1991, Butler escorted contingents of public hospital workers to demonstrations in Washington, D.C. to support extensions of unemployment benefits. On July 24, he brought a busload of Local 420 members to join a rally and lobbying day of some 2,500 unemployed demonstrators organized by independent unemployed groups from Baltimore, Long Island, New York City, Philadelphia, and Pittsburgh, all of whom were seeking to extend federal unemployment benefits.[61] On October 4, Butler again accompanied a vanload of Local 420 members to a rally with some 300 unemployed workers outside the White House to protest George Bush's third veto of a bill passed by Congress to extend unemployment benefits. The July 24 rally was organized by the New York Unemployed Committee and Philadelphia Unemployment Project, along with the Baltimore Unemployed Council, Long Island Progressive Coalition, and Mon Valley Unemployed Committee. Local 420 was the only New York-based union to attend the rally formally. Some 2,000 construction workers from Philadelphia building trades also attended the rally. Butler addressed the demonstrators at both the July and October 1991 events.[62] In addition, in the summer of 1992, Butler sent a busload of his members to support a picket organized by rank-and-file workers protesting the closing of Taystee Bakery in Queens, which had displaced 510 workers from their jobs.[63]

Local 420's mobilization strategy in neighborhoods encourages local community activism and exposes Butler to potential challenges avoided by other unions who disregard the unemployed inside and outside of their organizations. Butler, however, views the union's local activism as essential for organizing unskilled and semi-skilled workers represented by Local 420:

> I represent the nonprofessional workers. People who get up early in the morning and mop the floors, people who take the soiled linen and reproduce it into clean linen, nurses aids, assistant professional nurses, food service who work in the kitchen with the dieticians to make sure the correct diet is prepared for the patient who is on that particular diet. That's their job, that's their skill, that's what they know about.[64]

Butler dismisses opposition that may result from political action on the local level, arguing that inaction poses a greater threat: "When you mobilize you have smooth sailing, when you don't you've got bumpy roads."[65] Failure to mobilize can lead to complaints that the union is doing little to benefit workers. As Butler puts it:

> I believe in taking action on behalf of the members so that [they] won't go in the locker room or lunch room and say the union ain't shit, you can't say that when your union is out on the street on the battlefield fighting for you, no way you can say that.[66]

Of course this raises a question as to whether some of the demonstrations are cosmetic attempts to satisfy the immediate rage of the rank and file. Butler, however, sees the demonstration of activism on behalf of worker and community as a real source of social change and as a must for union leadership. "That is part of the responsibility of the drum major, to educate. Some people say 'oh that's just the union' but the union is hospital workers, and they're part of the community."[67]

## DC 37: Detached Leadership and Limited Participation

But despite the enthusiasm of its leadership, Local 420 is no match for the unemployment crisis that it periodically faces. As sole collective bargaining representative in negotiations with the Health and Hospitals Corporation, DC 37 outranks Local 420 and other affiliated local unions covered by the citywide contract. Notwithstanding the active role played by Butler on the executive board of DC 37, the power of constituent unions like Local 420 is limited by the bargaining agreement with New York City that designates the parent union as exclusive representative of hospital workers.

The framework for union representation in New York stems from the consolidation of municipal contracts signed with small unions into major contracts signed with large unions through the Office of Collective Bargaining created by Mayor Wagner in 1965.[68] Consolidating union power among designated centralized union organizations like DC 37 considerably reduces competition with other trade unions for membership. In the case of the Healthcare Workers Union, centralizing the union collective bargaining structure with the City of New York, as done under the firm leadership of Victor Gotbaum, substantially reduced the importance of local labor union leaders. Following consolidation of collective bargaining, DC 37 policies tended to accommodate the City.[69]

While other union leaders seem content with the surrender of authority to the centralized leadership of DC 37, Butler still maintains a degree of control over the union. "Butler is a main player in making decisions for the union," according to Evelyn Seinfeld, DC 37's research director. "He is one of the few people that knows what is going on. He knows more than anyone about his Local." Mr. Butler's power base stems from his long tenure as president of Local 420, the large number of workers represented by the union, and his important political contacts.[70]

## Organizational Structure and Union Activism

Centralized municipal labor bargaining at the district council level, then, reduces the power local leadership has over rank-and-file membership.[71] Consequently, members of DC 37 locals tend to identify with the central authority of DC 37 rather than with their local unions. The preeminence of DC 37 threatens to render local presidents obsolete. Yet Butler encourages and organizes rank and file and community activism in support of job security and local services, thus preserving the relevancy of his leadership in Local 420. His preference for collective action is illustrated in his skepticism about formal labor-management bargaining arrangements.

> I get very impatient when it takes time for other groups to make up their minds. In government, you like to go to conferences and talk all

day. I believe in taking it to the streets, beating the drums, mobilizing, protesting, demonstrating.[72]

Mobilizing Local 420 membership for political action has increased loyalty to Butler and reduced challenges to his leadership from the district council. In addition, Butler's capacity to organize rank-and-file members gives him a decisive voice in collective bargaining with management. For Butler, then, community mobilization and action has also served as a buffer against both management and union officials who would prefer dispassionate negotiations of labor-management disputes.

Local 420's militant activities have been the result and source of tension between Butler and DC 37 leadership. In 1978, Butler clashed with Gotbaum over the parent union's attempt to supervise and control local finances of the union.[73] From the late 1970s to the mid-1980s, Gotbaum struggled with him for control of Local 420.[74] In 1978, Gotbaum and senior DC 37 officials charged Butler with misappropriating union funds for personal use. Gotbaum contends Butler subsequently forged ties with progressives and supported social causes as a cover for this alleged unlawful activity only after District Council 37 attempted to remove Butler from office.[75] Gotbaum speculates that Butler's zeal may be at least partially attributable to residual opposition he faced from DC 37, stemming from the charges in the late 1970s that he participated in illegal financial transactions with his union. Butler disputes Gotbaum's charges as baseless. Whatever the truth may be in this case, the struggle faced by Local 420 in its efforts to mobilize the unemployed illustrates the obstacles posed by the structure of centralized labor organizations in New York to dealing with the worsening problem of unemployment.

## CONSTRUCTION: IBEW LOCAL 3

The International Brotherhood of Electrical Workers (IBEW) Local 3 is a New York-based union representing electrical workers in the building trades. The union represents predominantly white male workers, although it has recently been forced to diversify its membership to include people of color and women. Local 3 also represents workers who manufacture and process electrical components, utility and repair workers, off-track betting workers, employees of Madison Square Garden, and other maintenance workers.[76]

Like the other unions discussed here, IBEW Local 3 has recently faced crisis levels of unemployment. In the aftermath of the stock market crash in October 1987, the decline in financial, real estate, and insurance industries lessened the demand for luxury residential and office construction, the backbone of the building industry during the 1980s regional economic boom. As a consequence, the New York construction industry experienced its deepest setback since the fiscal crisis of the mid-1970s. The 1990s decline in private construction was intensified by a simultaneous cutback in public sector construction.[77] By the early 1990s, official figures for unemployment among construction workers approached 50 percent, while unofficial estimates were in the range of 60 percent to 70 percent.[78] Among black construction workers in the New York market during the early 1990s, unemployment was even higher, in the range of 80 percent.[79]

Seasonal unemployment and insecure employment are commonplace in the construction industry. Erlich observes that most construction workers leave the industry primarily due to the stress of job instability rooted in the boom and bust cycle of the industry.[80] Union officials have been forced either to endure high unemployment and the prospect of organizational instability or devise strategies addressing the needs of their unemployed members. Regulating access to employment in the industry is essential to organizing workers in the building trades and is a device used by construction trade unions to control the consequences of unemployment affecting both union and non-union workers in the building trades. In the late 1960s, union construction workers comprised 80 percent of all construction activity in the United States. By the late 1980s, organized workers represented only 22 percent of the total construction workforce.[81] One reason Erlich sites for the declining power of building trades unions is shortsighted resistance to organizing new members, many of whom are African Americans, Latinos and women.[82]

## Standard Responses of Unions to Unemployment

Direct influence over the local labor market is what gives trade unions economic and political power. Unions operating in industries with a scarcity of workers tend to be stronger than unions in markets with surplus labor. By increasing the supply of labor, high unemployment typically poses a relentless economic threat to the labor market power of unions and their members. While variation in the number of workers and jobs is normally associated with the ebb and flow of unemployment, trade unions effectively regulate the labor supply in industries and create artificial shortages even in situations where there is a plentiful supply of workers. In the building trades, volatile labor markets are the norm rather than the exception, and unions attempt to control access to jobs as a means of decreasing labor competition and maintaining high wage and benefits for their own members. IBEW Local 3 exerts a certain amount of bargaining power by restricting access to employment. By organizing both training and referral processes, IBEW determines who is and who is not eligible for employment in the higher paying electrical jobs of the building trades. Local 3 operates a referral system through a Joint Industry Board, an employment department managed by the union and employers. The JIB allows employers to maintain 750 employees that are exempt from the union's rotation system, which strives to provide jobs to workers through a work sharing system.

Rising unemployment in the construction industry during the early 1990s posed a genuine challenge to such policies. Most New York City construction industry analysts speculate that the industry will not rebound until the end of the decade. Anticipating a new round of seasonal and cyclical unemployment in the early 1990s, IBEW Local 3 redesigned a standard policy to ameliorate sudden and rising joblessness for "core" members that might lose work without finding new jobs in the industry. The following account of policies affecting employment and unemployment at Local 3 demonstrates the scope of influence the union asserts in controlling access to work in an industry with a surplus of labor.

IBEW's position as primary referral agent for unemployed workers is unique among most unions in the building trades. In most industrial and public sector unions, the employment relationship is also the sole determinant of union membership. Typically, when workers are laid off from a union shop, they also surrender their union membership. Unions have negligible interest in maintaining association with unemployed workers who are not contributing dues to the organization and may be hostile to leaders over their joblessness. But in the case of construction unions like IBEW, which have the capacity to control access to employment in segments of an industry, workers tend to maintain their affiliation to unions long after they lose their jobs. By retaining ties to the union, construction workers maintain access to the high wage jobs typically associated with the unionized sector of the construction industry.

Local 3 has a long-standing policy governing access to employment in the industry. This policy is aimed at reducing unemployment among core members and resolving conflicts among the rank-and-file that might lead to opposition to union leadership and stability. Essentially, Local 3 tries to minimize consequences of unemployment for electrical workers who are members of the union. To achieve this goal, the union operates as a gatekeeper to jobs, maintaining employment for workers considered "core" members of the organization, and limiting access to "outsiders" (minorities, immigrants, and women) and newcomers who are likely to oppose leadership. By enforcing job-sharing schemes and using the federal unemployment insurance system to its advantage, Local 3 minimizes the impact of joblessness in the electrical industry even during high unemployment in the industry.

### Regulating Unemployment in the Electrical Industry

Employment in the electrical industry parallels seasonal and cyclical trends in the New York City construction sector. In response to widespread unemployment, Local 3 uses two standard procedures to help members to cope with joblessness—a work sharing plan and a supplementary unemployment program. Local 3's work sharing was established in the 1930s by Harry Van Arsdale to distribute the burden of unemployment among all members when the construction industry is relatively idle. Every February, union and management leadership determines an average number of weeks that electrical workers must be unemployed during the following year. Under work sharing, electrical workers are required to stop work for a specified number of weeks established by the union. The work sharing rate fluctuates according to the ebb and flow of unemployment in the construction industry.

One goal of the work sharing program is to guarantee that all workers experience unemployment, according to Vincent McElroen, a business representative of Local 3.

A certain percentage of workers would never experience unemployment because they are part of basic core network. But we

believe that all our members ought to experience unemployment to
have an understanding and . . . so they would have some hardship.[83]

In 1977, Local 3's work sharing program was challenged by
construction industry contractors. Members of Local 3 were locked out
for 11 weeks before the dispute was resolved. As a result of the work
sharing program, McElroen claims, unemployment is not as damaging
to Local 3 members as it is for workers in other building trades unions.

> At other building trades unions you get unemployed for two years at
> a tremendous cost to the employee. In our union, members aren't
> happy that there is even any unemployment to experience. Now the
> member is pissed off because he has to lose 8 weeks of work. At the
> height of the recession there were 16 weeks of unemployment. The
> fact is that it (work sharing) is the most envied benefit in all the
> building trades unions.[84]

However, while the union designated 16 weeks as the average number
of work sharing time off for its members in 1992, some workers were
unemployed for longer periods. Under the currently instituted work
share program, McElroen says, no worker was unemployed for longer
than 39 weeks, during the worst of the decline of the New York City
construction industry recession of the early 1990s.

Although the plan is supposed to distribute downtime equally
among all union members, the program tends to protect a nucleus of
core employees considered most important to employers. Under the
current rules, employers may designate particular workers exempt
from layoffs. At smaller shops with fewer than 50 employees, up to 14
IBEW members can be designated exempt. Since the industry is
dominated by small shops, a core of electrical workers tend to be
protected from job loss even during periods of high unemployment.
These protected workers tend to be union members for a longer period
of time.

The second provision against unemployment is an unemployment
security program that provides supplementary income to workers who
lose their jobs. Jobless benefits are provided by the union to
complement government unemployment benefits, thereby reducing the
economic threat of local recessions to rank-and-file members. Under
the plan negotiated with management, contractors contribute money to
the security benefit plans of individual members. When members

become unemployed, they can withdraw up to $450 per week from funds in their unemployment security accounts. The supplemental security system resembles the federal unemployment insurance system, to which employers make contributions based on the number of hours worked by their employee. However, under the plan administered by Local 3, contributions are made directly to the accounts of individual workers rather than to a general union fund for distribution to all workers.[85]

Local 3's work sharing plan and supplemental security program allow union members to cope with periods of high unemployment, when they are most vulnerable to economic hardship. The fact that electrical workers tend to maintain membership between jobs attests to the success of these programs, which has contributed to support of the union leadership. Building trade unions with no mechanisms to cushion unemployment for their members have more difficulty in controlling opposition to their leadership.[86]

But while Local 3's supplemental security program ostensibly protects all workers during times of high unemployment, the program tends to protect disproportionately the members who have accumulated considerable funds in their accounts; these are the "core" workers least likely to experience extended unemployment. Workers who are unemployed frequently are much less likely to have amassed funds to tide them through long periods of unemployment, rendering the program largely worthless to those who need it most.

### Response to High Unemployment

The recession of the early 1990s generated extended unemployment for a larger than usual segment of Local 3 members. For during the construction boom of the mid-1980s, some 2,000 electrical workers from other unions across the nation had come to work in New York under the jurisdiction of Local 3.[87] When the economic expansion came to a sudden halt in the late 1980s, some union members experienced unemployment exceeding the 26 weeks of federal unemployment insurance coverage.[88] The union supported legislative proposals sponsored by the AFL-CIO leadership to extend benefits beyond the basic 26 weeks, but did not take an active role in organizing or mobilizing its own membership around the issue.

The union channels political action through established labor organizations over which it exercises considerable influence. Its leadership on the New York Central Labor Council and the New York State AFL-CIO affords IBEW Local 3 considerable influence in New York labor politics. Thomas Van Arsdale, president of the New York Central Labor Council is business manager and *de facto* leader of IBEW Local 3, and Ed Cleary, president of the New York State AFL-CIO, is a member of the union. The prominent position within state and local branches of the AFL-CIO occupied by Local 3 allows the union to engage in political action through the organized labor movement. As a leader in this movement, the union rarely joins with other ad hoc coalitions of labor, especially coalitions that seek to transcend AFL-CIO moderate policies and conservative strategies.

Nevertheless, the union is periodically persuaded to take part in events organized by outside groups. For example, Ed Cleary testified at Senator Moynihan's Finance Committee field hearing New York City in June, 1992 on behalf of unemployment insurance benefit extensions. The New York field hearing was arranged by the New York Unemployed Committee, which threatened the Senator with public denunciation if he did not promote a bill to extend federal unemployment benefits.

In response to rapidly rising unemployment within the union, leadership invited members to meetings at Local 3's headquarters in Flushing, Queens, to inform unemployed electricians about their rights to unemployment benefits. The union assigned a business representative to counsel members who became unemployed or were having difficulty collecting unemployment benefits.[89] According to member testimony, unemployment in the electrical industry tended to hurt minority members more harshly than the union's white male workers.[90]

After the federal government finally enacted a temporary extension of unemployment insurance in November 1991, Local 3 established a union-based program to help unemployed members collect additional weeks of benefits. Since the new federal benefit extension included a provision requiring unemployed applicants seeking extended benefits to apply for work at a minimum of three firms, the union had to revise its unemployment registration policy to allow workers to seek work at outside non-union shops. To qualify for the first 26 weeks of benefits, Local 3 members were only required to register as unemployed with the union's employment department, located at union headquarters. Members unemployed for more than 26 weeks were compelled to search for work outside of the union. The new regulation posed an obstacle to union members and a threat to the strength of the union, since members would be required to register with low-paying non-union contractors not offering comparable wages and protections, undermining the electrical industry and union wage and benefits benchmark.[91]

IBEW Local 3 responded to the new federal restrictions on the long-term unemployed, collecting an additional 13 weeks of benefits by establishing a rather misleading "Salting Program" that purported to attempt to place jobless union members in jobs at non-union work sites whenever possible. Under the program, Local 3 steered unemployed members to apply to non-union contractors for jobs on public works projects. While the nominal objective of the program was to place unemployed members of the union in non-union public building projects, the underlying intention of the program was to furnish additional job search references for unemployed union members to qualify for federal supplementary benefits. As Vincent McElroen, director of the plan, put it:

> Our workers ordinarily register with our employment department so they don't have to go out and search for work. Many of the other jobs are lower paying positions that are nonunionized . . . The Salting Program that we had going on was very beneficial to members in getting extended benefits. Once people knew you were Local 3 they didn't want you. The Salting Program was primarily beneficial in getting our members unemployment benefits.[92]

Such actions on behalf of unemployed members, however, had an extremely limited effect on the unemployment problem, even in the union itself. The union's programs for unemployed electrical workers in the construction industry were not available, for instance, to IBEW workers employed in electric industry plants, who, as a rule, have no protections at all, and rely on federal unemployment benefits when they are laid off.

## Internal and External Opposition to Local 3 Hiring Policy

The ability of Local 3 to minimize the severity of unemployment among its own building trades members through expanded supplemental unemployment benefits and the work sharing program has silenced internal criticism of leadership. Still, the union is exposed to "outsider" threats from electrical workers who are not part of the core membership, and from workers not affiliated with the union at all. Local 3 president Thomas Van Arsdale contends that the exclusion of minority members from the union results from the "limited number" of these groups who apply for jobs and the reluctance of employers to hire them.

> We publicize openings in the program. Although we might take 1,000 or less, 4,000 or 5,000 apply for that apprenticeship. A very limited number of minority men or women apply, but the opportunity is clearly there . . . When an individual gets a job, the employer has the right to determine whether the employee is satisfactory to them. [When they have to cut back on the size of their workforce], they decide which employees are least needed by them. Because of the atmosphere that has developed over the years in regard to [equal employment] requirements for electrical contractors, [African American, Latino, Native American and Female] individuals have been kept in the workforce on particular jobs even though they are not the most valued employee on that job.[93]

Nevertheless, some minority members of Local 3 publicly charge the union with favoring white, male workers in the apprenticeship program and the employment referral program administered by the union.[94] In a report released in December 1993, Local 3 was charged with improperly excluding minority members who registered with the union's employment department's "out-of-work" list maintained by the Joint Industry Board, an organization representing both union and management.[95] Unlike most building trades unions, Local 3 operates as a hiring hall, where work crews are organized by the union, and not by contractors. Jobless members who sign up at the union hall are allegedly placed on the "out-of-work" list, with those workers unemployed the longest receiving priority.[96] However, the "out-of-work" list permits the Joint Industry Board great discretion in hiring employees, particularly since the union has not allowed members access to the list. According to Van Arsdale: "The list is generally not available to individuals who wish to review it."[97] At the New York Commission on Human Rights, the union was criticized for irregular practices by Local 3 workers: "Numerous workers in Local 3 stated they were denied access to the union office to sign the out-of-work list."[98] In many cases these practices denied equal treatment to minority electrical workers. Despite the apparently unbiased makeup of the union's work sharing program, the New York Commission on Civil Rights found discrimination to be a recurrent problem at Local 3: "Allegations of discrimination were made repeatedly by members of Local 3 with regard to the Employment Director, Mr. McCormick, of the JIB." Testimony revealed minority members to be out of work "at least 12 weeks out of the year—a much higher downtime than white workers."[99] Some minority workers, claiming that the union operates on "a corrupt system of favoritism" and that no list exists, filed appeals with the National Labor Relations Board against the union.[100]

That workers believe there is unfair access to jobs at Local 3 is illustrated by the following electrical worker's complaint:

> As a minority, you are the last to be hired and the first to be fired. They put you to work for one or two days at a job that is finishing, you get laid off and you end up back at the union. You have to wait weeks, a month and a half. So you're lucky if you get three months of work a year.[101]

Such accounts of discrimination reflect patterns of disparate access to jobs. The restriction of access to the "out-of-work" list betrays the union's concern that members may discover inconsistencies between referrals for minority members and referrals for white males. The union may also be trying to protect core workers who have seniority.[102] Union control over employment referrals appears to translate into patterns of unequal access on the basis of race, immigrant status, and gender.

**Patterns of Minority Exclusion at Local 3**

The New York City Commission on Human Rights recognizes the disparity in employment for minority workers to be a serious problem in Local 3:

> While the acceptance rate of black males is in need of improvement, the overwhelming problem is that in a union whose jurisdiction encompasses New York City, with a population that is more than 50% persons of color, more than 80% of Local 3's applicants to the apprenticeship program are white. This strongly indicates that outreach to minority communities is insufficient, and that the

union's reputation in communities of color is negative. For this
reason, many people of color don't bother to seek entry into the
union.[103]

A survey by the New York Commission on Civil Rights found that
unequal access continues to be preserved among apprentice workers
entering the electrical trade. While people of color make up 27.6
percent of the 7,212 in the trades of plumbing, electrical work,
operating engineer, carpentry, sheet metal work, steamfitting, and
bridge, structural and ornamental iron work, few are advanced to
journey-level status. The problem is particularly acute at Local 3, in
which white men make up a larger share of union membership than in
the building trade industry as a whole. Tellingly, only 16.4 percent of
Local 3's apprentices are minorities.

## United Third Bridge

Patterns of discrimination by Local 3 are widely recognized by
minority construction workers, both inside and outside the union.
African American, Latino, and Asian construction workers who are
frequently unemployed or excluded entirely from union work attempt
to increase minority representation in the industry through the
formation of minority coalitions. Two of the most prominent of these
coalitions are United Third Bridge (UTB) and Harlem Fight Back.
(See chapter 5 for a detailed examination of Fight Back actions with
respect to unemployment.) While building trades unions have charged
some minority coalitions with disrupting construction sites and
extorting jobs and money from contractors, The New York
Commission on Civil Rights considers the two groups as legitimate
activist organizations advocating greater minority representation on
the job,[104] but the leadership of Local 3 claims that United Third
Bridge is an unlawful organization that seeks to undermine the gains
that it has made through collective bargaining process by disrupting
work sites and exploiting racial tensions that may exist in the union.[105]

United Third Bridge was formed in 1975 to promote the rights of
minority workers who did not have equal access to jobs in the
electrical industry, particularly well-paying electrical jobs in the
construction industry. In its early years, UTB efforts centered on filing
complaints of employment discrimination against Local 3 with the
State Equal Employment Opportunity Commission. UTB charged

Local 3 with blackballing, intimidating, harassing and blacklisting minority members of the union that criticized union hiring policies.[106] Local 3 officials have repudiated charges of favoritism in the union and have in turn charged UTB and other minority coalitions with weakening the power of construction workers of all races. Both United Third Bridge and Fight Back recommend that the City of New York create its own hiring hall to allow equal access to lucrative public and private construction jobs.

Keyssar's view that minorities and immigrant workers shoulder the disproportionate burden of unemployment is demonstrated by the case study of the resistance of IBEW Local 3 to inclusion of United Third Bridge members into the union. These divisions among core union members, marginal members, and the non-union employed and unemployed workers in the electrical industry also support Arrighi's argument that intraclass racial and gender divisions relegate minority workers to the lowest paid and least secure echelons of employment.

## CONCLUSION

Two factors can be drawn from the four case studies of trade union unemployment policy presented in this chapter to explain their inadequate responses toward unemployment: (1) The importance that trade union leaderships place on organizational stability and maintaining control over their organizations; and (2) the exclusive or inclusive organizing strategies of unions (See Table 4.1 for a schematic analysis of occupational communities and forms of union political action).

First, organizational stability plays a critical role in determining how, and to what extent, trade unions respond to base level and unexpected rapidly rising unemployment. An omnipresent feature of all four unions is the importance that trade union leaderships placed on asserting control over their organizations. Officials from each union proclaimed a concern about the rise of internal and external unemployment and an interest in an organizational response to alleviate the problem of unemployment. Local 420 and Local 259 directly organized their members and unemployed former members, and participated in mobilization actions with the remote unemployed organized at government jobless centers by the New York Unemployed Committee, but union officials exerted tight control over the direction of these efforts. Organized unemployed workers did not represent an ongoing antagonistic force to these unions.

**Table 4.1: Occupational Communities and Forms of Union Political Action**

---

**UAW Local 259**
  Market Sector: Service Semi-skilled Auto
  Membership Category: Inclusive Class Workplace
  Unemployed Effort: Moderate
  Political Action: Narrow
  Labor Mobilization: Narrow

**ACTWU Joint Council**
  Market Sector: Manufacturing Semi-skilled Textile
  Membership Category: Inclusive Class Workplace
  Unemployed Effort: None
  Political Action: Extensive
  Labor Mobilization: Narrow

**AFSCME Local 420**
  Market Sector: Public Semi-skilled Hospital
  Membership Category: Inclusive Class Workplace
  Unemployed Effort: Narrow
  Political Action: N/A
  Labor Mobilization: Moderate

**IBEW Local 3**
  Market Sector: Building Skilled & Semi-skilled
  Membership Category: Exclusive Craft Union
  Unemployed Effort: Moderate
  Political Action: Extensive
  Labor Mobilization: Extensive

---

Note: **Market sector** indicates the occupational labor markets of unions and their members; **membership category** indicates the pattern of union organizational affiliation and identifies the locale of representation (workplace/union); **unemployed action** indicates union has assembled unemployed members committees. Unions that organized unemployed members to engage in political action or other forms of support such as job search, access to retraining, and service needs were determined to have taken more prominent action; **political action** is defined as union actions to mobilize support for desired social policy; **labor mobilization** indicates if union participated in mobilizing working and nonworking members for demonstrations in support of jobs or social benefits.

Local 420 president James Butler has a reputation of being an activist. While Local 259 seemed to be worried about alienating themselves from management, Local 420 aggressively challenged hospital management, especially in efforts to cut the workforce. Butler said that he was held accountable by a membership who would oppose him if he did not resolutely oppose layoffs.

Local 259 president Sam Meyers met no opposition inside or outside of his union, yet the prospect of a mobilized unemployed with ties to the working members was a potential nuisance to a union with limited resources. Meyers spurned proposals to form a more active unemployed committee in his union because it may have mobilized opposition to his leadership position. The union's employment crisis limited the resources allocated by the union to the embryonic organization formed by outside activists. Also, the actions of the organization were narrowed to social services rather than political mobilization, in part because participants in the union's unemployed council began to criticize union leadership's failure to defend their jobs.

The ACTWU Joint Board did not deviate from its political strategy to defend and expand union jobs. Organizing the disorganized jobless was not a part of the union's approach to relieving unemployment. However, the union was slightly more responsive to joining labor and community-based issue campaigns on unemployment than UAW Local 259 or IBEW Local 3. As a union that represents large numbers of women, minority, and immigrant low-wage workers, ACTWU does not have an internal or external force competing for power against the union, which may have mitigated any independent union-based organizing effort. However, the benefits and protection provided ACTWU members are also inferior to those of craft and professional unions. On average, full-time ACTWU workers earn an average of 10 percent to 25 percent of the $75,000 to $150,000 average annual wages of Local 3 workers. Leaders of the union did not consider mobilizing the unemployed during the recession, most likely because they believed the unemployed would pose a nuisance to a union that was short of funds and resources. The long-term unemployed that could not find work ultimately left the union.

Internal organizing efforts by IBEW Local 3 were limited to informational meetings for unemployed members on available union and government services. The union did not independently mobilize its membership around jobs and unemployment extensions, but did join larger coalitions through the New York buildings trade unions and the Central Labor Council (See chapter 5). Local 3 is faced with internal and external opposition to its leadership. Internal challenges come from minority members who charge that there is discrimination in referral practices. External challenges come from large contingents of minority workers who seek equal access to high-paying jobs controlled by Local 3, which regulates its membership.

Second, the policies enacted by individual unions indicate that organizing strategies specific to each union influence the ways in which unions respond to job loss. Inclusive unions that organize workers directly through the workplace tend to be less vulnerable to membership disapproval, while exclusive unions that organize the labor market by recruiting workers before they enter the labor market are subject to greater membership disapproval.

With high levels of unemployed union members who were active in the union, the exclusive Local 3 was forced to mobilize its members when growing unemployment strained its ability to provide work for jobless workers who remained members of the union. We also observed that exclusive membership attributes influenced the specific ethnic form and class boundaries of organizing that construction union officials followed in response to unemployment. Local 3 was not concerned with the fate of minority, immigrant and women workers. Nor did it consider the fate of its members who were employed outside of the construction industry. However, unemployed construction worker members actively participated in meetings and union organized events. Union officials joined together to develop a strategy to protect members to the exclusion of minority and immigrant workers who were not core members of the union. In turn, leaders of minority and immigrant workers formed independent "minority coalitions" to defend the interests of workers who considered themselves to be excluded by Local 3 and other building trades unions dominated by white, male workers.

Unlike Local 3, the three other unions considered in this chapter that organize members directly through employers were not compelled to respond to the concerns of unemployed former members who lost their jobs. While all three unions do not formally exclude workers from employment in their respective labor markets, they are less accountable to their members who become unemployed. Local 259 demonstrated concern for unemployed workers through two efforts to mobilize former members into unemployed councils, but the workers found this demonstration shallow and inadequate. ACTWU leadership, which enjoyed only limited rank-and-file participation, experienced limited internal pressure to organize its members for political action. The seasonal nature of employment in the textile and apparel industry caused the union's members to rely on federal unemployment insurance as a source of income during long periods of unemployment and so the union terminated the membership of those workers who lost their jobs as a consequence of permanent shop closures. In Local 420, where rank-and-file members were more active, union leaders tended to be more likely to engage in more vigorous policies in response to unemployment. Jim Butler, president of Local 420, acknowledged that the active membership of his union was a factor in his decision to respond to unemployment. But his efforts were hampered by the policies of the parent union, DC 37, which was less concerned with broad social problems than Local 420.

The three inclusive unions analyzed in this chapter (UAW Local 259, ACTWU, and AFSCME Local 420) did not face active opposition to their leaderships. The absence of an organized opposition is associated with the organizing strategies of these unions. Workers in all three inclusive unions are not recruited into the organization, but are organized directly through their places of work. When these workers are laid off, they are shunted back into the general labor market. Latent opposition to Local 259's union leadership was engendered through the union's internal unemployment efforts. Union leaders quickly discontinued the unemployed efforts when it became evident that the organizing provided a forum for disgruntled workers. Local 420 leaders may have resorted to an active policy toward members in response to desire to maintain some relevance within a centralized DC 37 union structure that opposed local efforts for autonomy. The union's president maintained that if he did not speak out and organize against unemployment and municipal layoffs, he would subject himself to greater rank-and-file opposition. Where a union controlled a substantial portion of the labor market (IBEW Local 3), leaders faced intense opposition from minority coalitions of workers who were not members of the union and from unemployed members who considered themselves to be excluded from job referrals.

The research recounted in this chapter suggests that union officials will respond more resolutely when rising unemployment is associated with higher levels of conflict in their organization and that rising instability is directly associated with the organizing strategies of individual unions. Inclusive unions that organized workers directly through the workplace had weak attachments to their members when they became unemployed. The exclusive union (IBEW Local 3) that recruited workers before they began to work in the industry remained accountable to members after they became unemployed. The next two chapters will explore in more detail the impact of exclusiveness and inclusiveness of unions on their capacity to build and exploit coalitions that might deal with the problem of unemployment.

## NOTES

1. Although unions are unable to decide the workers who will keep their jobs in closings of entire shops, they are usually able to determine the sequence of this process of job loss, if all the workers are not simultaneously laid off.

2. In the building trades unions, as opposed to many industrial unions, union members depend on their union to supply available jobs to them. In most industrial unions, workers are first hired by a firm and subsequently become members of the union.

3. From 1990 to 1993 salaries of the Local 259's executive officers were reduced by 25 percent to $304,209, both through attrition and salary cutbacks. During the same period, the union laid off members of its office staff. Data derived from Local 259's Form LM-2, (Labor Management Report) filed with the U.S. Department of Labor, 1991, 1994.

4. Margo Nash, *Local 259: United Automobile Workers of America*, New York, UAW Local 259, 1983.

5. Margo Nash, 1983.

6. See Nash 1983.

7. Miriam Thompson, former education director of United Auto Workers Local 259, indicated a strong desire to help form an authentic union-based unemployed action program similar to the organizing efforts of the 1920s and 1930s. Interview, Miriam Thompson, January 21, 1994.

8. Among the benefits that Local 259 has offered laid-off UAW members are job placement assistance, extended medical coverage that is mandated under federal guidelines, membership in good standing for up to six months, and free copies of *Local 259 Unity News*, the union newspaper. To maintain membership in good standing, laid-off members must request withdrawal cards to avoid paying an additional initiation fee when they return to the union. But note that *Local 259 Unity News* ceased publication when

Miriam Thompson left the union in 1992. The union also claims that it will help members obtain unemployment insurance and other benefits. (Local 259 Standard Letter to Laid-Off Union Members, 1991, 1992).

9. Interview, Marcella Perry, jobs referral director, United Auto Workers, Local 259, December 13, 1994.

10. The union organized a local bail fund for Martin Luther King Jr. and participated in Freedom Rides. According to Nash, Local 259 members joined an AFL-CIO demonstration in New York in 1959 to picket Woolworth's because the store chain refused to serve blacks in its Southern stores. Under Meyers's leadership the union developed consumer education programs for Spanish-speaking workers, mental health programs for blue-collar workers, and support for Advocates for Children, an organization promoting child welfare. The union mobilized members to oppose American involvement in the Vietnam War during the early 1970s. The union's tradition of concern for the poor continued under the direction of Miriam Thompson from 1984 to 1992. According to Thompson, Meyers maintained a progressive posture and respect within the union movement in the late 1960s and 1970s, as public service unions expanded. In the school teachers strike in 1968, Thompson recalls that "Meyers spoke for community control while protecting the interests of striking teachers." Interview, Miriam Thompson, education and political director, United Auto Workers, Local 259, January 21, 1994.

11. Meeting with Sam Meyers, November 1993.

12. Meeting with Sam Meyers, November 1993.

13. Sam Meyers, Local 259, Region 9A, International Union, United Automobile, Aerospace and Agricultural Implement Workers of America, UAW, *Proceedings of Thirtieth Constitutional Convention*, June 14-18, 1992, San Diego, California, 96.

14. Sam Meyers, Local 25, Region 9A, International Union, United Automobile, Aerospace and Agricultural Implement Workers of America, UAW, Proceedings of the Thirtieth Constitutional Convention, 263, June 14-18, 1992.

15. In addition to Local 259's support for unemployment benefit extensions and job creation programs, the union participated in coalitions in support of universal health insurance and solidarity groups fighting South Africa.

16. Thompson attended an organizing meeting on unemployment on December 27, 1990 Association for Union Democracy Conference, in Philadelphia. The informal strategy session was called by the New York Unemployed Committee and attended by the Philadelphia Unemployment

Project and activists of union locals from New York, Boston, and other eastern cities.

17.  One rationale for including the NYUC was that it offered free organizing support for the union, which was short on resources. During this period, the union had laid off staff and terminated publication of its newspaper. Miriam Thompson, education and political director, who left the union in the summer of 1992 to become director of the Center for Constitutional Rights, was not replaced.

18.  Minutes of Local 259 unemployed organizing meeting recorded by the author, January 1991.

19.  Sam Meyers, minutes of unemployed meeting recorded by author, January 1992.

20.  Interview, Sam Meyers, December 1993.

21.  The union had also held consultations with union stewards of International Electric Hardware, a Brooklyn-based industrial plant that produced component parts for the Defense Department, about rapidly rising unemployment in the union. As a result of declining government business, the shop eliminated 118 of 200 positions in the late 1980s. In January 1992, Meyers and Thompson agreed to send NYUC organizers to the shop in Brooklyn, but these plans were later canceled due to concern about worker sensitivity to discrimination by plant management. Those who permanently lost jobs were not contacted by the union. Still, Meyers told union stewards:

> The big thing to know is that we have people who are dedicated to organizing those at the bottom of the barrel. People that are interested in helping. This fulfills responsibility that the union has . . . We are going to do everything we can to help the unemployed. (Minutes of January 13, 1992 meeting recorded by the author.)

22.  Local 259 letter, April 15, 1992, from Sam Meyers to unemployed UAW auto workers, informing them of the first meeting on May 8, 1992.

23.  A review of subsequent unemployed support group meetings by Local 259 unemployed organizers produced a consensus that jobless workers came to the meetings seeking jobs: "Discussion ensued noting that when the service was first offered to our unemployed, many who came to the meeting were coming with the impression that they were going to get work. However, this did not prove to be the case. What was being offered was information about what is or may be available, i.e., services, resources, etc. to them." (Minutes of February 12, 1993 meeting attended by Shlosko, Marsella Perry,

the union's job placement Counselor, and Sylvia Aron a social worker and union consultant.)

24. These observations are based on discussions of unemployed workers contacted during 1992, 1993, and 1994.

25. Interview with Roberta Shlosko, a mental health counselor who was director of the Local 259 unemployed organizing effort, and Sylvia Aron, a social worker who ran the union's job club, June 1992. When Shlosko was appointed director of the effort, she had been involved in the union for about 40 years. She appeared to be a trustworthy supporter of Meyers.

26. *Local 259 Survey of Unemployed Members, 1993*. The author responsible for drafting the survey, which required the approval of the new unemployed committee. Participants returned their surveys by mail to Marsella Perry, Local 259's job referral representative. Results of the union's confidential survey are in Appendix D.

27. At the outset the author served as a participant observer, organizing unemployed members under the direction of union leadership. The author subsequently became director of the effort in April 1993 and continued through February 1994.

28. The Local 259 Unemployed Hotline was discontinued in December 1994. While few people called the hotline, Marsella Perry, the union employment referral agent, told me that the union was receiving an average of 150 calls a week from former members seeking job referrals to auto dealerships. A majority of these calls, according to Perry, were coming from relatively unskilled B mechanics. Meyers, who confidently said that the union's unemployment had stabilized in the last months of 1994, was not aware of the large volume of calls the union had received from unemployed members. Interview, December 13, 1994.

29. Interview between the author and Roberta Shlosko, January 1993.

30. According to Dubofsky, in 1914, New York garment manufacturers produced 69.3 percent of all women's clothing made in the United States and 38.4 percent of U.S. men's wear production. See Melvyn Dubofsky, *When Workers Organize: New York in the Progressive Era*, (Amherst, Massachusetts: University of Massachusetts Press, 1968).

31. Dubofsky, 5.

32. Interview, Nick Unger, ACTWU, New York State Political Director, April 5, 1994.

33. Unger argues that the unemployment benefit program was inspired by the union's leadership who were committed to the development of a socialist or social democratic change. The belief was based on having "the union set up things with the understanding that government will take them

over." By providing a modicum of support, the program also deterred unemployed garment workers from bidding down the price of their labor. Unger maintains that the unemployment benefit program was an initiative of leadership and did not spring from membership demands for such a program. Interview, Nick Unger, April 5, 1994.

34. Unpublished data, U.S. Bureau of Labor Statistics, New York, 1994.

35. Amalgamated Clothing and Textile Workers Union, AFL-CIO, *Report of the General Executive Board.* Sixth Constitutional Convention, Las Vegas, Nevada, June 7-10, 1993, 136-137. ACTWU predicts a decline in all basic occupations with the possible exception of nongarment sewing machine operators.

36. On February 20, 1995, mainly as a consequence of dwindling membership and political clout, The Amalgamated Clothing and Textile Workers Union agreed to merge with the International Garment Workers Union (representing approximately 150,000 women's apparel workers) to form UNITE, the Union of Needletrades, Industrial and Textile Employees. According to *New York Times* reporter Leonard Sloane, a chief motivation of the merger was to become "a major political force in New York." See Leonard Sloane, "The Two Big Apparel Unions to Outline a Merger Today," *The New York Times*, February 20, 1995.

37. For a discussion of the implications of seasonal, cyclical, and secular unemployment trends, see Chapter 2.

38. Nick Unger, Political Director, ACTWU, Interview, April 5, 1994.

39. Nick Unger, Interview, April 5, 1994.

40. On the state level, ACTWU's political lobbying efforts include attempts to augment regulation of "hot shops" that employ undocumented workers and to persuade the state to provide funds for training textile workers.

41. In the early 1990s ACTWU actively supported the Jobs With Justice Campaign for Universal Health Insurance, a labor and community coalition that is directed by the Communications Workers of America.

42. Nick Unger, Interview, April 5, 1994.

43. The field hearing, held at Federal Plaza in New York City by Senator Moynihan, who was a key member of the Senate Finance Committee, was the result of intensive lobbying by members of the New York Unemployed Committee. NYUC members initiated a campaign in February 1991 to protest the conspicuous indifference of local members of the House of Representatives and the Senate to the issue of the escalating numbers of unemployed who exhausted their government jobless benefits. NYUC organizers asked that local unions participate in the campaign. NYUC members prodded Senator Moynihan and his staff to conduct a field hearing

on joblessness and the deficiency of unemployment benefits in New York City to demonstrate his empathy with the problem. But Moynihan and Senate Finance Committee members were opposed to extensions on principle, since they would interfere with the October 1990 budget accords between President Bush and Congress, under which no new appropriations would be authorized, unless offset by a corresponding cut in the budget or an increase in taxes. The testimony of Clayola Brown was one of the results of the effort by the NYUC to encourage Moynihan to hold a hearing in New York City. Other labor leaders to testify included Ed Cleary, leader of the New York State AFL-CIO.

44. Clayola Brown, Vice-President, ACTWU, *Our Members Need Unemployment Insurance Reform Now!*, Testimony, Hearings of the Subcommittee on Social Security and Family Policy, Senate Finance Committee, New York City, June 24, 1991, 3.

45. Clayola Brown.

46. See Chapter 4 on ACTWU's goals, political strategy and bargaining towards the New York Labor Campaign on Unemployment.

47. Interview, Nick Unger, political director, ACTWU, August 24, 1994.

48. Interview, Nick Unger, political director, ACTWU, August 24, 1994. The CP model referred to by Unger represents the American Communist Party's strategy of organizing the unemployed in the 1930s and 1940s.

49. In the early 1990s, the International Ladies Garment Workers Union challenged a company dominated union at the Domsey Trading Company, a used clothing distributor in the Williamsburg section of Brooklyn. Both ILGWU and ACTWU continue to challenge company-dominated unions.

50. District Council 37. *22 Years: Local 420 Hospital Division of District Council 37: We Want Our Jobs Not Welfare*, New York: DC 37 American Federation of State County and Municipal Employees, 1975, 4.

51. *22 Years*, 4.

52. Key leaders in the campaign were Jerry Wurf, executive director of DC 37, Carrie Miller, then president of Local 420, and James Butler, then Chapter Chairman of Fordham Hospital. Union leaders said their primary motivation in the campaign to save Fordham Hospital was to preserve a vital community service serving a low-income community. The union also contended that the decision to close Fordham would have disproportionately negative consequences on low-income Black and Puerto Rican residents in the Fordham area of the Bronx. See *22 Years,* 1975.

53. Conflict between the Office of Collective Bargaining and DC 37 (and other members of the Municipal Labor Committee) tends to heat up

during contract negotiations. During the early 1990s, Mayor Dinkins and management representatives said it was contemplating layoffs as a means to help balance the city budget. While some DC 37 members lost jobs, according to one union informant, all of Local 420's members who were laid off were redeployed in new jobs. The union's ability to preserve jobs may be explained in part by its willingness to engage in direct confrontation against the city and the Health and Hospitals Corporation. Yet the union is regularly threatened with mass layoffs by administrators and political officials seeking to cut budgets for public hospitals.

54. See Todd S. Purdum, "Dinkins Says He Is Considering Laying Off 15,000 City Workers," *New York Times*, October 5, 1990. Confirming the suspicion of many labor leaders, Mayor Dinkins formally linked municipal wage increases to layoffs three weeks later by warning that the city would have to lay off 25,000 to 35,000 workers if the city agreed to give municipal workers an equivalent 5.5 percent wage increase previously awarded to public school teachers. See Todd S. Purdum, "Dinkins Links a Loss of Jobs to Pay Raises," *New York Times*, October 27, 1990.

55. Simon Anekwe, "Union to Protest Plans to Close City Hospitals," *Amsterdam News*, April 21, 1990.

56. The 1995 New York City budget includes $46 million in cuts for the Health and Hospitals Corporation, exposing Local 420 members to layoffs. See Jonathan P. Hicks, "After the Deal, the Pain Eases for Some Agencies, But Cutbacks Loom," *New York Times*, June 22, 1994.

57. James Dao, "Pataki Proposes broad Reductions in State Spending," *The New York Times*, February 2, 1995.

58. Interview, James Butler, President of Local 420, and March, 14, 1994.

59. Interview, James Butler, March 14, 1994.

60. On March 15, 1994 Butler's union reported that it organized approximately 2,000 workers and their families in a demonstration against Mayor Giuliani's suspension of the expansion of Kings County Hospital in a primarily African-American neighborhood of Brooklyn.

61. The Philadelphia unemployed contingent that participated in the December 24, 1991 rally in Washington included approximately 2,000 jobless construction workers organized through their building trades unions. Interview, John Dodds, executive director, Philadelphia Unemployment Project, December 25, 1991.

62. See *AFL-CIO News*, July 29, 1991 and October 14, 1991.

63. Interview, Lynn Bell, director, Community/Labor Campaign to Save Taystee Jobs, September 14, 1994. The campaign to save the bakery was

actively opposed by Bakery Workers Local 65, the union that previously represented the rank-and-file workers. According to Bell, a union activist before the Taystee plant was closed, the Local 65's leadership did not want to jeopardize a small number of distribution jobs that Taystee planned to keep in New York. She added that she believed that Local 65's leaders did not want to create an image that it was a militant union because they feared antagonizing management at other regional bakeries where its members were employed. Local 420 was the only union to actively mobilize members in support of the drive to save the Taystee bakery. The fight to save the Taystee plant was also supported by New York Unemployed Committee under the direction of Keith Brooks. While other unions, including Hospital and Health Care Local 1199 and Bakery Workers Local 3, supported the effort, other groups did not organize their members to protest the closure.

    64. Interview, James Butler, March 14, 1994.

    65. Interview, James Butler, March 14, 1994.

    66. Interview, James Butler, March 14, 1994.

    67. Interview, James Butler, March 14, 1994.

    68. Mark Maier, *City Unions*, 78-84, contends that city contracts were consolidated by Mayor Wagner in 1965 to reduce the militancy of unions competing for new members by striving to negotiate superior contracts. From 1968, when the Office of Collective Bargaining was created until the end of 1975, the number of city bargaining units declined from over 400 to 114.

    69. Maier notes that the one exception was the short-lived 1971 walkout, 88.

    70. Interview, Evelyn Seinfeld, director of research, AFSCME, DC 37, May 31, 1994.

    71. Gotbaum discounts the argument that local leadership is suppressed by DC 37, maintaining that the local derives meaningful benefits in the form of collective bargaining and grievance services that cannot be provided on the local level. Interview, July 13, 1994.

    72. Interview, James Butler, president, Local 420, March 14, 1994.

    73. In 1978, Gotbaum and Butler squabbled over Local 420's independent control of its financial records in violation of the international union's policy. Gotbaum tried but could not oust Butler from leadership of the local union. For an account of the dispute between the two union leaders see Jewel Bellush and Bernard Bellush. *Union Power & New York: Victor Gotbaum and District Council 37*, New York: Praeger Publishers, 1984, 433-434. Gotbaum maintains that his effort to remove Butler from the union stems from sound information he received about misappropriation of union finances by Butler. In an attempt to weaken Gotbaum, Jerry Wurf, former DC 37

executive director and then leader of International AFSCME, formed an alliance with Butler.

74. *22 Years*, 2. In an introduction to a monograph on the union's first 22 years, Gotbaum credited Lillian Roberts, a key organizer in the union election victory in 1965, for her role in the union without referring to Butler:

> In the election for union representation, there was no single individual who gave as much and accomplished as much as she did. After 420 won the election, it was Lillian's vision and dedication that launched, nurtured and expanded the education and training programs mentioned before.

75. Interview, Victor Gotbaum, former executive director of AFSCME District Council 37, July 13, 1994.

76. Bylaws of Local Union No. 3.

77. Unlike previous recessions, the decline in private construction was not offset by public sector building. This unprecedented downturn in both public and private construction in New York City brought high unemployment to the building trades industries.

78. Unpublished data, Bureau of Labor Statistics, U.S. Department of Labor, New York, NY, 1992.

79. Interview, Gil Banks, assistant director, Harlem Fight Back, June 23, 1994.

80. Mark Erlich, Who Will Build the Future," *Labor Research Review*, (12), Vol. VII (2), Fall 1988.

81. Erlich, 1.

82. Erlich argues that in an industry with no provisions for seniority older union members believe that job security can be achieved only through restricting membership (15-16).

83. Interview, Vincent McElroen, business representative, IBEW Local 3, June 7, 1994.

84. Interview, Vincent McElroen, June 7, 1994.

85. Gerald Finkel, *History and Organization of the Joint Industry Board of the Electrical Industry: 50 Years of Labor-Management Relations 1943-1993*, Flushing, NY: Joint Industry Board of the Electrical Industry, 1993. Under the Joint Industry Board supplemental security plan agreement, employers contribute 7.65 percent on the first $57,600 of total wages and 1.45 percent on wages of $57,600 to $135,000. The supplemental security fund was considered indispensable for Local 3 members during the decline in the construction industry of the late-1970s. According to the report: "The

participants of the Additional Security Benefits Plan have been able to draw on the fund for the relief they needed and still do need in these recessionary and inflationary times" (Finkel, 50-51).

86. For instance, according to Peter Brennan, former president of the Building and Construction Trades Council, the leadership of unions representing heavy construction workers that depended on large building and infrastructure projects faced severe internal opposition in the early 1990s as a result of the union's unemployment rate of 25 percent. This internal opposition composed of unemployed workers, threatened the leadership positions of some of these union officials. Interview, Peter Brennan, December 1, 1994.

87. Interview, Vincent McElroen, June 7, 1994.

88. Interview, Vincent McElroen, June 7, 1994.

89. At each meeting of the union's unemployed, business representative Robert McCormick was delegated to describe procedures of appeal and advise members on specific problems with the system. Van Arsdale addressed unemployed electricians on the bleak outlook of the construction industry. See *Electrical Union World*, December 19, 1991.

90. Testimony to New York City Commission on Civil Rights against Local 3's restrictive hiring practices were given by members of United Third Bridge, Inc., a coalition of minority electrical workers.

91. Local 3's bylaws direct members to inform the union of any other member who is working below its wage scale: "Any member who has knowledge of another member working for less than the recognized wage scale of this Local shall immediately report the same to the Business Manager. See International Brotherhood of Electrical Workers New York. *Bylaws of Local Union No. 3*, Article XIII, Section 16(b), 26, Flushing, New York, February 14, 1985.

92. Interview, Vincent McElroen, June 7, 1994.

93. Testimony of Thomas Van Arsdale, President, International Brotherhood of Electrical Workers, New York City Commission on Civil Rights, Local 3, April 26, 1990.

94. While the union claims to strive for the incorporation of minorities into its apprenticeship program, it accepts 600 out of 2,544 white male applicants (23.6%), 46 out of 295 black applicants (15.6%), 52 out of 234 Hispanics (22.2%), and 11 out of 21 Asian Americans (52.4%). None of the 12 Native American applicants were accepted (New York City Commission on Civil Rights, December, 1993). Local 3 is also criticized by minority coalitions such as United Third Bridge, Inc. for maintaining a discriminatory

membership policy that tends to restrict employment to white workers and exclude minorities and women.

95. New York City Commission on Human Rights, *Building Barriers: Discrimination in New York City's Construction Trades*, New York, 1993.

96. In referring workers to job sites, the Joint Industry Board may also evaluate workers on the basis of their skills, experience, and past job performance. See New York Commission on Civil Rights, 25.

97. New York City Commission on Civil Rights, December, 1993, 196. This practice was in violation of state labor law, which mandates that if 10 percent of workers receive employment through a union referral system, the union is required to make the list available to those workers that are affected.

98. New York City Commission on Human Rights, December 1993.

99. See New York Commission on Civil Rights, December 1993.

100. See Elizabeth Kadetsky, "Minority Hard Hats: Muscling in on Construction Jobs," *The Nation*, July 13, 1992.

101. New York Commission on Civil Rights, 26.

102. Testifying before the New York Commission on Civil Rights, union leader Thomas Van Arsdale was unaware that Local 3 was legally required to make their "out-of-work" list available to all members. New York Commission on Human Rights, 25-26.

103. New York Commission on Civil Rights, 190.

104. According to Kadetsky, minority construction coalitions were involved in 542 disruptions at construction sites in 1991. Some of these coalitions are being investigated by the government for fraud, extortion, and murder. Kadetsky finds that some minority coalitions are organized by "a few hungry leaders and not necessarily their community-based work force." Often these leaders extort huge profits and generate few jobs for their members. The New York Commission on Human Rights, 2, concludes that the rise of minority coalitions in the construction industry is linked to discrimination. The Commission argues that minority coalitions "undermine the efforts of legitimate groups like Fight Back and United Third Bridge, who are indeed seeking to open the trades to people of color.

105. Interview, Vincent McElroen, June 7, 1994.

106. In 1993, UTB president Samuel Lopez charged Local 3 with nepotism in hiring union representatives and referring out-of-town workers to jobs, even though Local 3 members remained out of work. According to Lopez, over 2,000 out-of-town workers were employed in union construction jobs. See Building Barriers, 93-96.

# CHAPTER 5

# Organized Labor Responds to Rising Unemployment

The case study of the "Jobs Now!" coalition of exclusive unions in this chapter will show that building trades union policies toward their unemployed members are constrained by the unions' accountability to their workers. Construction workers remain active union members of these exclusive unions even after they lose their jobs. It will be demonstrated that the catalyst for the march and rally was angry workers demanding that the building trades unions respond decisively to the high unemployment in the construction industry that persisted in the late 1980s and early 1990s. Ordinarily, many building trades unions are expected to provide job referrals to these members who complete work assignments. The intensified rank-and-file anger over the unions' failure to provide jobs was displaced through the "Jobs Now!" march and rally, which directed hostility away from union leaders and contractors to government officials. While the building trades union mass demonstration described in this chapter indicates the militancy of unemployed workers, it also displays the shallow and exclusive demands of unions and contractors bent solely on improving conditions in the labor market for construction workers. It will be clear that the building trades rally's demands were limited to the revitalization of a lucrative segment of high-profile construction projects. The construction coalition virtually excluded demands for the construction and rehabilitation of low- and middle-income housing programs that would have also advanced the interests of minority construction workers as part of a broad jobs program for low-income workers in other sectors of the economy.

The principal plank of the building trades rally, "Rebuild New York: Jobs Now!" was a demand for state and local jobs programs to create at least 15,000 new jobs for unemployed construction workers. More than 50,000 employed and unemployed construction workers from some 200 building trades unions marched across the Brooklyn Bridge on December 19, 1991 to a rally calling for government creation of construction jobs.[1]

The building trades rally was perhaps the largest unemployed workers demonstration since the 1930s.[2] During the Great Depression, massive mobilization of jobless workers pushed the federal government to create work programs and a system of unemployment protection that laid the foundations for the current American welfare state. Similarly, the December 1991 rally seems to have prompted city and state officials to declare public support for capital spending programs that produce jobs for unemployed construction workers.[3] Construction industry and union officials maintained that the construction rally persuaded Mayor Dinkins to speed up $225 million in capital construction projects. The Mayor also agreed to convene a "summit meeting" to address concerns of the city's construction trades.

Surprisingly, the building trades unions were much more active in organizing both working and unemployed members in direct political confrontation aimed at unemployment than other, more progressive unions in New York. Unlike unions that took part in the ad hoc New York Labor Campaign on Unemployment in 1991 and the New York Labor Coalition to Rebuild New York in 1991 and 1992, the building trades unions effectively elicited cooperation and a collective response to unemployment through direct political action. The march and rally by about 50,000 working and unemployed construction workers demonstrate that trade unions—or, at least construction unions—can mobilize members if they choose to do so.

The construction unions' decision to organize their members in a march across the Brooklyn Bridge and to rally for two hours at City Hall Park had to do, in part, with the special relationship that building trades union members have with their union. Construction unions often act like guilds and, in some ways, employment agencies. Unlike members of unions organized through collective bargaining agreements with their employers, building trades unionists often first become associated with their unions while acquiring their specific skills in apprentice training programs, and continue to remain affiliated during periods of unemployment. Membership in the union is not an afterthought once the worker has been hired, but rather a critical determinant in obtaining a skill and a job. A majority of workers in the building trades unions are recruited into long apprentice programs before they become journeyman members of their organizations. Apprentices enter training programs lasting from six to eleven years before they become journeymen. Once a construction worker becomes a journeyman, he remains dependent on a referral agency that is often also administered by building contractors. In this way, trade union leaders assert considerable influence over the shape that workers' lives take even after they are unemployed. Construction workers, in turn, exert pressure on their union officials to furnish an ample number of jobs. This system differs considerably from the nebulous association of workers who are members of industrial, service, and government unions.

During periods of unemployment, workers represented by the building trades are also in a different relationship with their unions than workers in other industries. Most union-worker relationships are quickly severed after workers lose their jobs. For most unions, representing working members takes precedence over ministering to the troublesome and often demanding needs of workers who are laid off. The formerly supportive association between union and worker is usually disrupted permanently following unemployment as unions cut ties with their former members. Most unions see their responsibility to working members as representing them in collective bargaining, handling grievances, and maintaining health and pension plans. Finding a new job is usually not considered a union responsibility for industrial, service or government union members, but as something for which the individual atomized worker is responsible. At this point, the worker ceases to be an autoworker, textile worker or hospital worker.

Conversely, construction workers tend to retain affiliation to their union even after they are laid off. In short, they retain their identity as construction worker even without the job. This is not surprising since building trades unions recruit and train members and often refer them to employers. Building trades unions are considered to have some responsibility in finding jobs for membership after they are laid off. This expectation, held by both members and leadership, is not present in unions representing semi-skilled and unskilled workers.

The bonds between construction workers and their unions are solidified by the unsteady and temporary nature of construction that produces frequent bouts of unemployment. In this industry, the erratic and temporary character of employment tends to engender a closer relationship between members and their unions than between members and management. When construction projects are completed, jobs with specific contractors are often terminated and workers rely on their unions to provide referrals for new jobs at prevailing wages. As a function of the referral system, unions have more control over their members' lives than exists in other unions.[4] Such control derives from the unique position that building trades unions occupy in the structure of the construction industry.

The close relationship between construction workers and their unions can be both beneficial and harmful to trade union power. On the one hand, building trades unions command greater loyalty from members recruited individually into their organizations; on the other hand, when the industry undergoes periodic economic decline and therefore has fewer jobs, building trades unions are often unable to provide employment referrals anticipated by their members. When this happens, the possibility of discontent and rebellion in the rank-and-file increases.

## Trade Union Influence in the Construction Industry

Activism in the building trades began in the early 1990s, in an environment of escalating political and economic adversity towards unions. Construction unions no longer had the labor market power to command high wages for their members that they had in the 1960s, when labor unions dominated the construction industry. The decline in influence resulted from a sharp rise in non-union building contracting, reduced demand for skilled craft workers, and more minority and immigrant workers in the industry. Expansion of the non-union segment of the construction industry in the 1970s and 1980s weakened the capacity of unions to maintain high-wage union jobs for a decreasing membership.[5] Many high-wage union jobs were already displaced by construction industry jobs requiring fewer skills. According to Erlich:

> The feeling of craft pride and a sense that union membership was a badge of craft competence were once the glue that bonded organized craftsmen. These appeals will no longer function as effectively with

a body of workers who are less skilled and semi-industrial in nature. Organizers now have to operate in an industry in transition and therefore must tailor their messages to workers with widely disparate levels of skills, expectations of job security, and long-term commitment to the industry.[6]

In a shrinking construction industry, however, building trades unions are reluctant to organize new workers who will compete for fewer and fewer jobs with existing members, particularly new members drawn from minority and immigrant populations. Still, non-union contractors employ these disdained workers in larger and larger numbers at lower wages. According to Susan Jennick, executive director of the Association for Union Democracy, building trades union opposition to organizing new workers has further concentrated high-profile construction projects in the hands of a small labor aristocracy while conferring a larger number of low-wage jobs on minority workers.[7] "The larger issue is control," according to one analyst of New York labor. "Unions are reluctant to bring in new workers who may oppose them and members will be opposed to bringing the unemployed in. Employed people are against new unemployed workers because they will bring competition."[8]

Even as the power of building trades unions in New York declines, construction workers continue to value their union cards as a means of access to high-wage jobs. Without membership in an established building trades union, workers are virtually excluded from such jobs. Thus, construction unions tend to segment into low-wage, moderate-wage, and high-wage jobs. The low end of the industry tends to be dominated by smaller housing and commercial building projects utilizing non-union, minority, and immigrant labor. The high end of the industry consists of heavy construction jobs (highways, bridges, subways, and other infrastructures) and mechanical trades employment (electrical, plumbing, steamfitting) in the construction of large buildings.

## Unions in a Declining Industry

The economic recession of the early 1990s hit the construction industry the hardest. While the number of all jobs in New York City decreased by 12 percent from December 1989 to January 1993, jobs in the construction industry declined by 37.4 percent, more than any other industry in New York and more than the 1969-1976 decline of 36.8 percent in the construction industry.[9]

The capacity of building trades unions to give their members access to the jobs they had come to rely on was therefore severely curtailed during the New York City economic recession of the early 1990s. Tens of thousands of construction workers were put out of work by the steep drop in private residential and commercial construction following the collapse of the local real estate market. A simultaneous drop in public sector construction projects intensified the effect of the loss of private sector jobs, historically a dependable safeguard for building trade unions during economic recessions.

Since the late 1960s, building trades unions have had to defend their members' high-wage jobs in an environment of shrinking demand and increasing labor competition from new, unorganized construction workers. While it is common for the industry to experience cyclical recessions, fewer workers have regained steady jobs following revival of the local economy during the most recent economic downturn. In addition, more high-profile luxury construction projects, which provide fewer jobs than low- and middle-income residential housing development, further impaired job growth in the industry since the late 1970s.[10] Thus, although construction unions have weathered cyclical swings of joblessness between recessions and recoveries, employment stability in the industry as a whole has gradually declined in the two decades since the early 1970s.

More immediately, unions in the early 1990s faced the serious predicament of unemployment rates exceeding 50 percent. Although all building trades unions suffered from high rates of unemployment, some were hit harder than others. Building trades unions that limited the labor supply by restricting membership experienced lower levels of unemployment than unions with fewer barriers to membership. And as we observed in chapter 4, while continuing to shield core workers from unemployment, Local 3 cushioned the severity of unemployment for workers in the union's construction division by creating a work-sharing program and annuity benefit plan that provided supplemental benefits for out-of-work members. Many building trades unions, however, lacked Local 3's union-based unemployment protections that were developed over decades under the stewardship of past president Harry Van Arsdale. These unions tended to represent workers that were employed in heavy construction projects that were held up during the recession: operating engineers, carpenters, concrete workers and truck drivers.

## Appearance of Unemployment in the New York Building Trades

The construction union referral mechanism was damaged by the early-1990s recession. A large pool of unemployed construction workers was created by the long duration of joblessness that resulted from the economic downturn. As in previous recessions, the inability of unions to find new jobs for unemployed members strained the political credibility of union leadership. Construction workers who lost jobs were unable to find new work before exhausting their 26 weeks of federal jobless benefits. Some officials facing high unemployment encountered electoral challenges to their leadership. For example, unemployment rates exceeding 50 percent put pressure on the leaders of unions representing operating engineers, carpenters, and haulers of concrete and other materials. Union halls were filled to capacity by hundreds of members demanding that their unions provide jobs. In response to these insurrectionary tendencies, union officials turned to political action to deal with unemployment in the industry.[11] Building trades unions also contemplated collective strategies to address the needs of their unemployed members. Both these strategies resulted, in part, from growing disaffection among the membership.

## Managing Discontent: Organizational Apparatus of the Labor Movement

The December 1991 "Rebuild New York: Jobs Now!" rally called for removal of bureaucratic government obstacles to local construction projects and pushed for federal legislation to create a "National Infrastructure to Rebuild America." The rally was organized and sponsored by building trades unions and contractors, and while the vast majority of demonstrators who attended the rally were both working and unemployed trade union members, the action was also endorsed by employers associations. These groups wanted to expedite construction projects requiring government consent and funding. The rally was sponsored by The New York Building and Construction Trades Council, the local coordinator of political action for construction unions; the New York Building Trades Employers Association, representing the interests of large building contractors; and the New York Building Congress, a joint labor-management association promoting economic development through construction projects in New York City. Formally sponsored and organized under the auspices of established building trades unions, no dissident community groups or labor organizations representing minority, immigrant, and women workers were invited to participate in the rally. As a result, the goals of the construction workers' rally did not extend beyond the immediate demands of building trades union members and their employers.

What follows is an examination of key organizations participating in the December 1991 building trades rally, their rationales for involvement, speculation of their leaders on the feasibility and effectiveness of political mobilization of their members, and examination of divisions among construction workers that tended to limit broader political action.

### Building and Construction Trades Council

The Building and Construction Trades Council of Greater New York, a coalition representing the political and economic interests of building trades unions, organized the December 1991 rally. The Council rose to prominence in the early 1970s as a result of their staunch support of President Nixon's Vietnam War effort. Peter J. Brennan, the president of the Council, brought building trades unions together in May 1970 to march in support of Nixon's war policy. Police estimated that 150,000 construction workers marched up Broadway to City Hall on May 20, 1970 in support of Nixon's expansion of the Vietnam War.[12] Two weeks prior, several hundred marauding bands of helmeted construction workers using metal wrenches and pipes broke up student anti-war demonstrations in the financial district, leaving about 70 persons injured.[13] While Brennan said the demonstrations by the construction workers were a spontaneous response to the anti-war protests, in his estimation the violence may have been justified. "Perhaps a few ruffians opened the door to let the light in . . . violence opened the door to some sanity."[14]

A week later, Nixon invited Brennan and Thomas Gleason, general president of the International Longshoremen's Association, to the White House to congratulate them, calling their support for his Vietnam policy "very meaningful."[15] In a prepared statement to Nixon, Brennan reiterated construction workers' support for Nixon and the Vietnam War.

It is our fervent hope and prayer that you will be successful in your efforts and we call on all Americans to cooperate with you in giving your plan a chance. . . . The hard hat will stand as a symbol, along with our great flag, for freedom and patriotism to our beloved country.[16]

He added that he hoped Vietnam War veterans would eventually return to construction jobs: "We pray that our fighting men will be able to exchange their steel helmets very soon for hard hats and join with all of us in building a greater America, morally and physically for all Americans."[17] These words ironically foreshadowed the deepening crisis of unemployment in the building trades industry that would develop over the next 20 years, forcing Brennan to organize a rally calling on government to provide jobs for construction workers.

With the same objective of influencing government through a mass display of organized members, Brennan said he organized the December 1991 jobs rally to demand that city and state officials accelerate public construction projects. However, according to Brennan, the primary impetus for the rally was to vent the frustration of unemployed building trades workers who were putting pressure on union officials to take more tangible action in response to the jobs crisis in the construction industry:

It probably was the most impressive show of force we had since the Vietnam War. I would say the motivation for the rally was jobs and frustration among the men and their families. It not only sends a message to elected officials, but it also allows the rank-and-file people to blow some steam off. The officers of unions in the building trades were very happy when we organized the rally. Unemployed people were turning up filling halls of several hundred members. There was frustration. People were asking questions. Wives were looking for paychecks. And union leaders needed to show that they were concerned with their unemployed members.[18]

According to Brennan, the rally was welcomed by union leaders, particularly heavy construction unions, who were experiencing high levels of unemployment and criticism from their members:

There was a lot of pressure from union officials for us to do something. That is what I meant by letting some steam off. It was a serious rally, but [the workers] also had some fun. Some of the heads of unions were very happy. If it was just one union doing it by themselves—that doesn't mean much. We had cooperation from many union leaders.[19]

Construction workers who participated in the demonstration broke into chants of "We want jobs! We want jobs!" and rally organizers channeled these sentiments into support for a 10-project action plan to spend public funds for new construction projects to rebuild New York, thus actualizing the release of government funds for unionized construction jobs.

At the demonstration, Brennan expressed his confidence in direct action as a political strategy to defend what he called union jobs in New York. He warned that if "government doesn't pay attention" to the demands made at this rally, the Building and Construction Trades Council would organize other rallies in support of jobs for unemployed construction workers: "We will do it over and over again as long as they are needed." However, in an interview, Brennan confided to me that he considered rallies and demonstrations to be a final recourse to be used only on rare occasions when demanded by members:

> I think overall that it was successful to let the men and women express themselves. We know we can get them out in big numbers—but we don't usually call for demonstrations. . . . Same as in the rally in 1970 to support the troops and get them home safe. You can't do it everyday because it loses its impact. . . . You can't pull them off all the time or you wear the members out. They ask 'What are they marching around?' So you don't call these things every week. The men have things to do with their families. If you have a plan they follow you. Plus they know you're out there too.[20]

According to "Rebuild New York: Jobs Now!" building trades rally organizers, about half of the demonstrators were unemployed construction workers called by their unions to attend the rally. Most of the other protesters taking part in the demonstration were employed construction workers who exchanged a day's pay to participate in protesting the steep unemployment rate in their industry.[21]

Although the "Rebuild New York: Jobs Now!" demonstration was limited to defending the narrow interests of the construction industry, the mobilization of rank-and-file members for political action showed that building trade unions were willing and able to use direct action as a means to mollify agitated workers and partially achieve their goals. And according to Brennan, the political objectives of the rally were partially realized.

> By putting those people on the streets, and we kept politicians out of it, it was [intended to] shake up politicians. We didn't think that everything would suddenly happen by having a rally. . . . [But] sometimes politicians don't take it seriously—they think that we have to do this to allow our workers to let some steam off. We had meetings with the mayor, the head of the Port Authority and quite a few other people. . . . City, State and other officials can't always do things. But the rally showed them that you don't just sit by.[22]

Control over the angry workers at the demonstration was exercised by issuing finite and limited demands to the city to expedite government approval of public construction projects. All the speakers were officials of established labor unions, representatives of construction industry contractors, political officials, and religious leaders. No rank-and-file union members or leaders of activist minority organizations were invited to speak at the rally.[23] Larger issues surrounding unemployment, the pressing need for low- and middle-income housing in New York City, the right to work or job security, and the role of industry or municipality in job security and worker retention were not addressed at all.

The Building Trades rally also indicated that union officials wanted to steer rank-and-file anger from leadership to government officials. The primary motivation of the rally, according to Brennan, was to "allow our workers to let some steam off." Because membership is not contingent on employment, union officials remained accountable to their members even after they were laid off from work. According to Brennan, the sharp decline of the construction industry in the early 1990s drew attention to union leaders' failure to supply jobs to members.[24]

**New York Building Congress**

While the union-controlled Building and Construction Trades Council was responsible for organizing most of the building trades union members at the demonstration, the New York Building Congress worked with employers and their interests and developed demands compatible to both business and labor. The "Action-Plan" put forth at the rally called for ending red tape and delay of 10 government construction projects, and for incentives to spur public and private housing and renovation projects. The Congress also called for city and state government officials to participate in a "Rebuild New York Summit" in early 1992. The demands to "Rebuild New York" paralleled the demands of the Labor Coalition to Rebuild New York, the ad hoc organization formed by progressive unions calling on local and state government to revitalize the manufacturing base in New York City (see chapter 6). Most of the latter group's demands would have helped the specific concerns of the labor unions participating in the coalition. While the demands of construction unions were articulated through mobilizing over 50,000 construction workers, the most that the Labor Coalition to Rebuild New York could do was have a meeting at the Yale Club in New York attended by labor officials, economists, and sympathetic politicians. The result was an agreement by the New York State AFL-CIO to support the 15-point program. The demands of the construction unions were considerably more focused and would benefit the coalition of some 200 unions in 17 building trades. Organizers proposed that the summit should examine speeding up public and private projects, enforcing workplace safety and the prevailing wage. These demands addressed concerns of both contractors for new construction sites and of labor unions for new jobs. The Building Congress estimated that the proposed projects would create about 15,000 new jobs for construction workers.

In reference to the rally, Building Congress president Louis J. Coletti said the demonstration was effective in compelling city, state, and federal political officials to expedite new public and private projects.

> . . . to their credit, the officials were listening. Rally organizers and participants knew their message had been heard when Mayor Dinkins quickly announced that he would hold a "Summit Meeting." The Summit agenda was going to include discussions of how City Hall and the private sector, as well as State and Federal agencies, could work together to ensure that the City received its fair share of capital spending. And ways of expediting the City's Capital Program would be taken up. . . . Within several weeks of the rally, several major projects that had been stalled began to move through the

approval pipeline with the help of City Hall, some to the point where they could be started soon.[25]

This assessment of the outcomes from the rally indicates that even officials representing management consider direct action an effective means to influence government officials. Construction industry leaders found this method of political negotiating palatable because they agreed with the building trades union demands to remove government obstacles to new construction projects.

**New York City Central Labor Council**

The New York City Central Labor Council (CLC), the local affiliate of the AFL-CIO that is customarily responsible for initiating political strategy for organized labor, actively participated in the building trades rally. Thomas Van Arsdale, president of the CLC and IBEW Local 3 brought 9,000 of his members to the demonstration and was a prominent speaker at the rally.

The CLC generally takes conservative positions on political issues. Election to the CLC is not based on democratic rank-and-file participation of members of New York City locals. Instead, each local New York trade union affiliated with the AFL-CIO is allocated a single vote. Industrial and public sector unions are not allocated additional voting rights based on their larger membership; consequently, the CLC is dominated by conservative leadership elected by the more numerous but far-smaller craft and building trades unions. No formal established collective opposition currently challenges CLC leaders on their positions. Theoretically, CLC's leaders are considered by trade unions affiliated with the AFL-CIO as the political arm of the local labor movement, responsible for local policy and political action. Usually, however, the organization does little more than organize the traditional Labor Day March up Fifth Avenue.[26] (See chapter 6 for a discussion of the CLC in relation to various ad hoc trade union and activist efforts to address the unemployment problem in New York during the early 1990s.)[27] But while the New York CLC usually projects a conservative, passive stance toward government policy, the extent and depth of the recession in the early 1990s compelled more urgent action. Perhaps the most notable show of concern with the unemployment problem was the CLC's support of the "Rebuild New York: Jobs Now!" rally.

Up until this action, the CLC had not entirely ignored the unemployment crisis in New York City. Competition from independent ad hoc labor groups, in response to rising unemployment, prompted the CLC to make several moves on unemployment. There was political action in the form of monthly meetings of the Human Services Providers Advisory Committee (HSPAC), an organization of union-based social workers. HSPAC efforts typically involved education advocacy, job referral services, seminars, and other meetings for political, education and social service directors of labor unions to consider strategies to minimize the effect of unemployment on affiliated trade unions and their members. These efforts culminated in the fall 1992 conference that included a workshop on "Job Loss and Survival."[28] The outcomes and recommendations tended to focus on individual financial security during unemployment and did not advocate social or political responses to the crisis. The CLC was not willing or interested in taking a more conspicuous role in the struggle for jobs or expanded unemployment benefits.

The Central Labor Council rarely promotes any form of political action that it does not initiate. In particular, it avoids association with any action that smacks of militancy. Harry Kelber, coordinator of the Trade Union Leadership Institute of the Central Labor Council from 1985 to 1990, suggests that the reluctance of CLC leadership to support independent labor action creates obstacles for conscientious labor leaders who decide to take militant action against employers.

There are some very sophisticated labor leaders who are trying to do the best for their members. They are honest, sincere, but they are limited in what they can say and do. They are limited, for example, if they went out now on strike. Technically the CLC would support them. But if the CLC felt they were a little too radical for their tastes they would issue a statement of support but would do nothing for them.[29]

Kelber points out that CLC and prominent labor leaders shun these people "because they don't want anyone to come forward in leadership" and compete against them for their members' allegiance.[30]

The Building Trades Rally proved to be an exception to the rule, mainly because it was organized by established union officials with dominant positions in the New York labor movement. Outsiders were not invited to participate in the rally. Historically, there is a relationship between the CLC and New York building trades unions, and the leaders of both the CLC and the New York State AFL-CIO have come from the building trades unions. As a consequence, they would not oppose a union-sanctioned demonstration uniting the interests of building trades union workers with construction industry management.

The CLC supported demands made at the December 19th rally for government support in creating union-based construction worker jobs. Van Arsdale told the rally participants:

> We are here this morning to protest the high level of unemployment in our building and construction industry. We are here to remind the public officials of our city, state and nation that unemployment causes great hardships and threatens us and the stability of our families.[31]

Van Arsdale's address to the rally emphasized the narrow interests of building trades unions and construction employers without reference to the larger problem of unemployment in New York:

> We are here to say that we expect those public officials to do many things to solve the problem. There are capital improvements which are needed which are being delayed which should be put on a fast track. There is the building of our infrastructure which is being neglected. There is the continuing need for building of 100,000 affordable units of housing.[32]

While it is true that the construction industry was enduring one of its worst recessions, it is nevertheless significant that Van Arsdale did not expand demands to provide jobs for all unemployed New Yorkers. Van Arsdale's unexpected demand for building affordable housing was welcomed by minority leaders that had advocated such housing construction for three decades.

### Minority Coalitions: Harlem Fight Back Jobs Creation Proposal

The December 19th building trades demonstration, "Rebuild New York: Jobs Now!", focused attention exclusively on unemployment among rank-and-file members. The rise in joblessness among minority and immigrant construction workers, many of whom are not building trades union members, was ignored by the organizers of this demonstration. Nevertheless, the principal demands of building trades unions and the construction industry as a whole for the creation of government jobs were largely congruous with long-standing demands made by labor and community organizations representing minority and immigrant workers in the industry. Organizers of the "Rebuild New York: Jobs Now!" demonstration proposed that government provide funding and incentives for public and private housing and renovation projects, and push for federal legislation to create a national infrastructure fund.

Harlem Fight Back, a minority coalition of construction workers formed in 1963 to promote black and Hispanic worker representation in construction projects, also supported these general proposals. Over the years, Harlem Fight Back has endorsed housing construction and revitalization projects benefiting workers and residents in minority communities. Since its inception, however, Fight Back has been shunned by the building trades unions as an unlawful group aimed at taking union jobs away from their members. The organization has used pickets and demonstrations at construction sites to publicize discrimination in the industry and to persuade contractors and unions to hire more minorities.[33]

In the wake of the building trades unemployment rally, Harlem Fight Back director James Haughton drafted a proposal to revitalize the economy through building and housing rehabilitation in New York and throughout the country. In early 1992, the activist group promoted a strategy to unite building trades unions, contractors, and workers in the non-white community in the "struggle for jobs." The strategy included a plan to mobilize 50,000 construction workers for a demonstration in Washington, D.C. and a lobbying campaign, including a "total work stoppage in New York City." Fight Back promoted a federal program to build 500,000 homes for low- and middle-income families nationwide and a rehabilitation program for another 100,000 homes inhabited by these same groups. The organization proposes forming a coalition that would link building trades unions and activist groups like Fight Back in supporting such a program through political advocacy and demonstrations in Washington, D.C.[34]

But building trades union officials were not interested in forming a coalition with Harlem Fight Back for affordable housing, nor were they interested in adopting Fight Back proposals for a nationwide "struggle for jobs." The "Massive Jobs for Housing Program" would have been "a major step against racism in the construction industry," according to Haughton, "but building trades unions were never serious about creating jobs for unemployed African American and Hispanic workers."[35] He contends that the building trades rally was designed to benefit the large ranks of unemployed white workers. The construction union seniority systems shut out long-term unemployed African American and Hispanic workers. Haughton argues that:

> The history of racism in the labor movement has impaired building trades unions from seeing beyond the immediate confines of their unions. Once a minority worker becomes unemployed, you become a non-person. You don't exist. Building trades unions don't behave like labor unions in the basic meaning of the term.[36]

Since building trades unions defend the narrow interests of their immediate unions and members, Haughton argues that they are useless in strengthening the labor movement as a whole. This analysis of the rally reflects the general ideology of Fight Back. The activist group maintains that its primary function is "educating black and white workers in the interest of all working people."[37] Gil Banks, assistant director of Fight Back, characterizes the organization's approach as aimed at developing an accurate understanding of social and organizational structures that oppress workers in poor communities:

> Our primary role is education—don't pray to Jesus—go out there to talk to the boss. The understanding and education of workers in their struggle—they only read one side of the story in the media— they are not exposed to the real struggle that labor is involved in against capital.[38]

Fight Back leaders believe that construction contractors employ the race card as a means to push wages down in the industry. According to Banks:

> And when black workers can get jobs, prevailing wages are usually not paid. The problem is that contractors hire Black and Hispanic workers because they don't have to pay the wages that go to white construction workers who are union members.[39]

Fight Back views the exclusion of non-whites and other minorities from good union-based wage construction jobs as an attempt to maintain a segregated labor market for white and black workers. One result of this pattern of worker segregation is the bidding down of all workers' wages by contractors. Since black workers are excluded from high-paying union jobs in the industry, they are forced into exploitative nonunion jobs with subminimum wages and poor work conditions.[40]

The "Jobs Now!" rally was, in some respects, an example of success in the mobilization of unions in response to the problems of unemployment. Nevertheless, that success was severely limited by the very phenomenon that made it possible, the exclusiveness of the unions involved.

**CONCLUSION**

The building trades unions' function as a hiring hall for members produces stronger ties with unemployed members than exist in most other unions. Construction unions maintain an ongoing relationship with members even after they become unemployed. As a consequence, a large body of unemployed members is a risk to the leadership of building trades union officials who are concerned with maintaining their authority. The social connection of the unemployed to most construction unions forces them, unlike most class-based unions, which terminate membership with the termination of employment, to grapple directly with the problem of unemployment.

Yet these unions' willingness to deal with unemployment comes at a cost: construction unions protect core members by restricting the admission of new workers. While union leaders encountering the entry of diverse workers in most other industries have reluctantly supported incorporation of these new members, building trades unions have doggedly resisted their full admission as core members. As a consequence, a huge labor force of minority and immigrant workers stands at the margins of construction unions. Controlling unemployment in the building trades unions is achieved by limiting entry of new workers. The exclusion of these large segments of construction workers from established unions has become an enduring structural feature in the building trades industry. By confining membership to a smaller number of workers, construction unions limit opposition and competition for an inadequate number of available jobs. However, the inflexible building trades unions strategy of providing high-paying jobs for favored union members has made them increasingly irrelevant as non-union contractors enter the industry in larger numbers.

## NOTES

1. Information and details on the December 19, 1991 building trades demonstration were collected through interviews with rally organizers, participants, union newspapers, and other sources collected from labor and employer associations. The author attended the rally as an observer.

2. See Franklin Folsom, *Impatient Armies of the Poor: The Story of Collective Action of the Unemployed 1808-1942* (Niwot, Colorado: University Press of Colorado, 1991) for a historical review of the New York City unemployed rally on March 6, 1930. Folsom adopts the Communist Party's estimate of 100,000 demonstrators at the rally while *The New York Times* accepted the police department estimate of 35,000 demonstrators. See "The Great Response" (March 6, 1930), chapter 16, 245-260. *The New York Times* estimated that 50,000 people attended the December 19, 1991 march and rally of construction workers. The New York Building Congress, representing both building trades unions and the construction industry, estimated that 75,000 people attended the rally, while the New York Central Labor Council calculated that 65,000 demonstrators participated in the rally.

3. See *Building Congress Update*, New York Building Congress and the Council of Business and Labor for the Economic Development of New York (Special 1992). See also Calvin Sims, "Idle, Angry Hard Hats Tell off City Hall: Protesters, Many Unemployed, Want More Public Works Projects," *The New York Times*, December 20, 1991, B2.

4. See Mark Erlich, "Who Will Build the Future," *Labor Research Review*, 7 (2) Fall 1988, for an examination of the declining power of building trades unions in the construction industry and its effect on union-member relations.

5. See Mark Erlich Fall 1988.

6. Erlich, 18.

7. Interview, Susan Jennick, executive director, Association for Union Democracy, September 21, 1994.

8. Interview, Harry Kelber, former director, Union Leadership Training Institute, August 18, 1994.

9. See Robert Fitch, *The Assassination of New York*, (London: Verso, 1993). See Appendix 1, Appendix 2, and Appendix 14. In the seven-year period from 1969-1976, construction industry employment fell by 39,000 jobs

or 36.8 percent; the industry lost 46,000 jobs in the three years between December 1989 and January 1993.

10. Fitch 1993.

11. Interview, Neil Madonna, Vice President, Teamsters Local 282, December 8, 1994. The union represents haulers of excavation, building, and construction material workers. According to Madonna, unemployment in the union has lingered in the 50 percent range from 1989 through 1994. This trend continues a steady decline that began in the early 1960s. Unlike other construction unions, Local 282 has experienced a secular decline in membership, from 12,000 in 1959 to 3,500 in 1994. "We've been slow for four years," according to Madonna. "This high unemployment was of serious concern to our union leadership." Following a federal corruption investigation, the union was taken over by the U.S. government, the leadership was dismissed, and the union was put under federal trusteeship.

12. Homer Bigart, "Huge City Hall Rally Backs Nixon's Indochina Policies," *The New York Times*, May 21, 1970. The rally was joined by hundreds of policemen in riot helmets marching at the rear of the parade. According to police estimates, 150,000 construction workers participated in the parade, more than the 125,000 demonstrators who attended an anti-war demonstration in 1967. Brennan told the throng of demonstrators that "History is being made here today because we are supporting the boys in Vietnam and President Nixon."

13. The workers stormed City Hall and forced policemen to raise the American flag to full staff after it was left at half-staff in mourning for students killed in anti-war demonstrations at Kent State University. See Homer Bigart, "War Foes Here Attacked by Construction Workers," *The New York Times*, May 9, 1970.

14. Edward Hudson, "Building Trades Set Rally Today," *The New York Times*, May 20, 1970. In apparent support for the rioting construction workers, Brennan has also said "violence by them [anti-war protestors] can bring violence by our people or others disagreeing with them. Therefore, it's a two-way street."

15. Robert B. Semple Jr. "Nixon Meets Heads of 2 City Unions; Hails War Support," *The New York Times*, May 27, 1970.

16. Prepared statement, Peter J. Brennan, president of Building and Construction Trades Council of Greater New York, May 27, 1970.

17. Prepared statement, Peter J. Brennan. May 26, 1970.

18. Interview, Peter J. Brennan, former president Building and Construction Trades Council of Greater New York and former Secretary,

United States Department of Labor during the Nixon administration, December 1, 1994.

　19.　Interview, Peter Brennan, December 1, 1994.

　20.　Interview, Peter Brennan, December 1, 1994.

　21.　*Electrical Union World*, January 28, 1992, reported that virtually every construction job involving building trades union workers had closed for the day. "Workers on those jobs agreed to give up a day's wage to draw attention to the industry's problem. Many union officials also forfeited their wage for the day to be in solidarity with their membership."

　22.　Interview, Peter Brennan, December 1, 1994. Neil Madonna, vice president of Teamsters Local 282, who said, "I think the rally fell on deaf ears, we've been slow for four years", disputes this view. He argues that there has not been any noticeable increase in heavy construction, upon which Local 282 depends. Interview, Neil Madonna, December 8, 1994.

　23.　Cardinal John O'Connor of the New York Archdiocese told demonstrators who attended the rally that "Workers want jobs, not welfare. . . . " adding that "[g]overnments . . . should not be balancing their budgets on the backs of the poor, sick and aged." He also said that he supported the cause of organized labor and the aims of the rally for ending restrictions on public and private construction projects. "Construction Jobs Rally Draws 65,000 from Labor, Management and Civic Groups," *Labor News*, New York City Central Labor Council, January 1992.

　24.　Interview, Peter Brennan, December 1, 1994.

　25.　Louis J. Coletti, "Is the 'Jobs Now' Rally Working?" *Building Congress Update*, Spring 1992, 3. In summing up the consequences of the rally, Coletti noted that " . . . we do know that, after the rally, doors opened and officials listened to our message at public hearings and private meetings where we urged they take the steps that lead to jobs." Coletti said that organized labor should be given most of the credit for "making the rally a success."

　26.　Even the previously sacrosanct Labor Day Parade is considered to a big undertaking for the Central Labor Council, which decided in 1994 to hold the Labor Day Parade down New York's Fifth Avenue once every two years rather than every year. "We're a victim of our own success," explains Ted Jacobsen, secretary of the CLC, as a rationale for changing the Labor Day Parade in New York to a biannual event. "We've created this big middle class, and it likes an extra day's rest at the end of the summer like everyone else." This vision of a victorious and ascendant labor movement in New York is debated by Michael T. Kaufman, "Labor Day Approaches for Harvard," *The New York Times*, September 3, 1994. Kaufman argues that a more accurate illustration of the circumstances of organized labor in New York can be found among hotel and restaurant workers, who were waging a defensive strike against the Harvard Club in New York to protect their health benefits, job titles, and job security. Perhaps Jacobsen's observation reflects the reality that construction unions and other craft and professional unions form a predominant part of the Central Labor Council leadership.

27. In some localities, such as Milwaukee, Central Labor Councils dominated by more radical unions have taken militant policy stances and active roles in worker protests.

28. The workshop focused "on problems of the unemployed and underemployed in the current economic depression." Topics discussed by panelists from the Workers Defense League, New York State AFL-CIO, and State government officials included ways to access the unemployment system and effectively advocate for the unemployed, financial survival, money management and helping strategies. As noted in Chapter 5, CLC efforts did not include mobilization of rank-and-file trade union membership for legislative or social action.

29. Interview, Harry Kelber, former director, Union Leadership and Training Institute, August 18, 1994.

30. Interview, Harry Kelber, former director, Union Leadership and Training Institute, August 18, 1994.

31. Participant observation of the "Rebuild New York, Jobs Now!" march and rally and transcript of Central Labor Council president Thomas Van Arsdale's address to the City Hall rally on December 19, 1991.

32. Transcript of Thomas Van Arsdale's address, December 19, 1991.

33. Harlem Fight Back was founded in the summer of 1963 when black construction workers protested exclusion from jobs at the construction site for Harlem Hospital and Downstate Medical Center in Brooklyn. According to Gil Banks, a leader in Harlem Fight Back, the protests led to 1,500 arrests at construction sites in July and August 1963.

34. See James Haughton, *Coalition for Massive Jobs Through Housing: Proposal for a Mass Mobilization of the Building Trades and Non-White Community for a Massive Jobs Through Housing Program to Revitalize the Economy and Put New York City to Work*, a project proposal prepared by Fight Back in the Spring of 1992.

35. Interview, James Haughton, executive director, Harlem-Fight Back, May 27, 1994.

36. Interview, James Haughton, executive director, Harlem Fight Back May 27, 1994.

37. Interview, Gil Banks, assistant director, Harlem Fight Back, June 23, 1994.

38. Interview, Gil Banks, assistant director, Harlem Fight Back, June 23, 1994.

39. Interview, Gil Banks, assistant director, Harlem Fight Back, June 26, 1994.

40. Interview, Gil Banks, assistant director, Harlem Fight Back, June 23, 1994. Banks thinks that discrimination in the New York construction industry is built on established patterns of corporate race-baiting that have their roots in early industrialism, where black workers were recruited workers to break strikes in mining and manufacturing.

# CHAPTER 6

# Inclusive Labor Issue Coalitions on Unemployment

This chapter chronicles a partial alternative to the narrow efforts of union coalitions to defend the parochial economic interests of their industries. This alternative was an attempt on the part of a coalition of diverse, organized, inclusive labor unions, in alliance with grass-roots and other activist groups, to take action against unemployment among workers in unions of all kinds in New York City during the recession of the early 1990s. The chapter also analyzes the motivations of the unions and union leaders who, encouraged by a grass roots activist organization called the New York Unemployed Committee, embarked on tentative efforts to form a coalition to extend unemployment benefits known as The New York Labor Campaign on Unemployment. That campaign was an effort to ameliorate unemployment for all workers and build working class solidarity across craft, skill, and income categories. It included militant efforts to mobilize the unemployed for political action, modest lobbying efforts by union leaders of political officials, limited actions promoting education, and alternative programs. The reactions that these efforts elicited from union leadership will confirm the argument that the fragmented labor markets and occupational communities of unions in New York tend to influence organizational responses to unemployment. In contrast to the narrow unemployment policies of exclusive building trades unions, inclusive unions representing a broad spectrum of low-income workers tend to support government policy change. However, the dispersed and segmented nature of the New York City labor market for low-income labor makes it difficult for workers who become unemployed to maintain their ties with their unions and fellow workers.

## ISSUE COALITIONS

What happened to the New York Labor Campaign on Unemployment should provide some indications of the problems facing issue coalitions trying to deal with unemployment by uniting unions operating in sharply differing labor markets.[1] Union leadership often wishes to minimize criticism of current policy, regardless of its effectiveness. This is especially true with regard to job security issues that tend to generate intense responses from membership. On the one hand, unions need to expand political power by mobilizing membership; on the other hand, membership mobilization can destabilize union hierarchies and interfere with leadership strategies as UAW Local 259, ACTWU, and other union leaders themselves point out.[2] Mobilizing working membership with recently laid-off workers and the masses of unorganized unemployed might incite protest over the failure of leadership to safeguard jobs. According to Harry Kelber, an observer of labor union officials in New York, the activation of the jobless can create a new power base among disgruntled workers within the unions reflecting concerns of unemployed workers. Jobless workers could expose trade union officials to unwanted criticism from members and the unemployed that could jeopardize their positions of authority.[3] Inclusive class-based unions that have fewer attachments binding members to their unions are therefore particularly averse to mobilizing their unemployed former members for political action.

## FORMATION OF THE NEW YORK LABOR CAMPAIGN ON UNEMPLOYMENT

By the fall of 1990, the labor community had embarked on several independent and collective responses to the disturbing increase in unemployment. A coalition of some 25 New York unions and several activist groups came together in the winter of 1991 to form the New York Labor Campaign on Unemployment. This campaign was planned by the New York Unemployed Committee (an independent organization formed by labor activists) and local New York labor unions to deal with the combined problems of rising unemployment and loss of government safeguards for the jobless.[4] Most trade unions taking part in the *ad hoc* labor campaign had worked together before, forming alliances around other progressive, social agendas related to labor and the community. These are trade unions that frequently work together to promote social change beneficial to workers. According to Jonathan Bloom:

> These people are very active to the extent that their jobs allow. A lot of these people include educational, research and political staff who are assigned to political action. So you'll get the same people who are active on NAFTA, Jobs with Justice Health Care Campaign, and hot strikes in New York City. It's their job to be active on issues that concern their unions.[5]

Other trade unions that joined the coalition had experienced high unemployment over a long period of time or were embroiled in strikes.

Key members of the coalition included unions affiliated with the Amalgamated Clothing and Textile Workers; Amalgamated Lithographers, American Federation of Musicians; United Auto Workers; Communications Workers of America; and American Federation of State County and Municipal Employees, American Transit Union, and American Lithographers Union. Other participants were affiliated with the Teamsters; New York State Public Employees Federation; Hotel, Restaurant & Club Employees and Bartenders; Hospital and Health Care Workers; Actors Equity Association; and the Screen Actors Guild.[6] The most important activist groups involved in the campaign were the New York Unemployed Committee and Corporate Campaign. The Long Island Progressive Coalition, which organized jobless workers in New York suburbs, also participated in some coalition meetings.

### New York Unemployed Committee

Formation of the New York Labor Campaign on Unemployed was spurred by the efforts of the New York Unemployed Committee. Members of the NYUC are jobless workers directly recruited from unemployment offices and organized to support legislation extending unemployment benefits. NYUC was not affiliated with any union, and claimed to represent unemployed workers as a whole; as such it was free to urge trade union officials to take militant action in organizing members for federal and state unemployment benefit extensions.

Keith Brooks and this author, two union organizers with the American Federation of Musicians Local 802 formed NYUC in November 1990.[7] As unemployment rose in New York City and throughout the region, Brooks, a veteran unemployed organizer during the 1970s and 1980s, debated the prospect of forming an unemployed organization to respond to high levels of unemployment and inadequate levels of unemployment benefits. Brooks was best known for the formation of the United Committee of Unemployed People in Baltimore during the summer of 1982, an organization that was instrumental in compelling the State of Maryland to extend unemployment benefits for thousands of unemployed workers during the height of the recession.[8]

During the fall of 1990 and winter of 1991 Brooks and this author felt that the impending regional and national recession represented a new opportunity to organize jobless workers to demand an extension of unemployment benefits beyond the 26 weeks available through much of the 1980s. Brooks initiated a campaign to publicize the fact that jobless workers in the United States were facing a recession with a fraction of the unemployment benefit protections available to workers in previous recessions, including the recession under Ronald Reagan from 1980 to 1982.[9]

As the recession deepened in the New York area during 1990 Brooks decided to test jobless workers' receptivity to a demand for an extension of unemployment benefits. On Monday morning, December 3, 1990 Brooks and two labor organizers distributed leaflets at the Hempstead, Long Island unemployment office calling for the extension of unemployment benefits. By the next Monday, December 10, the group leafleted the largest unemployment office in the nation, on Dean Street and Fourth Avenue in Brooklyn, an office that had long lines of unemployed workers queuing up around the corner. According to Alan Ring, manager of the claims department, the office would have 2,000 unemployed workers claiming benefits on a typical Monday morning during 1991.[10] The efforts by the NYUC were received enthusiastically by jobless workers who were filing claims for unemployment benefits, and unemployment recruitment efforts were expanded at other centers. The New York Unemployed Organizing Committee in December 1990, and redoubled our effort to sign up jobless workers at unemployment claims offices, primarily in Brooklyn, but also in Manhattan.

The organizing efforts at the unemployment centers had a two-pronged strategy: to encourage jobless workers to sign a petition calling on federal and state government to extend unemployment benefits; and to develop a cadre of unemployed workers to organize at unemployment offices to attend demonstrations and protest events publicizing the declining availability of unemployment insurance benefits. By January 1991, the effort was in full swing; NYUC became a regular presence at the unemployment offices on Dean Street and recruited large numbers of minority and immigrant unemployed workers. The vast majority of the unemployed workers recruited into the organization were West Indians (from Guyana, Jamaica, Trinidad, and other islands), Latinos (from Puerto Rico, the Dominican Republic, Mexico, and Central America), and African Americans.

A primary impediment experienced by the unemployed committee from its origins was inadequate resources. As full-time organizers for Local 802, Brooks and this author had to alter work schedules to continue a regular presence at unemployment centers in Brooklyn, especially when support for our organizing efforts increased. Brooks and this author were encouraged to intensify the advocacy effort at the Brooklyn unemployment office, organizing demonstrations for better treatment of the unemployed. On February 19, 1991, for instance, after a membership meeting in a local church a group of some two dozen unemployed workers marched six blocks to the unemployment center to demand immediate payment of checks for claimants who had been denied benefits. Along the way other claimants joined the procession, and by the time they reached the office a large enough group had amassed that the management was compelled to schedule a meeting with the group. Following the demonstration, management acknowledged the New York Unemployed Committee's right to organize inside the center, the group's right to present grievances on issues like late checks, and the need to treat the unemployed with greater respect. NYUC consequently formed a grievance committee that continued to keep the pressure on the center to honor the agreement. From then on, when the committee brought late checks to the attention of management, action was relatively prompt and in general the center processed claims more rapidly. NYUC had put them on notice that, if the situation didn't improve, stronger actions would be taken. NYUC also took up advocacy on the national front, working primarily on extending the length of time unemployment benefits were paid. The group frequently organized members recruited from the unemployed center to testify in Congress, together with groups from Baltimore, Philadelphia, Pittsburgh, and Long Island, in an effort to bring the issue to national attention. The committee lobbied congressional representatives directly, and stepped up its media campaign in the newspapers, radio, and television.

Our stated goal was to bring the jobless to life as a social movement, encouraging them to join other groups, such as trade unions, in the struggle for full employment and social and economic justice.[11] A NYUC statement published in Social Policy explained the group's primary objective:

> We believe that no drive for social change can succeed without including the unemployed as a constituency, and the right to a job or to survive if you can't get one as part of its agenda. By directly recognizing the immediate survival needs of the jobless workers through unemployed organizing, people out of work can become a vital force in defending not only their rights, but also the rights of all workers.[12]

By organizing unemployed persons recruited from jobless centers in demonstrations and rallies, NYUC hoped to focus national and local attention on extending the duration of unemployment benefits to the jobless. NYUC hoped to empower the unemployed as a social group and develop a lasting constituency devoted to these goals. Through much of 1991, NYUC continued to help organize unemployed people from New York City to join other unemployed groups from eastern cities in demonstrations supporting unemployment benefit extensions in New York, Long Island, Albany, Washington, D.C., and Kennebunkport, Maine, the summer home of President George Bush.[13]

During 1990 NYUC recruited 500 workers from unemployment centers as active members of its organization, and at its peak, mobilized nearly two hundred people for a demonstration and lobbying day in Washington D.C. (July 24, 1991) urging Congress to pass legislation to extend benefits. Thousands more unemployed workers signed a petition circulated at unemployment centers throughout New York City appealing to the president and governor to extend unemployment benefits. Other jobless workers joined demonstrations at the unemployment center on Dean Street without actually becoming active members of the organization. Our initial efforts involved lobbying local members of the House of Representatives and Senate to support the benefits extension. Congressman Thomas Downey of Long Island, who chaired the House Human Resources Subcommittee of the Ways and Means Committee, and was an early target of our efforts, played an integral role in drafting and promoting legislation to extend unemployment benefits.

From 1991 to 1993, NYUC regularly held demonstrations for benefits extensions, improved treatment, and swifter claims processing at the unemployment office in downtown Brooklyn.[14] Demonstrations in Washington, D.C. and other east-coast locations focused national media and political attention on the problem. The campaign culminated in November 1991, when President Bush finally signed a federal act into law after vetoing two similar bills on separate occasions during the year. The new law provided temporary extensions of unemployment benefits in states where unemployment exceeded the national average. Thereafter, NYUC branched out to unemployment offices in other boroughs, and also joined worker protests in the wake of mass layoffs.

After passage of the federal extension in November 1991, NYUC dedicated itself to educating and informing the unemployed. In 1993, NYUC held forums near unemployment offices to familiarize laid off workers of their rights to unemployment insurance and other compensation.[15] Along with other unemployed groups, and newly formed unemployed organizations from Southern New Jersey and Connecticut, NYUC continued to go to Washington, D.C. to lobby Congress for continuation of the temporary benefit extensions. NYUC joined forces in demonstrations with the Community/Labor Campaign to Save Taystee Jobs in an effort to keep open a bakery in Flushing, Queens, which had been moved by Stroehman's Bakeries to production facilities in Pennsylvania during 1992.[16]

Despite these successes NYUC was limited in its capacity to organize jobless workers at the unemployment offices. The NYUC didn't have the staff or money to sustain or expand our effort, so turned to labor unions for help. In January and February 1991, Brooks and this author discussed with union presidents, union officials and labor consultants three strategies to include labor unions in the fight to extend unemployment insurance:

1. Encourage trade unions to participate directly in the formation of unemployed committees at unemployment offices by assigning staff to the effort. Brooks and this author hoped to be assigned by Local 802 to promote this effort. Harry Kelber, a former official with IBEW

Local 3 and the Central Labor Council, suggested that individual unions assign staff to particular unemployment offices in the area. This effort would include both advocacy and service support for unemployed workers.

2. Propose that trade unions form rank-and-file unemployed committees of their laid-off former members. Unions would provide resources and logistical support for these committees. Each union would develop guidelines for its own committees (some would establish autonomous committees, others would enroll their unemployed workers as associate members).

3. Formulate a community-labor coalition to lobby political officials for the extension of unemployment benefits. Under this proposal labor unions would join forces with committees of the unemployed. Unions would decide on individual means of organizing their former unemployed members, while unemployed organizations would continue their autonomous efforts. Unions would contribute financially to the efforts of unemployed committees at jobless centers.

NYUC organizers viewed the creation of a New York Labor Campaign on Unemployment as critical to building a solid base of support for those directly affected by unemployment, and thus increase both the visibility and effectiveness of the effort to extend jobless benefits and other social protections. "Programmatically, I am looking for a society of work or income," said NYUC's coordinator Keith Brooks. "While fighting for jobs, my goal is also to establish a vehicle for the defense of the living standard of the unemployed that would influence real policies covering people's lives—income, housing, and medical care."[17]

Brooks considered unions a critical reservoir of working and unemployed workers available for recruitment into the NYUC organization. In fact, some of the more active members of the NYUC were laid off trade unionists from unions that would eventually join our coalition. Brooks underscored the importance of building alliances between trade unions and the unorganized unemployed:

> Central to our project is the organization of the unemployed themselves. A petition to extend benefits has already gained widespread support at unemployed centers and a growing number of union halls. A growing number of the unemployed have already expressed their support to participate directly in meetings and demonstrations.[18]

The initial efforts by NYUC organizers were well received by a number of trade unions. By the end of 1991 NYUC reported that eight unions had contributed $3,050 to its organizing efforts.[19] These funds were used primarily to print pamphlets and charter buses and vans for the organization's lobbying and protest demonstrations in Washington. Trade union members of the Labor Campaign publicly supported mobilization and organizing efforts by NYUC at unemployment offices and in Washington. However, beyond their limited financial contributions, they did little to support directly the group's initial activities. Nevertheless, by February 1991, many agreed to meet to discuss the possibility of forming a community-labor coalition to support and advance the cause of extending federal and state unemployment benefits.

**Trade Union Participants**

The NYUC gained the support in part because of the failings of the Central Labor Council, which was supposed to be the political wing of the labor movement in New York. Though CLC officials acknowledged the devastating consequences of this growing body of jobless workers for New York trade unions, they took a passive approach to unemployment, trying to ameliorate consequences rather than affect causes. Workshops organized by the CLC covered such "self-help" topics as access to unemployment insurance, health insurance, and job retraining.[20] In practice, the CLC prefers to show as little hostility as possible to management, government officials, and business leaders. Concern for the unemployed former members and the unorganized unemployed did not seem to be a priority for them. Hence, while the CLC and its members publicly endorsed legislative efforts of the AFL-CIO to extend government unemployment insurance benefits, they did not make unemployment insurance extensions a priority, nor did they support direct action to extend benefits by activist groups of rank-and-file and unemployed workers.

    Three incidents in particular illustrate the CLC's reluctance to initiate or take part in broad campaigns. First, in a March 1991 meeting with Local 259 trade union officials, rank-and-file members facing layoffs and the New York Unemployed Committee (NYUC), Howard Van Jones, director of employment and training for the New York CLC, suggested that unions should maintain constructive relations with employers and government leaders rather than antagonize employers by mobilizing members.[21] By preserving amicable relations with employers, he argued unions would be able to monitor changes in the economic condition of firms that might be planning to move or close.[22] Second, In June 1992, the executive board of the Central Labor Council's Human Services Providers Advisory Committee opposed suggestions by members to organize "an action type of program" on unemployment at a conference on workplace challenges in the 1990s that was to include a panel on job loss and survival.[23] Third, the CLC's aversion to political organizing and direct action is conveyed openly in federal and state authorized forums in accordance with the Federal Worker Adjustment and Notification Act (WARN Act). CLC held seminars for workers thrown out of work by mass layoffs and plant closings to advise them about aid like unemployment insurance, other federal and state benefits, and retraining programs.[24] Basic information on jobless services was presented, but the CLC did not encourage workers to resist mass layoffs or support unemployment benefit extensions by forming community-labor coalitions.[25] As Van Jones concedes, unemployment insurance benefits were usually exhausted long before those displaced workers completed the retraining programs advocated by the CLC, which in any case, provides uncertain job prospects.[26]

Many unions were frustrated with the inactivity of the established labor movement, as represented by the CLC, in the face of worsening unemployment. They believed that the CLC was making only perfunctory efforts to help trade unions deal with the high numbers of unemployed in the early 1990s. The coalition of unions that participated in the New York Labor Campaign on Unemployment had frequently united in the past against what they saw as the restrained political response of the CLC to concerns that distressed their members. Key members of the Labor Campaign Coalition included ACTWU New York Joint Board; American Federation of Musicians Local 802; United Auto Workers Local 259; Communications Workers of America Local 1180; Amalgamated Lithographers Union Local 1; AFSCME District Council 1707; AFSCME District Council 37; Amalgamated Transit Union Local 1202; Hotel and the Motel Trades Council.[27]

In addition to the New York Unemployed Committee and sympathetic trade unions, Corporate Campaign, an activist organization seeking to expand the effort for extended benefits into a national movement, also participated in the New York Labor

Campaign on Unemployment. This is an organization that runs public action campaigns for labor unions that are involved in fierce labor disputes against employers. Its executive director, Ray Rogers organized a nationwide boycott in support of the successful effort of the Amalgamated Clothing and Textile Workers Union to organize several J.P. Stevens Textile plants in the South in the 1970s. Rogers and Corporate Campaign had assisted leaders of local P-9 in coordinating the strike against a Hormel meat packing facility in Austin, Minnesota in 1984-1986.[28] More recently, in 1993-1994, Corporate Campaign directed a campaign to defend locked out union workers employed by A.E. Staley Manufacturing Company, a corn processor in Decatur, Illinois.[29]

In working with the New York Labor Campaign on Unemployment, Corporate Campaign proposed a mass effort to expand unemployment benefits involving sympathetic unions across the country. Under the plan, Corporate Campaign would mobilize support through Central Labor Councils, trade unions, and independent organizations nationwide. It would also lead a media campaign and help implement organization of the unemployed in public demonstrations. Rogers proposed an independent effort by New York unions participating in the Labor Campaign to push the AFL-CIO into action: "[We are proposing] a mass educational campaign to generate media activity like Keith and Manny are doing."[30]

As a result of his support for unauthorized strikes Rogers developed a reputation as an independent player often in conflict with established union leadership. According to one analyst of labor in New York, union leaders are "on the outs" with Rogers. "Some unions figured out the Corporate Campaign principle and decided to do it themselves. . . . A program on unemployment insurance coming right off Hormel was not a propitious time."[31] While some trade union officials who were members of the campaign considered Rogers a folk hero of the labor movement, they were cautious about embracing his proposals in the community-labor coalition.

The Labor Campaign, then, was joined by unions from industrial, service, and public sectors, including unions with large numbers of minority members, women, and immigrants. All these organizations endorsed the principle that a weak unemployment benefit system acts as a restraint on the organizing power of unions by increasing the pool of potential employees. According to William Henning of the Communications Workers Local 1180:

There is no question that [unemployment] is a factor when you look at all the strikes that occur and the employer tactic of using permanent replacements to scab on the strike. I can't think of a single strike where the employer has employed that as a tactic where they haven't had an ample supply of scabs ready, willing, and able to take the jobs of striking workers. If the social safety net were high enough so that folks who scab would not be positioned nearly so well by scabbing, then I think you might have less of it going on. To the extent that the social safety net either doesn't reach, or the benefits aren't high enough . . . if you have a choice between $200 on unemployment and $400 a week with benefits, I think you'll take the $400 and scab. You know $200 is hardly enough to live on for an unemployed worker. The reality is that many fewer people even have that $200. So that folks who for a variety of reasons are not collecting unemployment benefits are much more apt to scab.[32]

Trade unions representing semi-skilled and unskilled workers were doubly vulnerable to the peril posed by high levels of unemployment and a declining unemployment benefits system. First, according to Jim Guyette, former organizing director of AFSCME DC 1707, which represents low-wage child care and home health care workers, a weak unemployment insurance system hinders the union's ability to negotiate with management and ultimately infringes on the power of unions representing low-income workers on the economic playing field because the availability of unemployment insurance benefits deters people from becoming replacement workers. Second, according to Guyette, a weak unemployment benefit system contributes to low wages in the industry, which fails to lift most incomes above the poverty line. "There isn't much of a difference between our workers making $4 to $5 an hour and an unemployment check. People who we were representing were barely eking out a living."[33] This sentiment by trade union members of the Labor Campaign may have influenced their decisions to further the cause of disenfranchised unemployed workers in an active and potentially visible way. They may also have seen the Campaign as a means to alleviate the impoverished economic condition of some unemployed former members.

## RISE AND FALL OF NEW YORK LABOR CAMPAIGN ON UNEMPLOYMENT

The New York Labor Campaign held its first formal meetings and collaborative sessions during the first nine months of 1991. During this developmental phase, various labor union responses to rising unemployment were considered and discussed. Recommendations ranged from plans to build a national movement for the extension of unemployment insurance to organizing groups of unemployed persons for direct action at unemployment centers. Activist organizations and trade unions introduced proposals for action. However, full employment advocacy groups, independent non-profit organizations, and academics also contributed to Campaign deliberations. Some of the members of the coalition had been involved in the unemployed movement during the 1920s and 1930s.[34]

Activists in the coalition said they saw the Campaign as an effort to connect political lobbying to demonstrations.[35] They advocated three forms of action:

1. Organizing of jobless former members through the creation of associate membership and the formation of unemployment committees at union locals. Associate membership would allow members who had lost their jobs to retain affiliation with their unions. Unemployed committees would work on maintaining formal relationships with these workers for possible mobilization and political action.
2. Mobilizing current members by calling attention to the issue of unemployment and inadequacies in the unemployment insurance system that would affect members threatened by impending layoffs.
3. Supporting demonstrations at unemployment offices and other mobilizations of the jobless at different sites (drop-in-centers, shelters, food kitchens, and welfare offices) to extend organized action beyond unions and into communities affected by high unemployment. Demonstrations would be part of the campaign to increase public awareness of looming unemployment coupled with the weak unemployment insurance system. This action would put political pressure on government officials to reform the system by providing extended benefits to the jobless. (In July 1991, in fact,

members of the Labor Campaign on Unemployment proposed petitioning the state legislature for use of the New York State Unemployment Reserve Fund to extend benefits to the long-term unemployed).[36]

Initially, labor union members of the coalition favorably received these activist proposals. But over time, labor leaders proved unwilling to become directly involved in organizing the unemployed or expending resources to support the effort.

**Conflicts Within the Labor Campaign**

One of the early problems encountered by the Labor Campaign on Unemployment was the division that emerged among members. Trade union officials, leaders of activist organizations, and individuals brought independent and competing agendas to each meeting. Most trade union officials taking part in the coalition told me that they saw the campaign as an effort to stem the threat posed by unemployment to their members. Participants in the Campaign also told me that they saw the effort as a means to show that they were minimally responding to the problem of rising unemployment in their unions.[37] While the unions participating in the coalition saw the effort as a way of ameliorating the pain of extended unemployment on their members, NYUC and Corporate Campaign saw the campaign as the beginning of something bigger, a long-term effort to build broad-based labor support and increase trade union membership. The campaign was viewed by the activist groups as a means to increase bargaining power for labor with management, and to reclaim the unions' role as guardian of low-income organized and unorganized workers. However, some of the participating labor officials also saw the campaign as a way of revitalizing the labor movement. Harry Kelber, a consultant to the CLC, saw the coalition as a means to encourage and educate trade unions, so they can create their own organizations of jobless workers at unemployment offices.[38] He proposed that "the campaign set up a phone and office and pay staff through union contributions."[39] Miriam Thompson of Local 259 visualized the campaign as a possible means to replicate the unemployed organizing drives of the 1930s in the 1990s, but no concrete effort was mapped out at the beginning to achieve that objective.[40]

The absence of a clear agenda at meetings was a salient factor in the decline of the organization. One participant, Jonathan Bloom, executive director of the Workers Defense League, concluded that trade unions may respond to specific requests, but "Unless you ask them to do something particular you'll have a hard time getting them to do it. . . . If you have to tell them what to do they'll say yes or no— but you have to ask for something specific."[41] According to Bloom, NYUC and Corporate Campaign efforts to gain labor's support for building a movement of unemployed workers were too broad for most of the unions who were grappling with difficulties in their individual industries. Discussions and subsequent follow-up interviews with participants indicate that the majority of trade union leaders were initially enthusiastic about the goals of the campaign but became largely unresponsive when they discovered that it aspired to become a militant nationwide movement. On the whole, union leaders were wary of the ambitiousness of the effort that was being planned by the New York Unemployed Committee and Corporate Campaign. They demonstrated both a hesitancy to usurp the leadership position of AFL-CIO and established labor movement through the Labor Campaign, combined with a anxiety about the financing of the organizations activities and showed a reluctance to organize autonomous unemployed members and to participate in a campaign that included activist outsiders.

A bloc of trade unions in the labor campaign worried that the coalition would overstep the bounds of the federal and New York State AFL-CIO, and New York Central Labor Council as national, state, and local political representatives of organized labor. This faction continued to hold out hope that labor's established political bodies could be persuaded to support political action through legislative channels. Local 802 advocated ties to established labor bodies who preferred lobbying to political mobilization and direct action. According to Bloom, labor officials affiliated with the AFL-CIO and its subordinate groups try to avoid local activists capable of instigating dissension that might encroach on their political influence:

> Central Labor Councils were set up by the AFL-CIO to be weak. The real power and clout is held by international unions affiliated with the AFL-CIO. They are potentially working class organizations. But these trade union leaders consider lobbying and organizing to be the same thing. The prestige union officials do 'politics.' For them

doing politics is electing politicians, passing bills, and mobilizing their existing membership base through telephone banking and mass mailing. Some have good technical skills in political lobbying but few skills in direct organizing. This is one reason that they fear union organizers who often have closer ties to their members, or otherwise have the ability to mobilize workers.[42]

While some trade union officials in the campaign expressed a desire to push the AFL-CIO to support their causes they were actually reluctant to oppose the AFL-CIO's conciliatory and compliant stance. Members of this conservative contingent were also uneasy about forming an ad hoc organization because of their limited financial resources. Turning leadership of the Campaign over to the AFL-CIO or New York City CLC, they believed, would grant the effort greater prestige, not to mention financial and organizational resources needed to build a national campaign. John Glasel, president of Local 802, expressed concern over the limited financial solvency of the coalition, along with reservations about the effect a local group would have in exerting significant influence over national policy: "We are a local group—but it seems like we are talking about a national campaign—we haven't got the money. If we can get the money from each city that is a lot easier."[43]

Trade unions who wanted to appeal to the AFL-CIO as overseer of the campaign also felt it would be impolitic to embarrass the AFL-CIO into taking more vigorous action to support coalition goals. Members of this bloc saw independence from the AFL-CIO as counterproductive to the goal of extending unemployment benefits. These members felt that by pressing the AFL-CIO into action, the Campaign would alienate dominant forces in the trade union movement. Glasel believed that a confrontational policy would obstruct development of a broad-based trade union movement for extension of national unemployment insurance benefits. He claimed that unions participating in the Labor Campaign could be identified by the public as "left and radical" and marginalized. In a meeting of the Campaign, Glasel noted the following:

If we get identified on a grass-roots level, we are going to ruffle feathers. Ed Cleary [president of the New York State AFL-CIO] said it wasn't necessary. We have lobbyists in Washington, D.C. . . .

Organizationally it would be better to get [the Central Labor Council] back on board.[44]

This group was distrustful of the leading role activists held in the Labor Campaign and were concerned that the coalition would encroach on the authority of established political bodies of organized labor (The AFL-CIO and the CLC). John Glasel warned the campaign "if we jump too soon, the AFL-CIO may wonder who the hell are those guys screaming."[45] Harry Kelber, who had close ties to building trades unions, warned that the organization should avoid being pigeonholed as radical. He recommended that established union leaders take over and direct the organization.

> A number of things need to be done. You have to start a conversational thing with the AFL-CIO. You have to have top people who they will not challenge. How will they check it out—'is this bad, will it create a problem for you?' If it's left and radical unions—you're not going to get support from the AFL-CIO.[46]

Kelber was suggesting that leaders of leftist unions (many who represent low-income workers), the NYUC, Corporate Campaign, and other activist groups should not be given leadership positions in the organization because established figures in the AFL-CIO and Central Labor Council would mistrust their motives, as did these union leaders.[47] NYUC and Corporate Campaign were viewed by some labor officials as outsiders and usurpers exploiting the ad hoc issue campaign on unemployment. According to one trade union participant in the campaign:

> What we need is a three-track approach, one centered on the unemployed committees, second in the labor unions, and finally a legislative campaign. We have to make it AFL-CIO policy to get on board to fight for benefits. The New York Unemployed Committee cannot be a primary leader if we are to achieve this.[48]

The argument to exclude the New York Unemployed Committee and Corporate Campaign from active participation in the coalition was strengthened by uneasiness of interfering with the political domain of the AFL-CIO and union leadership, which, unlike activist groups, had knowledge and expertise of lobbying on Capitol Hill.[49] Although the

AFL-CIO and international unions lobbied Congress and testified in the House of Representatives and Senate about the need to extend unemployment benefits, they did not sponsor, or organize any formal campaign.[50] This reluctance to act on unemployment on the local level is illustrated by Judy West, political director of Local 802, who expressed her wariness over the issue:

> Everybody I have spoken to thinks it's a great idea to get on with the extension of unemployment benefits. But they put the issue aside and say lets get on with other things because they feel beleaguered by this. They say you can do this through the Central Labor Council.[51]

## Unions' Hesitation to Participate in the Campaign

The diversity of unions in the coalition, which contributed to its initial vitality and enthusiasm, was also responsible for its inability to choose specific actions and get anything done. Early on, a clear difference of opinion emerged regarding the objectives of the coalition, both among the trade union officials, and between trade union officials and activist group leaders. Eventually, all the union officials agreed on one thing: the campaign had to be scaled back in order to succeed.

Moderate labor leaders believed the Labor Campaign should be turned over to the state and national AFL-CIO, and urged the organization to make unemployment insurance reform a key part of their 1991-1992 legislative program. "I don't think each union has the resources for this effort on their own," repeated John Glasel, president of Local 802, in response to the proposals of NYUC and Corporate Campaign. "Do we have the names of people around the country that support the program? Can we work with them to promote Ray's thing?"[52] William Henning, vice president of CWA Local 1180 also questioned the ability of the group to raise funds for the effort:

> I am concerned about the ambitiousness of this group. I would propose that we reach out to other organizations and try to get this a major focus of the IUD, I am concerned that we can't get the $45,000 that is necessary in start-up costs.[53]

Nick Unger, political director of ACTWU said he was unwilling to commit his union to support a mass action, but would be willing to take more moderate action to extend unemployment benefits:

> What kind of coalition will form? We need much tighter proposals. The ad hoc nature makes it difficult. It is possible that pushing the IUD to promote the issue at the Solidarity Day II demonstration on August 31 is the hook for the union. We need political proposals we can work with so that our union can discover the terrain better. We no longer describe our union as 70 percent unemployed, but 70 percent smaller than it was. . . . We can't do general unemployed work in mass education forms. In addition to money for a general campaign, we would be interested in working on politicians. We aren't going to [Washington], D.C., but we may go to Moynihan's office in New York City.[54]

In June 1991, ACTWU vice president Clayola Brown testified at a field hearing held by Senator Moynihan in New York on the impact of declining unemployment insurance benefits on jobless members of the union. However, ACTWU officials did not deviate from a policy of excluding unemployed workers from political action.

### Activist Response to Efforts to Shift Campaign to AFL-CIO

NYUC and Corporate Campaign measured the Labor Campaign's success by its ability to compel the AFL-CIO and larger established labor bodies to take direct action in reconstructing federal and state unemployment benefits systems. Rogers of Corporate Campaign said he wanted to build on the organizing efforts of the Labor Campaign by appealing to national unions to back a media and public relations effort and by supporting autonomous efforts to organize unemployed workers in communities around the nation. This strategy contrasted sharply with the timidity of individual labor unions regarding both direct action and solicitation of support from the established labor community. While many unions were troubled by rising unemployment they were not threatened by former members who lost their jobs since these workers were no longer members. Ray Rogers maintained that the primary objective of the coalition should be starting a movement that would ultimately pressure organized labor into concrete action:

We need to put a fire under the Central Labor Councils. . . . The
AFL-CIO started out not interested in the striker replacement issue,
but now they are running with the thing. One of the problems is that
the AFL-CIO says they support it but they don't run with it.[55]

But most union officials were less willing to test the limits of policy set
by their own union leaders, international unions, and local units of the
AFL-CIO labor confederation. While local union officials in the
coalition often favored more decisive tactics by organized labor, they
were disinclined to clash with leaders in the established union
movement.

Both Corporate Campaign and NYUC had distinct plans to build
a national movement independent of organized labor: Corporate
Campaign proposed a dual approach, first, developing support among
trade unions on a national basis, and second, implementing a publicity
campaign culminating in a national "Economic Justice for
Unemployed Americans Day." This event would coordinate national
demonstrations of jobless workers with mass media outreach.
Corporate Campaign, proposed Rogers, would

prepare an action plan that encourages unions and other groups
individually or in coalition to establish ad hoc support groups across
the country to participate in a variety of events. Coordinated
demonstrations could be planned in conjunction with a goal of
distributing one million pieces of campaign literature or getting a
quarter of a million postcards delivered to the President saying:
'Please let me know what the administration plans to do about this
matter.' The date for mass coordinated actions would provide
opportunities for getting national media exposure.[56]

As activist groups, Corporate Campaign and NYUC were willing to
build a national campaign without endorsement from the AFL-CIO,
but hoped eventually to prod the labor movement to back direct action
to extend unemployment benefits and provide other worker
protections. By developing a national grassroots political organization
of unemployed and organized workers outside the AFL-CIO and its
mainstream labor organizations, NYUC and Corporate Campaign
hoped to create an effective movement to extend unemployment
benefits. Presumably, by engendering compassion for the unemployed
and other marginal workers, they would encourage the AFL-CIO to

lend its support. If that failed, they would consider mobilizing progressive and militant trade unionists and union officials to confront the conservative policies and tactics of the AFL-CIO leadership.

## Unions' Reluctance to Organize Members

A key organizational determinant that prevented unions from actively participating in the Campaign was their unwillingness to organize their members. Trade union leaders representing non-professional, industrial, and service unions did not seek close ties with the unemployed because they saw their relationship with their members as contingent upon employment, and the payment of dues. As Henning puts it:

> I think the reality is that unions didn't see themselves the advocates for those who were not paying dues to them. And the unemployed essentially are not dues paying members. Our plate was full taking care of the members we had a formal obligation to. Some of us attended meetings, helped strategize, and contributed money to the campaign. Most of the folks that I knew of [who participated in the New York Unemployed Committee] were not people who came out of organized union shops. At least that was my perception. Of the unemployed who were involved, it was not my impression that they were folks who had a relationship with organized labor. It seemed they were folks who lost their jobs in a nonunionized setting. This for many of them appeared to be the first time they had encountered organized labor.[57]

Nick Unger, who was a key trade union leader in the campaign, supported this sentiment. In an organizing meeting of the Campaign, Unger said that his union would not actively participate in the coalition until he knew the form that it would eventually take:

> We will be institutionally hesitant until it is resolved what kind of campaign this is. We will not form unemployment committees; we have a hard time working with the unemployed workers in closed shops. Organizing unemployed workers takes different forms in shrinking industries like textiles. They are no longer part of our base.[58]

An exception to the union practice of suspending members when terminated from employment exists among unions representing skilled craft workers. These are the performing arts unions—musicians, actors, scenic designers, etc. (many active in the coalition), printing trades, as well as the building trades—electrical workers, carpenters, and mechanical engineers (see chapter 5). Such unions are expected to provide jobs and deliver services to unemployed workers who remain their members while out of work. Still, these union leaders that represent craft and professional workers are under constant pressure of being defeated by a surge in the number of dissatisfied unemployed members eligible to vote in elections. For example, Bill Pike, former vice president of Amalgamated Lithographers Local 1, attributes his defeat in a recent election to his decision to cut supplemental unemployment benefits and health insurance of jobless members and pension benefits of the union's retirees.[59]

## Labor Campaign moderates its Stance

After the initial meetings of the New York Labor Campaign on Unemployment in February and March 1991, trade union members of the steering committee drafted a plan of action more modest than those envisioned by the NYUC and Corporate Campaign.[60] Three basic policies were determined: (1) decisions to organize the unemployed would be made on a union-by-union basis or through autonomous unemployed committees; (2) the Labor Campaign would be responsible for promoting the need for federal unemployment insurance extensions among trade unions; and (3) the AFL-CIO and its subordinate organizations would be responsible for legislative action.[61]

In May 1991, Unger of ACTWU proposed that the Labor Campaign push for unemployment extensions at labor events organized by the AFL-CIO and international unions as an immediate goal. The Solidarity Day II demonstration, organized by the AFL-CIO and constituent unions, and planned for Washington, D.C. on August 31, 1991 was viewed as a good place to show support through numbers and the display of posters. Strategy was drafted encouraging trade unions around the country to print placards and posters promoting unemployment insurance extensions. No plans, however, were made for direct involvement of organizations of unemployed persons, such as those organized by NYUC or jobless former members, for the Solidarity Day II national demonstration.

According to Unger, if the campaign to extend unemployment benefits was to enlist tangible support from the AFL-CIO, the unemployed could not play a major role in the coalition: "How are you going to organize the unemployed and get on board a coalition?"[62]

As plans to gain support for an extension of unemployment benefits became more modest, interest and participation in the New York Labor Campaign on Unemployment steadily declined. Some 40 participants, including 22 labor organizations attended the initial coalition meeting on February 25. Participation dropped to less than 30 at a breakfast meeting on March 23, the last general meeting of the group. The steering committee of the Labor Campaign continued to meet through the summer of 1991. Attendance at these meetings fluctuated between 6 to 12 trade union officials, along with members of the New York Unemployed Committee. These meetings focused on the modest goal of publicizing the need for unemployment insurance extensions to trade unions through a letter to be circulated to local and national unions. This was to be a first step toward a broader effort to make unemployment insurance benefits a central element of the AFL-CIO's demands. "There will be no labor campaign without signing up 20 to 30 unions, so we need to develop a statement that unions *can* sign onto," said Unger. "This group is either going to have a Campaign to publicize the need for unemployment extensions or it is not going to meet anymore." However, even these efforts to gain support of local labor leaders were largely unsuccessful. At a subsequent meeting, Unger said: "I don't see resistance to our effort out of Van Arsdale [president of the New York City Central Labor Council], I see inertia."[63] After several meetings consisting of squabbles over the division of tasks in the campaign, the effort to draft a letter appealing to national unions to support the Solidarity Day II plan was abandoned.[64]

Union officials stopped attending meetings called by the steering committee, or argued against expanding the effort. Established labor failed to commit resources to the Campaign and were reluctant to participate in the national drive for extension of unemployment insurance. By the summer of 1991, the Labor Campaign steering committee could not agree on a plan or strategy to resist unemployment, and participation in the coalition dwindled to a bare few. The group slowly disbanded, and trade union members considered other ways of responding to the New York City recession. No meetings were convened until January 1992, when NYUC called a meeting of former members of the steering committee to reconsider the campaign. Union officials underscored complications around the issue of incorporating the unemployed into trade union political efforts. According to Nick Unger, organizing for government jobs creation was more expedient than political action on behalf of the unemployed. In spite of the fact that unemployment continued to escalate in the early 1990s, the unemployed were perceived as a minority group of outsiders incapable of marshalling political support in a national election year. Unger asserted the importance of understanding "the rub between the militant minority and the majority position—if you are approaching a majority strategy, you can't show how many people you have if you can't mobilize membership."[65]

According to this view, unemployed workers symbolized a "militant minority" with whom the majority of employed workers do not identify.

In preparation for the 1992 presidential election, Unger and Henning said that the unions that took part in the Labor Campaign on Unemployment would stress the importance of creating new jobs over maintaining income supports through extended benefits. They perceived the two kinds of action as an either-or proposition, arguing that backing unemployed groups instead of promoting job growth would marginalize trade unions. The campaign to fight for extended benefits for individuals already unemployed was essentially abandoned. Unger and others agreed to serve as advisors to the NYUC but said that they no longer considered themselves major players in the trade union campaign to extend unemployment benefits.[66]

## TRADE UNIONS SHIFT FROM ORGANIZING TO LOBBYING: LABOR COALITION TO REBUILD NEW YORK

By the fall of 1991, the Labor Campaign on Unemployment was supplanted by the Labor Coalition to Rebuild New York, a group comprised of many of the same trade union officials who joined the New York Labor Campaign on Unemployment. Key participants in the Labor Coalition included CWA Local 1180, CWA Local 1150, ACTWU, UAW Local 259, UAW District 65, AFM Local 802, and International Ladies Garment Workers Union.

Union members agreed as they had in meetings of the Labor Campaign that organized labor's emphasis should be on jobs creation, not unemployment benefits extensions, and paved the way for the more "positive" goals of the Labor Coalition to Rebuild New York. The Rebuild New York Coalition favored a leadership and organizational program in response to the problem of unemployment in New York rather than direct organizing of rank-and-file or unemployed workers. They proposed a broad program to generate primarily industrial jobs. Trade unions participating in the Coalition to Rebuild New York adopted a 15-point program developed by economic and political advisors of CWA Local 1180, and other trade unions. Union leaders got support from the State AFL-CIO. Some wanted to seek the approval of government and business leaders, like investment banker Felix Rohatyn of Lazard Freres, before releasing the document to the general pubic. John Glasel, of Local 802, for instance, suggested that, in order to succeed, the plan would require the enthusiastic support of business leaders. Glasel's view was sharply contested by other labor officials at the meeting, including Bob Kirkman, political director of UAW District 65, who argued that "Our plan runs against their power and interests—we are looking at a document that runs directly opposed to people in power. That doesn't mean that we shouldn't battle it out for the interests that we support."[67]

The broad-based program called for a major plan to restart the city's economy.[68] Reconstruction of the port and railroad system, revival of the housing industry, improvements in public education, a public takeover of Con Edison (the local electric company) and other jobs creation programs were its principal features. In addition, the plan called for specific economic redevelopment and subsidy programs for all the key trade union members of the coalition. What made the Labor Coalition to Rebuild New York appealing was that it offered benefits to individual unions, which are organized on the basis of industry rather than class. According to Unger:

> Our legislative agenda is different than . . . city workers and the building trades who want the government to spend money on projects that will assist their specific industries . . . We would love to be narrow and selfish and have a single bill that would help us in Albany, but there ain't none.[69]

The fifty-page economic development plan was presented and debated at a symposium entitled "Making New York Work Again" on June 5, 1992 in New York City. The conference was attended by both mainstream and progressive trade union presidents and officials, labor economists, public officials, and business leaders. Among the participants was Edward Cleary, president of the New York State AFL-CIO, who commented that the 15-point plan was "asking the right questions" even though he was "not sure it had all the right answers."[70] The Labor Coalition's position paper on regional economic development was later adopted by the State AFL-CIO as part of the legislative agenda for revitalizing New York State. Little, however, has been heard about the program since it was turned over to the State AFL-CIO. The measure of success for trade unions participating in the Labor Coalition to Rebuild New York was gaining the endorsement of the AFL-CIO for its proposals. Yet, ironically, while the AFL-CIO accepted the economic revitalization plan, they failed to promote it seriously in the New York State senate and legislature.[71]

Unlike the specific proposal of the Labor Campaign on Unemployment to extend federal and state jobless supports, the effort to promote the job creation plan of the Labor Coalition was vague and conveyed an ambiguous message to rank-and-file workers. The plan did not call on unions to involve members actively in any events staged by the organization. William Henning of CWA 1180, conceded that the plan was "essentially leadership driven":

> There was an attempt on the part, certainly, of Local 1180 to proselytize about the plan among our rank and file. I think if I were to characterize it, we were really looking for them to cooperate in the promulgation and the adoption of this in the general public discourse but we really never . . . involved the rank and file as participants in crafting the plan.[72]

Moreover, the Coalition to Rebuild New York did not include a definite plan for grass roots support for job creation and economic development. From the very beginning, mobilizing employed and unemployed workers was not part of the plan. Officials taking part in the Labor Coalition wanted support from the established labor movement, the New York State AFL-CIO and the New York City Central Labor Council. What they gained was a vague, nonconfrontational position paper that was ultimately buried in the bureaucracy of the established New York labor movement. The initiative of the New York Labor Campaign on Unemployment to address the concerns of persons directly affected by unemployment was transformed by trade unionists in the Rebuild New York Coalition into an innocuous policy statement that had one, and only one, advantage: luke-warm endorsement by the AFL-CIO.

The central demands of the 15-point plan of the Labor Coalition to Rebuild New York were to encourage government to provide funding to resuscitate the individual labor markets of those unions participating in the coalition. While the proposals of the Labor Coalition to Rebuild New York would have potentially benefited a significantly larger coalition of workers than the narrower Building Trades Coalition, they paralleled the demands of the "Jobs Now!" Coalition because they were on the whole limited to the industrial labor markets of member unions.

## CONCLUSION

While trade unions often advocate fundamental social change, they are also often reluctant to take action necessary to bring about this change. The New York Labor Campaign on Unemployment unified trade union officials dissatisfied with the failure of the AFL-CIO and Central Labor Council to respond resolutely to widespread unemployment in the local economy. In fact, the impediments encountered by leaders of the Labor Campaign to unify the independent unions that participated in the coalition were analogous to those occurring in the CLC. Both coalitions were unable to unify independent unions from disparate sectors of the New York economy through a political strategy of organizing members for collective political action. The CLC officials acknowledge this failing, whereas members of the Labor Campaign were less realistic. Union officials participating in the Labor Campaign began with a vague concern about rising unemployment and ended with even vaguer lip service to economic justice for workers. The unions that formed the Labor Campaign came from far more diverse occupational labor markets than the construction unions that participated in the more successful building trades march and rally, though the building trade unions were also constrained by rising anger among their rank-and-file members.

A successful union struggle to extend unemployment benefits would have required union officials to activate latent conflict between their unions that not only had weak attachments among themselves, but also shallow connections with their members. The more inclusive unions who participated in the Labor Campaign were not accountable to their unemployed members who, upon losing their jobs, also lost their ties to their unions. Unlike the more exclusive Jobs Now! Coalition, unions in the Labor Campaign were not constrained by their members to respond to unemployment. Since most workers in manufacturing, service, and government unions tend to be organized through their employers and not their unions, most workers who lose their jobs quickly lose their union affiliation. These inclusive unions with narrow organizing strategies are reluctant to participate actively in coalitions that do not benefit the individual labor market interests of their members.

The New York Labor Campaign on Unemployment, then, was an issue coalition brought to a standstill by the difference of opinion between trade unions and activist organizations.[73] These differences were intensified by the diversity of labor markets that divided unions participating in the coalition. As is noted in chapter 3, labor market differences are deepened by the segmented and spatially dispersed nature of industry in the New York City economy.

The conflicting interests of individual unions that derived from labor market differences were intensified by the organizational distinctions and organizing strategies among activists, trade unions, and union coalitions that participated in the Labor Campaign on Unemployment (See Table 6.1). Membership of the activist groups, consisting entirely of the unemployed, was the most fluid and least organized of the three organizations. Moreover, activist organizations had the least to lose through political mobilization, since they did not depend on dues-paying members or contributions. Their power was directly related to their ability to recruit and mobilize the unemployed and interfere with established authorities. The rank-and-file members of these diverse trade unions that participated in the coalition, were more organized than the unemployed workers in the activist groups, but they were often disconnected from the economic and political affairs of their unions, and therefore had little power in the unions. This was particularly true of inclusive unions, which had relatively narrow organizing strategies based on shallow associations with members at their places of work, which ended with the termination of employment. Most union officials this author interviewed did not consider organizing their unemployed former members to be a viable strategy. Finally, the trade union members of the CLC were the most organized of the three groups, yet the least active. CLC leaders represented diverse labor organizations and highly bureaucratic and autonomous structures and were often in conflict over policy decisions. Minimizing conflict among unions in the coalition was their primary motivation, and this was achieved by stifling any form of dissent. Aside from marching in the Labor Day Parade, trade unions were generally antithetical to participating in any form of collective political action through the CLC.

**Table 6.1: Composition of Labor Coalitions**

| Organizational | CLC | Trade Unions | Activists |
| --- | --- | --- | --- |
| Form of Action | Limited | Moderate | Militant |
| Membership Base | Trade Unions | Rank-and-file Members | Unorganized Unemployed |
| Type of Action | Dispersed Leadership Training | Coalition Lobbying and Political Action | Unified Direct ActionMass Action |

While NYUC was the most militant of the organizations in the New York Campaign on Unemployment, they represented the least powerful of the three groups in the coalition—unemployed people, a disproportionate number of whom were minorities and immigrants. The powerlessness of the New York Campaign to take concrete action was related both to the unwillingness of activist groups to turn the coalition over to established forces who were least interested in building a movement of the unemployed and to the rigidity of the more staid, organized labor leaders. With the exception of Local 420, which did not formally participate in the meetings but joined NYUC in demonstrations, trade union leaders favored moderate approaches that did not include organizing their members for political action. Trade unions and the Central Labor Council (through the State AFL-CIO) subsequently supported even more restrained policies not involving the organized members of the trade unions or the unorganized members.

The New York Labor Campaign's failure to influence trade union officials to involve their members through direct action, demonstrations, and pickets with the unemployed reveals the organizational limitation of coalitions that form among diverse trade unions whose members are located in different occupational communities and discrete labor markets. The inertia of the Central Labor Council and the breakdown of the ad hoc Labor Campaign also indicates other impediments to unified action among larger, more established, labor bodies. The CLC does not have political authority to establish policy for individual unions that classify their members by sector, organizational, and skill categories, and are often divided along gender, race, and national status. The AFL-CIO is a loosely knit organization that, unlike trade union movements in Germany and Sweden, does not possess authority to make policy on a local or regional basis. Similarly, while the New York City Central Labor Council ostensibly coordinates labor action locally, it typically limits actions to meetings and conferences for labor union officials on local concerns.

In spite of these limitations, trade union leaders who participated in the Labor Campaign pursued efforts to secure support from the AFL-CIO to achieve a modicum of support for their causes. Various attempts by union officials in the Campaign to defer leadership to the AFL-CIO failed to consider organized labor's inability to move beyond lobbying for individual labor market interests of unions and narrowly-based politicking to direct action aimed at transforming government labor policies via mobilizing workers.

The New York Labor Campaign on Unemployment, formed in the winter of 1991, illustrates the organizational obstacles faced by trade unions in making alliances among dissimilar organizations with different constituencies in the labor market. In this case, complications resulted from the difficulty in unifying disparate organizational structures into a single cohesive body willing to make collective decisions for all members of the association. This analysis demonstrates that the trouble also lies within the individual trade unions themselves that participated in the coalition, where trade union officials interested in furthering their personal and organizational power saw mobilizing members as a threat. Trade union officials firmly resisted any strategy that would bind them to the work of the activist New York Unemployed Committee. For most of these unions, organizing unemployed former members for political action was not even a possibility to be considered.

Finally the fact that organized labor on most levels did not view the effort to extend unemployment benefits to be directly beneficial to their unions, and did not make it a real priority, weakened the campaign. Even though most labor unions are sympathetic to extending unemployment insurance, they preferred programs proposed by the Labor Coalition to Rebuild New York that would produce direct and targeted results in the form of benefits to their individual unions and members. Nationally, the AFL-CIO neglected extension of unemployment benefits as a major policy plank, favoring policies such as legislation against worker replacement and opposition to NAFTA instead. On the local level, even the plan to create jobs through revitalization of the New York economy did not gain either the financial or organizational support required to generate serious legislative action.

## NOTES

1. Research shows unions are disinclined to initiate or organize for controversial social causes like unemployment, but do participate in coalition efforts. Brecher and Costello (1990) identified recent efforts by some unions to unite around concerns affecting the broader community as *issue coalitions*. They argue that such coalitions enable union leaders to transcend the established, oligarchic structures of their organizations and join forces with grass-roots activists. Moreover, by deferring responsibility to an external coalition, union leaders protect themselves from internal opposition and the resulting conflicts that arise from organizing membership around a controversial issue such as unemployment.
Issue coalitions of labor and community groups are instruments with which union leaders can respond to social concerns and avoid directly activating their own membership, thus reducing chances of them being unseated by a discontented insurgency.

2. Union leadership perceives that rank-and-file support is tenuous and core members could feel threatened by a pool of unemployed workers ready and willing to work. Unions typically lack the political capacity to meet the needs of their dues-paying members, yet they protect leadership from criticisms that may be levied by unemployed former members. Interview,

Harry Kelber, former director, Union Leadership Training Institute, August 18, 1994.

3. Interview, Harry Kelber, former director, Union Leadership Training Institute, August 18, 1994.

4. As noted in chapter 1, the author was one of two key organizers of this effort to encourage labor unions to mobilize their rank-and-file membership around the issue of jobs.

5. Interview, Jonathan Bloom, executive director, Workers Defense League, May 11, 1994.

6. A full roster of participants in the Labor Campaign is provided in Appendix C.

7. NYUC was originally known as the New York Unemployed Organizing Committee. Keith Brooks and this author served as co-coordinators from November 1990 through March 1991.

8. There had been little direct organizing activity among the unemployed as area residents absorbed layoffs waiting for the turnaround that never came. According to Brooks, "It was a very rude wakeup call when it was announced by the State of Maryland that 11,000 workers would be abruptly cut off from unemployment benefits." Fueled by unemployed organizing by Brooks and other steelworkers, a protest and lobbying effort was launched with demands for the State of Maryland to use its $300 million state unemployment insurance fund to replace the lost Federal money. Following a week of protests in Baltimore and the state capitol in Annapolis, unemployed activists were able to get thousands of signatures on a petition at the unemployment offices. As a consensus emerged for the extension, Governor Hughes finally supported the use of the state surplus unemployment fund to provide extended benefits to the unemployed. As a result of this organizing activity, Maryland was the only state in the nation to implement such a program. It was through this successful first battle that the United Committee of Unemployed People was formed.

9. Articles and editorials were published in *The New York Times, Philadelphia Inquirer, Baltimore Sun, Dallas Observer, In These Times, The Nation*, and *Labor Notes* and disseminated information to regional newspapers, including the labor press. In addition one or both of us appeared at conferences on the problem of unemployment and on area radio programs. Over the next several months, Brooks became the primary spokesman on the problem of growing unemployment coupled with a weak system of unemployment benefits.

10. Interview, Alan Ring, manager, Dean Street and Fourth Avenue Unemployment Office, August 3, 1994. Since 1991, when the New York

Unemployed Committee began organizing the office on a regular basis, the State Department of Labor referred jobless workers to satellite offices in Brooklyn. The numbers of unemployed applicants declined significantly by the beginning of 1992 as workers were referred to other claims offices. By the beginning of 1994, Ring told me that the unemployment office was transformed into a claims processing center for unemployed workers with claims contested by their employers. Ring, who was planning to retire in a year or two, told me that the New York Unemployed Committee had an important effect on the administration of the office, including decisions to modernize the facility and install an air conditioning system.

11. A synopsis of the NYUC view can be found in Brooks, Keith and Manny Ness, "Jobless-Insurance Cuts: Out of Work? Out of Luck," *The Nation*, December 24, 1990.

12. Manny Ness and Keith Brooks, "Organizing the Unemployed," *Social Policy*, Volume 21 (4), Spring 1991.

13. Maureen Dowd reported that "Mr. Bush apologized to residents of Kennebunkport for any disruption caused by a demonstration today protesting the President's refusal to make available $5.8 billion in unemployment benefits for those who have exhausted the 26 weeks of eligibility." Dowd reported on the news conference and march to Walker's Point, Mr. Bush's home, in which "Some protesters held signs reading 'Robbing George steals from the jobless to give to savings and loans.' The same day, Bush also criticized the disruptive protests of anti-abortion demonstrations organized by Operation Rescue in Wichita, Kansas. See Maureen Dowd, "Bush Chides Protesters on 'Excesses,'" *New York Times*, Saturday, August 17, 1991. A larger demonstration of some 2,000 AIDS activists organized by ACT UP two weeks later was even less well received. According to Robert Massa, a reporter for the Village Voice, Bush contrasted the ACT UP demonstration to the protest of the unemployed: "That one hit home, because when a family is out of work, that's one I care very much about."(sic) See Robert Massa, Village Voice, September 17, 1991. Several weeks later, after Congress sent the President a new unemployment benefits bill, the Washington Post quoted Bush as saying that he was tired of Congress "sending me a bunch of garbage I will not sign." See Eric Pianin, *The Washington Post*, September 26, 1991. For more details of the successful fight of the New York Unemployed Committee and other groups to extend unemployment benefits, also see Merle English, "Drive for Better Jobless Benefits," *New York Newsday*, December 11, 1990; Joyce Young, "Jobless Eye Maine," *Daily News*, August 18, 1991; "A Successful Fight for Benefits," *New York Newsday*, November 25, 1991.

14. For accounts of NYUC demonstrations at the Brooklyn unemployment claims office see Chapin Wright, "Unemployed Overwhelm Brooklyn Claims Office," *New York Newsday*, December 31, 1991, and Joyce Young, "To Be Heard, Jobless Employ a March," *Daily News*, December 31, 1991.

15. For example, on March 22, 1993, NYUC conducted a "survival" workshop for the unemployed intended to advise applicants on unemployment insurance, tax issues, other public benefits, job retraining and utility relief.

16. Interview, Lynn Bell, chairperson, Community/Labor Campaign To Save Taystee Jobs, September 14, 1994.

17. Interview, Keith Brooks, coordinator, New York Unemployed Committee, August 2, 1990.

18. Keith Brooks, coordinator, New York Unemployed Committee, general letter to unions, December 30, 1990.

19. From January to December 1991, the New York Unemployed Committee estimated that it raised over $9,000, including about $3,000 from unions, $4,300 from foundations, and $2,000 from individual donations. Union donors included Mailhandlers Local 300, CWA Local 1180, District Council 37, UAW Local 259, and HERE Local 6, the Newspaper Guild, and AFM Local 802.

20. Meeting with Howard Van Jones, director, Employment and Training Division, New York Central Labor Council AFL-CIO, Local 259 officials, and members of the New York Unemployed Committee, March 1992.

21. Meeting with Howard Van Jones, director, Employment and Training Division, New York Central Labor Council AFL-CIO, Local 259 officials, and members of the New York Unemployed Committee, March 1992.

22. A New York City Central Labor Council forum on mass layoffs and shop closings on November 24, 1993 was attended by about a dozen officials from an array of unions. The meeting was administered by the Midwest Center for Labor Research, a Chicago labor research and consulting firm. On December 3 and December 4, 1992, the Central Labor Council sponsored the "Unemployment Insurance and the Law Conference" attended by over 50 officials from labor unions from all sectors of the economy. Union officials were introduced to various strategies to identify shops that were about to close and move to other areas.

23. Minutes of Human Services Providers Advisory Committee executive board, New York Central Labor Council, AFL-CIO, June 26, 1992.

Sylvia Aron, representing United Auto Workers Local 259 proposed suggestion for an action-oriented conference.

24. The 1992 meeting, held shortly after the U.S. government extended unemployment benefits was designed to train union staff and leaders to represent members in unemployment insurance cases. The seminar focused on the new federal benefit extension and questions related to employers contesting benefits requests. Few unions formally assign staff or assist the unemployed collect benefits, according to Jonathan Bloom, executive director of the Workers Defense League. He noted that the International Ladies Garment Workers was the only union that he was aware of in New York City to assign a full-time union representative to collect benefits. Interview, Jonathan Bloom, director, Workers Defense League, May 11, 1994.

25. The Midwest Center for Labor Research, a labor consulting and research organization, recommends that forming community ties is the best way for trade unions to resist plant closings. See Leroy, Greg, Dan Swinney, Elaine Charpentier. *Early Warning Manual Against Plant Closings, Chicago: Midwest Center for Labor Research*, Working Papers, 2 (no date).

26. Interview, Howard Van Jones, director, Employment and Training Division, New York City Central Labor Council, AFL-CIO, August 2, 1994.

27. Appendix E examines these unions, their interests in participating in the New York Labor Campaign on Unemployment, and their frequent reluctance to do so as vigorously as they might.

28. The campaign against Hormel's plan to cut employee wages involved the direct participation of rank-and-file members of United Food and Commercial Workers Union Local (UFCW) P-9 and other UFCW locals in the Midwest. The International UFCW opposed the strike, and supported the successful efforts of Hormel's management to defeat the insurgent workers.

29. According to Rogers' account, Corporate Campaign organized a mass demonstration of about 2,000 Staley workers in 1993 in Springfield, Illinois to petition and lobby the state legislature to extend unemployment insurance benefits to locked out employees affiliated with Allied Industrial Workers Local 837 of Decatur, Illinois. The demonstration and lobbying effort led to a seven week extension in unemployment benefits.

30. Meeting of the Labor Campaign on Unemployment, March 27, 1991.

31. Interview, Jonathan Bloom, executive director, Workers' Defense League, May 11, 1994.

32. Interview, William Henning, vice president, Communications Workers of America, Local 1180, February 16, 1994.

33. Interview, Jim Guyette, former organizing director, AFSCME District Council 1707, September 28, 1994.

34. For example, Julius Margolin, then a union official with the International Association of Theater and State Employees, said he was active as an unemployed organizer in the early-1930s.

35. Unpublished Draft Proposal for A Labor Campaign on Unemployment: Reform the Unemployment Insurance System, Extend Unemployment Benefits, May 3, 1991.

36. *Draft Proposal for a State Legislative Program for the Labor Campaign on Unemployment*, New York Unemployed Committee, July 1991. The NYUC's draft proposal called on Governor Mario Cuomo to extend unemployment insurance benefits for jobless workers in New York State. In the Spring and Summer of 1991, members of the NYUC lobbied the New York State legislature to extend benefits. A similar effort by New Jersey industrial unions persuaded the New Jersey state legislature to pass similar legislation to extend unemployment benefits beyond the 26 week federal standard. The effort to target state as well as federal government was based on the efforts of the United Committee of Unemployed People (UCUP) efforts to extend state unemployment insurance benefits. UCUP, an organization comprised of laid-off Bethlehem Steel workers and other unemployed workers, was formed by Keith Brooks. See Keith Brooks, "Organizing the Unemployed—Baltimore," *Labor Research Review*, Vol. 1, No. 3., Summer 1983; and Keith Brooks and Kwazi Nkrumah, "Unemployed Committee Wins Benefits Extension for Jobless Maryland Workers," *Labor Notes*, October 26, 1982.

37. Bill Pike, for example, told me he was interested in developing a strategy to extend unemployment benefits for his laid off members because the union was planning to cut its supplementary unemployment benefits. Concerns about extending unemployment benefits were also expressed by John Glasel of Local 802 and Laura Unger, president of Communications Workers Local 1150, a union representing 1,100 technical and clerical workers in New York and New Jersey that lost more than 900 members due to layoffs in the year form July 1990 and July 1991.

38. Interview, Harry Kelber, former director, Union Leadership and Training Institute, August 18, 1994.

39. Harry Kelber, former director, Union Leadership Training Institute, at meeting of New York Labor Campaign on Unemployment, March 9, 1991.

40. Interview, Miriam Thompson, former education director, UAW Local 259, January 21, 1994.

41. Interview, Jonathan Bloom, executive director, Workers Defense League, May 11, 1994.

42. Interview, Jonathan Bloom, executive director, Workers Defense League, May 11, 1994.

43. Minutes of New York Labor Campaign on Unemployment Coalition Meeting, John Glasel, president, Local 802, March 27, 1991.

44. John Glasel, Meeting of the New York Labor Campaign on Unemployment, March 27, 1991.

45. John Glasel, meeting of the New York Labor Campaign on Unemployment, New York, March 27, 1991.

46. Harry Kelber, meeting of the Labor Campaign on Unemployment, New York, March 27, 1991. For more than 25 years, Kelber was an educator of trade union leaders and claimed to have ties to influential leaders in the federal and state AFL-CIO. From 1985 to 1990 Kelber was the coordinator of the trade Union Leadership Institute of the New York Central Labor Council. Subsequently Kelber formed an independent consulting group known as the Union Leadership Training Institute. In February 1991 Kelber published the pamphlet *How Unions Can Increase their Political Power and Why They Must Do it Now* (New York: Union Leadership Training Institute, 1991) which included a six-step plan for union mobilization of the disorganized unemployed. Frustrated by the inaction of the AFL-CIO on social issues like unemployment and worker replacement legislation, Kelber, who is retired, launched a personal campaign to reform the AFL-CIO in 1994.

47. Kelber argues that one of the basic concerns of trade union leaders is to have control over their organizations, that it would be reckless for union leaders to open their organizations to outside activists like the New York Unemployed Committee. Interview, August 18, 1994.

48. Anonymous labor union official, New York Labor Campaign on Unemployment meeting, March 3, 1991.

49. Bill Cunningham, a lobbyist for the AFL-CIO in Washington, D.C., said he considered lobbying to be the most effective method of passing legislation. He said that the effort to extend unemployment benefits was not served by including jobless workers who were mobilized by NYUC and other unemployed organizations to testify in congressional hearings, because, unlike the AFL-CIO, these jobless workers were not familiar with the legislative complexities of the issue. Interview, Bill Cunningham, January 17, 1991.

50. Interviews and discussions with labor union officials and analysts of organized labor in New York City, January 1991 through September 1994.

51. Comments of Judy West, political director, American Federation of Musicians, Local 802, at a meeting of the Labor Campaign on Unemployment on July 11, 1991.

52. John Glasel, Meeting of New York Labor Campaign on Unemployment, March 27, 1991.

53. William Henning, Meeting of New York Labor Campaign on Unemployment, March 27, 1991. The IUD is the Industrial Union Department of the AFL-CIO.

54. Nick Unger, Meeting of New York Labor Campaign on Unemployment, March 27, 1991.

55. Comments of Ray Rogers, meeting of Labor Campaign on Unemployment, March 27, 1993.

56. Ray Rogers, Corporate Campaign, presentation to Labor Campaign on Unemployment meeting, April 1991.

57. Interview, William Henning, vice president, Communications Workers of America, Local 1180, February 16, 1994.

58. Nick Unger, Meeting of New York Labor Campaign on Unemployment, March 27, 1991.

59. Interview, Bill Pike, former vice president, Amalgamated Lithographers Local 1, October 14, 1994.

60. Meeting of New York Labor Campaign on Unemployment, July 11, 1991, attended by Laura Unger (CWA Local 1150); Nick Unger (ACTWU); William Henning (CWA Local 1180); Jim Guyette (DC 1707); Judy West (Local 802); Sylvia Aron (a professor of social work and consultant to UAW Local 259); and Manny Ness (NYUC).

61. The first and third elements of the plan were clarified earlier at a Steering Committee Meeting of the New York Labor Campaign on Unemployment on March 6, 1991.

62. Nick Unger, Steering Committee Meeting of the New York Labor Campaign on Unemployment, June 4, 1991.

63. Steering Committee Meeting, New York Labor Campaign on Unemployment, July 11, 1991.

64. Unions participating in the steering committee were each supposed to send out 150 letters to unions around the country. However, some members even objected to doing this without the endorsement of the New York State AFL-CIO and the New York City Central Labor Council. Judy West, public relations director of Local 802, recommended that Ed Cleary, New York State AFL-CIO's president, sign the letter. New York Labor Campaign on Unemployment, Steering Committee Meeting, July 11, 1991

65. Nick Unger, Steering Committee Meeting, New York Labor Campaign on Unemployment, January 16, 1992.

66. Informal meeting New York Labor Campaign on Unemployment Steering Committee Members Nick Unger (ACTWU); Miriam Thompson (UAW Local 259); Bill Henning (CWA Local 1180); and Keith Brooks and Manny Ness of the New York Unemployed Committee, January 16, 1992.

67. Minutes, Labor Coalition to Rebuild New York, January 12, 1992.

68. The principal architect of the Labor Coalition's 15-point plan was Robert Fitch, a consultant to CWA Local 1180 who also has worked as a union organizer and journalist, and Ed Ott, a political lobbyist and consultant to organized labor.

69. Interview, Nick Unger, political director, ACTWU, April 5, 1994. Even where workers are dispersed among a large number of firms, unions tend to join forces along industrial and sectoral lines. For example, in December 1991, over 50,000 New York City construction workers were organized by their unions to rally for jobs (see chapter 4); in July 1994, thousands of public hospital workers joined a demonstration to defend New York area hospitals from some of the consequences of health care reform.

70. Minutes of symposium, "Making New York Work Again," June 5, 1992.

71. While key organizers of the Labor Coalition to Rebuild New York were delighted that their agenda gained the approval of the State AFL-CIO, they conceded that the AFL-CIO did not pursue legislative action seriously on the proposals since it adopted them two years earlier. Interviews, William Henning, Communications Workers Local 1180, February 16, 1994; and Nick Unger, ACTWU, April 5, 1994.

72. Interview, William Henning, Communication Workers Local 1180, February 16, 1994.

73. This analysis is organized on the basis of three forms of advocacy and action: (1) public education and media campaigns (limited action); (2) lobbying and political action (moderate action); and (3) direct action such as mass demonstrations (militant action). These forms of action are drawn from a framework outlined by Brecher and Costello (1990: 195) on labor-community coalitions.

# CHAPTER 7

# Conclusion: Hiring Halls and Workplaces: Trade Union Organizing Strategies and Unemployment Practices

Unemployment is always a threat to trade unions and their leaders. It poses a serious challenge to unions by driving down bargaining power against management. It also heightens internal strife among members, disrupting organizational stability and leadership continuity. As a result all unions try to shun marginal and unemployed workers. This study has found basic differences in the abilities of various trade unions to cope with unemployment. Exclusive unions that organize members through hiring halls are more committed to their unemployed members than inclusive unions that organize members at workplaces. The organizational strategies that trade union leaders chose to respond to unemployment in New York City during the early 1990s suggest that these differences are rooted primarily in the exclusive and inclusive organizing strategies of trade unions. Exclusive unions that faced greater internal opposition to their leadership tended to respond more vigorously to unemployment than inclusive unions that were able to disregard their jobless workers.

The case studies of trade union and labor coalition responses to unemployment presented in this work should modify our understanding of the role of the relationships between trade unions and the unemployed by recognizing the importance of membership organizing strategies that are related to labor market variability of individual unions. The research indicates a need to generate more detailed explanations of union action that stress economic and political strategies of individual unions in distinct labor markets that constrain them to organize members differently.[1]

A major contribution of this study is its focus on unemployment policies, a branch of the social science literature on trade unions that is often overlooked. This omission contributes to a slanted treatment of union relations with members that accentuates organizing new workers and depreciates ongoing relations of unions to their members within dissimilar labor markets. This study attempts to enlarge understanding of trade union membership organizing strategies to encompass analysis of the various procedures employed by unions to manage unemployment. This study shows that trade union organizing strategies are decisive in union approaches to control the effects of unemployment. This chapter first draws together the empirical findings of chapters 3, 4, and 5 and then examines how these findings help illuminate the relationship between unions and the unemployed.

## EMPIRICAL RESULTS

In the case studies, three arenas of union responses to unemployment were identified: (1) autonomous trade union action; (2) joint trade union action through established labor bodies; (3) responses to unemployment through ad hoc coalitions of trade unions and outside activist organizations. Each of these arenas appears to hinge on the distinct relationship between the membership, union, or coalition of workers formed by labor markets. This book has discerned that trade union action in response to unemployment seemed to be related to trade union leadership interest in maintaining organizational stability and control over their organizations. Exclusive unions that organize members through hiring halls faced more opposition from their unemployed members than inclusive unions that organized members through workplaces. Ironically, inclusive unions tend to represent low-wage and minority workers with greater need for organizational assistance.

### Individual Trade Union Responses to Unemployment

The individual responses of four unions to expected and emergency levels of unemployment in chapter 3 demonstrate the imperative of hierarchies among both membership and leadership within each union. According to Golden (1992), equality of members interferes with the ability of trade union leaders to designate the process under which workers are protected from unemployment. A member's job security depends on a variety of factors that are determined by skills, job classification, seniority, relative influence in the union, and the relative prominence of the industry.

This exploratory study suggests that these attributes are reinforced by the institutional structure of union job security mechanisms: skilled "A Mechanics" who are members of Local 259 are less vulnerable to layoffs than semi-skilled "B Mechanics" and unskilled workers; skilled core members of IBEW Local 3 are more likely to keep their high-paying jobs even during major economic downturns (creating, in effect, a labor market limited almost exclusively to white male construction workers); African American, Latino, and other minority construction workers who are members of Local 3 experience frequent bouts of joblessness in this closed labor market; and industrial and service workers in the same union routinely lose their union membership after losing their jobs, usually never to be heard from again.

Thus, by taking part in the process of determining who will keep or lose their jobs, trade unions create, reinforce, and reflect the labor market as a whole. They selectively provide job security for some core members while denying job security to others, particularly low-wage, unskilled minorities and immigrants. The local evidence from the New York City economy confirms Keyssar's (1989) contention that African American and minority workers suffer higher levels of long-term joblessness than do white workers. Unions in New York City establish an uneven hierarchical system of protection that endows some workers with greater protection.

The diversity of the ways in which trade unions do this is demonstrated in the case studies of individual union responses to normal and crisis level unemployment. Individual union responses to unemployment are determined largely by the internal opposition generated by workers that were formed by union efforts to organize distinct labor markets.

Building trades unions that represent construction workers tend to function in closed labor markets that limit access to a restricted class of privileged workers. These unions have been designated "exclusive" in membership policies because they restrict entry into their organizations. Conversely, industrial and service unions that represent low-income workers function in open labor markets with greater competition for jobs. These unions have been designated "inclusive" because membership requirements are based only on the employment relationship (see Introduction). Attachments of members to exclusive unions are strong because membership in closed labor markets tends to pre-date and follow employment. This is not the case in open labor markets, where membership hinges on continued employment in a union-organized establishment. The contingency of union membership in inclusive unions influences their treatment of unemployed former members and has important implications for the way union leaders respond to unemployment.

Moreover, government unemployment insurance has different levels of importance to union leaders, based on the exclusiveness or inclusiveness of their unions. For example, this study suggests that unemployment insurance benefits were important to the organizational stability of IBEW Local 3, an exclusive hiring hall union in which workers remained members even after they lost their jobs. Ironically, this analysis of several inclusive workplace-based unions representing workers with a greater likelihood of experiencing long-term unemployment (UAW Local 259, ACTWU) shows that these unions do not fight as hard for unemployment insurance benefits for their members as did IBEW Local 3. The inclusive workplace unions almost always terminate the membership of laid off workers, and thus have fewer incentives to defend their former members' interests. These differences between UAW Local 259 and IBEW Local 3 illustrate the important influence of hiring hall and workplace organizing strategies in distinct labor markets on union unemployment policies.

*UAW Local 259.* Despite the compassion that UAW Local 259 officials showed for unemployed former members, and despite their authentic attempt to form an unemployed council to assist their unemployed members, the union was not constrained to address the problem of unemployed members in the union. UAW Local 259's president championed far-reaching government social policy changes for workers through unemployment insurance and jobs creation programs. Interviews with unemployed former members of United Auto Workers Local 259 demonstrated that these workers were dissatisfied with their union leaders over the loss of their jobs. After these workers were laid off from their workplaces, their union membership was also terminated. Thus, while UAW had an inclusive class-oriented organizing membership strategy, its organizing objectives were largely passive in responding to unemployment in the industry.

*IBEW Local 3.* Unlike Local 259, with its attempt to advance the power of marginal workers through government protection through social unionism, IBEW Local 3 favored a policy that advanced member interests through collective bargaining with management. The closely-knit occupational community of electrical workers in the construction industry allowed for more intimate ties between working and unemployed members of the union that flowed from its hiring hall organizing strategy. Construction workers who were members of IBEW Local 3 were union members even before local shops hired them. The union regulated the entry of workers into the industry. Most members of the union went through the union-administered training and apprenticeship programs. Moreover, periodic unemployment was normal for workers in the building trades industry. Of course, when joblessness increased during the economic downturn of the early 1990s, the union had to contend with a sharp rise of unemployed workers who remained part of the union. Local 3, unlike Local 259, responded by minimizing the pressure of unemployment among electrical workers through a negotiated work sharing program and helping to protect the economic security of members through a supplementary system of unemployment benefits.

Despite the union's established methods for dealing with unemployment, the recession of the 1990s revealed inequities in Local 3's treatment of the unemployed. Local 3's leadership came under severe criticism from members and non-members who could not find jobs in the industry; most union critics were women and minority workers ordinarily excluded from the union. The union's ability to provide protection for core white male workers came at the expense of those minority workers who were not represented by the union. Some of these excluded workers formed independent ethnically- and racially-based coalitions to challenge the legitimacy of the union in the industry.

## Established Labor Union Responses to Unemployment: Building Trades "Jobs Now!" Coalition

The diversity of trade union interests is also exhibited in the case studies of union coalitions seeking to unify their demands and political strategies in response to rising unemployment in New York City. The building trades "Jobs Now!" Coalition shows that unions tend to pursue a political strategy that is beneficial only to workers in their discrete labor markets.

The building trades march and rally in December 1991 shows that union leaders representing craft and professional workers in the construction industry prefer to work through predictable channels that preserve their positions of authority in the labor movement and limit access to outsiders. The "Jobs Now!" march and rally were organized by building trades unions leaders who aligned with construction contractors. The demands of the coalition did not extend beyond calls for state and federal revitalization of the construction industry. Representatives of minority coalitions who demanded jobs for African American, Latino, and Asian construction workers were prevented from speaking at the rally and were excluded from the resulting debate on jobs creation. Their exclusion from the rally mirrored their exclusion from the closed labor markets that were controlled by unions and employers in the construction industry.

The spark for the "Jobs Now!" march and rally was rising anger among growing ranks of volatile unemployed building trades workers who criticized their leaders for failing to furnish jobs as they had done in the past. Peter Brennan, organizer of the demonstration, readily admitted that "letting off some steam" was the most important motivation of union leaders for mobilizing construction workers around the December 1991 rally, the largest demonstration of unemployed people in New York City since the 1930s. The motivation of building trades leaders to mobilize a mass demonstration against unemployment came from disappointed members who had expected their unions to provide jobs and referrals.

## Ad Hoc Community-Labor Coalitions in Response to Unemployment: The New York Labor Campaign on Unemployment

The ad hoc New York Labor Campaign on Unemployment broke apart largely because the coalition of left-oriented unions could not agree on a unified policy to benefit the individual interests of their members. Moreover, union officials who formed the coalition said they did not consider the marginalization of former unemployed members and unorganized unemployed workers to be a dilemma for their individual unions. Ironically, the workplace-based character of union members allowed their leaders to abandon their unemployed members, who were observed as unfortunate outsiders for whom they had no responsibility.

The demands of the New York Labor Campaign on Unemployment to extend jobless benefits were more far-reaching than the narrower demands of the "Jobs Now!" building trades coalition to prod government to stimulate local construction. The initial motivation of trade union officials to participate in the New York Labor Campaign on Unemployment was to maintain some relevance to members and workers in New York City. However, the case study of the Labor Campaign on Unemployment reveals a reluctance among union leaders to participate in a coalition that also included insurgent trade union activists and jobless workers organized at unemployment centers. The failure of the campaign supports this study's speculation that trade union leaders are distrustful and suspicious of coalitions that might upset their established and secure relations with employers, government, other trade unions, and, most important, their own members. Union officials in the coalition represented workers from dispersed labor markets. Union leaders had no interest in arousing latent dissent within their organizations by mobilizing working members and unemployed former members. While these union officials were disenchanted with the inaction of the established labor movement in response to rising unemployment, they also saw leaders of the New York Unemployed Committee and those of the Corporate Campaign as potential interlopers.

Like the parochial demands of construction unions, the goal of the 15-point plan of the Labor Coalition to Rebuild New York that replaced the campaign on unemployment was intended to benefit the individual unions participating in the coalition by calling for government investment in their industries without addressing the immediate needs of unemployed workers. To achieve their goals of revitalizing the New York economy, the union leaders did not include mobilization of workers as part of their strategy; they preferred to persuade largely unsympathetic government officials of the elegance of their plan.

The New York Labor Campaign on Unemployment started as a movement for the extension of unemployment benefits and evolved into an effort to promote regional economic development that would benefit unions involved in the coalition. Unlike the building trades unions, these unions did not experience a groundswell of pressure to mobilize workers to back their demands for reviving the New York economy. The unemployed that lost their jobs in these unions endured their fate alone. The New York Unemployed Committee was the only activist group in New York City that sought to mobilize dispersed and isolated workers in an effort to extend unemployment insurance benefits for the long-term unemployed.[2]

My research shows then, that exclusive unions that organize their workers on the basis of craft tend to have deeper connections with their members than inclusive unions representing unskilled and semi-skilled industrial and service workers (see Figure 7.1).

**Figure 7.1: New York City Union Organizing Strategies and Organizing Objectives**

| Organizing Objectives | Organizing Strategy | |
| --- | --- | --- |
| | Inclusive | Exclusive |
| Deep | Militant Active Unions Who Pursue Social Policy Gains for All Workers SEIU, IBEW | Active Craft Unions Who Pursue Labor Market Gains for Members IBEW Local 3 |
| Shallow | Unions Composed of Low-Income Workers Doing Little Organized Political Action ACTWU/Local 259 | Passive Craft Unions Who Pursue Labor Market Gains for Members Printing Unions |

Exclusive unions recruit members before workers enter the labor markets (often on the basis of craft and skill), creating close attachments among members and strong defense organizations. These unions customarily seek economic gains for their members through collective bargaining with management rather than changes in government policy. By controlling the hiring process, hiring hall unions can exclude marginal workers within industries that often experience high rates of unemployment. Conversely, inclusive unions that represent unskilled workers organize their members at individual workplaces, thus creating more nebulous attachments among members. Such unions tend to pursue economic gains for their members by promoting government social policy protections such as unemployment insurance and the minimum wages and government health benefits.

## IMPLICATIONS OF THE STUDY

Theorists who use class as an organizing framework emphasize that enduring and deepening divisions within the labor markets based on race, gender, immigrant, national and regional status, skill, and industrial sector have frustrated efforts to build or sustain class-conscious movements. Partly because of the need for unions to defend their shrinking territory, internal divisions and economic paralyses ensue, and union power is severely weakened as a result of these divisions (Pontusson 1991; Touraine, 1986). Moreover, the divisions weaken the power of unions vis-a-vis capital in the labor market (Arrighi 1991). According to these theorists, unions must eliminate narrow, divisive intraclass objectives and unite members around broader causes in order to regain and expand their influence. This study confirms that organizing strategies that segregate workers on the basis of discrete labor markets inform union policies in New York City and contribute to their inability and unwillingness to seriously address the problem of rising unemployment.

Trade union leaders interviewed for this study generally attribute their declining power to rising labor market competition resulting from higher unemployment. However, they do not consider the mobilization of unemployed and unorganized workers a practical strategy for their individual unions. While these union leaders support efforts to respond to rising unemployment, they also tend, as this study demonstrates, to avoid a commitment of union resources to mobilize jobless workers independently through their unions or in association with union coalitions.

### The Moderating Force of Organizations on Political Mobilization

My study of individual and collective trade union responses to unemployment corroborates established arguments of theorists who stress organizational factors as the cause of the trade unions' failure to defend workers' interests. The research demonstrates that even when union leaders supported reformative policy goals on unemployment, they did not tangibly pursue these goals because they feared that, in doing so, they might also activate internal opposition to their leadership. This conservative sentiment among union leaders corresponds with that identified by Michels (1915), who studied working-class leaders in pre-war Germany, finding that as unions and parties expand, they become oligarchic and undemocratic and inevitably fail to defend all of their members' interests (334).

Since the primary objective of an organization is to expand its size, struggles dividing the existing and potential membership must be avoided: "there has resulted, *pari passu* with its growth, a continued increase in the prudence, the timidity even, which inspires its policy" (336). One repercussion of the tendency of leaders to pursue conservative policies in working-class organizations is that they are exposed to new opposition from competitors intent on gaining power (342). However, Michels argues that, in consolidating their power, these new leaders also become detached from their class interests as they gain effective control over their organizations (353).

Michels reserves his harshest criticism for trade union leaders. He believes that while political leaders tend to become autocratic, "trade union leaders of working-class origin tend to become despotic and indifferent to the democratic aspirations of members." Such leaders often sell out the interests of their members and the working class to form alliances with capitalists in their respective industries (277-292). This study has found that, while trade union leaders were averse to mobilizing their members politically, they could not simply be written off as selfish and acquisitive. Most union leaders who participated in the Labor Campaign on Unemployment, in fact, expressed an obligation to represent their working members and were disturbed with the plight of their former unemployed members.

Among unions whose leaders are not as devoted to their members, recognition of the real or latent opposition that may ensue from an organization's conservative policies may motivate some leaders to support the ideals of working-class power without necessarily taking the concrete actions that can further their interests. The present study shows that while few trade union leaders in New York City in the early 1990s responded convincingly to rising unemployment by mobilizing their working and jobless members, most union leaders supported the abstract objective of extending unemployment insurance benefits for jobless workers. The common factor among those unions that failed to respond to unemployment was their workplace-based organizing strategies. Since membership in these unions is based solely at the workplace, unions were usually free to ignore workers after they became unemployed.

Lipset, Trow, and Coleman (1956) specifically apply Michels's hypothesis of organizations to an analysis of trade unions. They maintain that union leaders are given a near monopoly of power, seek to stay in office indefinitely, and suppress membership participation in union politics. While Lipset et al. (1956) agree with Michels' general theory, they also state that the "iron law of oligarchy" must not necessarily exist in every trade union or organization. In a historical and sociological study of the International Typographers Union, they argue those specific attributes of organizations and their members may mitigate unions' overall tendencies toward oligarchy. The attributes of the International Typographers Union promoting democracy and greater membership control were high membership income; a small gap between leaders and members; small trade union associations or units; the presence of two political parties in the organization; and relatively advanced education and skills that encouraged participation in politics (448).

Lipset, Trow, and Coleman's case study of a deviant democratic union does not negate Michels' general observation that unions tend toward oligarchy. However, their detailed examination of the unique characteristics fostering union democracy suggests that research into distinctive features of organizations also may be a useful approach to understand the variations of trade union economic and political actions in response to pressures such as unemployment.

Still, if the general premise of Michels' and Lipset's arguments is accepted, we are left with a gloomy depiction of union leaders and their organizations. Michels considers union officials as generally corrupt and autocratic. When new leaders emerge, according to Michels, they too become obsessed with maintaining power by the same means as their predecessors. Lipset et al. agree with this hypothesis; however, they believe that some unions with enduring democratic traditions may escape these circumstances. Paradoxically, their study associates real internal democracy in unions with relative weakness and smallness, factors that would not promote the power of such unions to defend the working class and unemployed. Other theorists who place greater emphasis on the need of strong organization in building worker power recognize that these union bureaucracies inevitably create divisions that also blunt their ability to build labor's power by unifying disparate workers. Organizational imperatives help account for the unions' failure to mobilize jobless workers to defend their own deteriorating positions in the labor market. Davis (1986) elucidates this threat and Mills (1971) who regard trade unions to be subject to recurrent economic and political contingencies that recast their leaders in different roles. Thus, for example, union leaders and activists who were guardians of the disenfranchised working class and unemployed in the 1890s, 1930s and early 1940s became complacent leaders of cautious sclerotic organizations when worker unrest subsided in the late 1940s.

My research also suggests the advantage of analyzing individual trade union organizational strategies within the context of the specific labor markets in which their members work. This approach is informed by Marks' (1989) hypothesis that trade unions pursue independent economic and political strategies with members, employers, and the state. Marks argues that trade unions both help shape the character and demands of political parties and engage in politics independent of parties. He argues further that individual union political interests often deviate from those of trade union federations and political parties. Differences in union political strategy seem rooted in organizational strength and bargaining power within the labor market (8-9). This study has found that hiring hall and workplace organizing strategies influence the various forms of union responses to unemployment.

Although this study of trade union leaders in the early 1990s supports the general hypotheses of conservative tendencies among union leaderships of both Michels and Lipset et al., observations and interviews of union officials' also reveal that most union officials view the growing problem of unemployment and joblessness seriously. Most union officials consider rising structural unemployment and the decline of their members' industries as perhaps the most serious problem facing their organizations and the labor movement as a whole. But union officials respond differently to this problem, and the evidence gathered seems to support the hypothesis that their responses are influenced by the distinct labor markets in which unions operated.

## Union Organizing Strategies and the Unemployed

I began this study by suggesting that a plausible explanation for the ambivalence of union leaders to mobilize marginal and unemployed workers lies in their fear of opposition to their continued leadership. This book has also suggested that some union officials view marginal and unemployed workers as a threat to their bargaining power against management. These union officials also believe that unemployment insurance should be maintained because it reduces competition for jobs and thus the depressive effect of competition on wages. Some union officials also maintain that mobilizing unemployed workers is essential to recast the image of organized labor from a defender of the narrow parochial interests of a labor aristocracy to a defender of all workers.

The major contribution of this study, then, has been to extend the theoretical understanding of the ambiguous relationship of trade unions to the unemployed. Dealing with unemployment constitutes a vital economic function of trade unions. However, unions respond autonomously to unemployment—independently from union federation and coalitions. This book's findings demonstrate the importance of an analysis that highlights the influence of distinct labor markets and organizing strategies on individual union political action. This study shows, moreover, that the segmentation of unions on the basis of labor markets tends to create a diversity of organizational responses to unemployment. Segmented labor markets and organizational boundaries have been found to divide union members and unorganized workers in New York City on the basis of intraclass divisions. The labor market boundaries engender a range of responses to unemployment—from apathy, complacency, and restraint to membership mobilization.

The paradox is that inclusive workplace unions that organize members around class interests tend to refrain from political strategies in responding to the effects of unemployment on their members. They do not respond as forcefully to unemployment as hiring hall unions because there is often less pressure from members to do so. Industrial and service unions that represent low-wage and unskilled workers advocate government policy changes to protect their members. Their leaders, however, are more reluctant to mobilize their members for the purposes of building a mass movement to extend unemployment insurance benefits and/or create jobs than were the leaders of exclusive hiring hall unions whose members had closer ties to their unions.

The dispersed unemployed former union members of inclusive unions whose leaders are not provoked to respond forcefully to rising joblessness are inevitably integrated back into the turbulent local labor market to fend for themselves and bargain down the price of labor.

While workers organized through trade unions have always constituted a minority of American workers, their share of the labor force has precipitously declined from about 35 percent of the national workforce in 1955 to 15 percent in 1995 of the national workforce. The decline in the density of organized labor is accompanied by declining wages, unemployment insurance, and other labor market protections. The findings suggest that while union officials express concern with their declining clout against management, their responses to unemployment are patterned by the distinct organizing strategies within their industrial labor markets. Exclusive hiring hall unions that recruit their members individually are forced to respond more vigorously to unemployment in their industries than inclusive unions that organize their members collectively at their places of work. While unions that organize their members through the workplace tend to favor more comprehensive solutions to the problem of structural joblessness, their unemployed members are not organized for political action because they are usually not seen as sources of opposition to union leaders.

But the failure of inclusive unions to protect workers from the threat of unemployment suggests that, despite leaders' best intentions, unions serve little more than the interests of leaders and core members.

**NOTES**

1. This research approach is endorsed by Marks (1989, see chapter 2).

2. There were, however, participants from other localities. The Long Island Progressive Coalition was active in mobilizing workers at unemployment insurance offices on Long Island and joined the New York Unemployed Committee's demonstrations and rallies in support of national unemployment insurance benefits extensions in New York City, Long Island, Washington, D.C., and Kennebunkport, Maine.

# Methodological Notes

This study is based on participant observation of trade union officials, activist groups, and labor-community coalitions, as well as interviews with trade union officials, activists, and observers on their activities and attitudes about unemployment, unemployment insurance, and the mobilization of the unemployed in the early 1990s.

These case studies of the relationships of unions to the unemployed in New York City are intended to shed new light on the complex relationship between trade union leaders and the unemployed.[1] While there is much theoretical speculation about the ambiguous association of labor unions with the unemployed, there is insufficient empirical work exploring the complexities and particularities of this relationship. This book seeks to deepen understanding of unions and the unemployed by examining the attitudes of key union actors in different sectors of the labor market. This research illuminates the conditions that push some unions to mobilize the unemployed as well as the conditions that cause other unions to shun them. Consideration is given to the effects of labor market changes on different trade unions in New York City to explain the variety of attitudes and activities regarding the unemployed. Case studies of labor unions' responses to the recession of the early 1990s are used to explain the ambivalent responses of labor unions to the unemployed.[2]

One of the primary limitations in the literature on the relationship of unions to the unemployed is the lack of an empirical basis. In the following chapters, the relationship is qualified through a detailed empirical investigation of individual and collective trade union organizing strategies in New York City in the early 1990s, a time when unemployment was a serious challenge to them. A key focus of this analysis is the understanding of the central influence of labor markets on union action toward unemployment.

Chapter 2 discusses two dominant nineteenth and twentieth century approaches in the social science literature on the problematic relationship between trade unions and the unemployed. One set of theorists argues that labor unions have a compelling interest in the organization of the unemployed, and another set of theorists argues that labor unions are both unwilling and unable to organize the unemployed. This book suggests that while classical organizational arguments explain the motivations and actions of trade union leaders themselves, they tell us little about the individual differences among unions functioning in discrete labor markets. It is clear from the research that workplace and hiring hall labor market organizing strategies exert a significant influence on individual trade union responses to unemployment.

Before examining the material gathered in the case studies, however, it is helpful to survey the dominant nineteenth and twentieth century approaches to the problematic relationship between trade unions and the unemployed. By doing so, the limitations of largely theoretical approaches are demonstrated and thus help to explain why the case study method is important for understanding the complexities of this relationship. The next step is to broadly examine the uneasy historical relationship between trade unions and the unemployed in the United States. Then it is necessary to examine the unemployment problems in each of the major labor markets in New York City. Finally come the case studies themselves, which focus on particular unions and union organizations in each of these markets.

During the early 1990s (in 1991 to 1992 as co-founder and coordinator of the New York Unemployed Committee, and as director of the Local 259 Unemployed Council in 1993 and 1994), the author participated in union meetings on unemployment to observe union officials' attitudes toward unemployment from the inside. Participant observation in coalition work with trade unions facilitated interviews with officials with whom the author became familiar during the early 1990s. Moreover, as a result of this work, access was gained to union documents pertaining to unemployment. Although there was some difficulty gaining access to leaders in building trades unions that did not participate in the ad hoc drives on unemployment insurance, information was gained from interviews with officials and labor analysts who have had relationships with them. In general, the author had excellent access to the efforts of trade unions to address the problem of unemployment in New York in the early 1990s. These efforts represented three arenas of responses, including, most important: (1) autonomous trade union action; (2) joint trade union action through established labor bodies; (3) responses to unemployment through ad hoc coalitions of trade unions and outside activist organizations.

This study employed a semi-structured open-ended interview schedule that was designed to reveal the attitudes of unions and union leadership towards the following questions:

Are union leaders motivated to organize and form alliances with the unemployed?

Do union officials avoid involvement with the unemployed, and why?

What factors influence trade unions to form alliances with organizations of the unemployed, mobilize their own unemployed former members, or organize the unorganized unemployed?

How important to trade union leaders is the issue of organizational control? What is the independent influence of the unemployed and activist groups in these organizations?

What factors contribute to the success of trade union coalitions on unemployment?

What factors contribute to disintegration of trade union and activist coalitions on unemployment?

What are the causes of dissension and conflict?

What are the implications of such relationships with organizations of the unemployed that form on union political influence?

The case studies will focus on the actions of three kinds of union-based organizations that have taken an interest in the problem of unemployment: (1) autonomous trade unions in four sectors of the economy including the service, manufacturing, government, and construction sectors (Chapter 4); (2) established union coalitions— exclusive coalitions of craft-based building trades unions that pursued narrower goals to revitalize the construction industry (Chapter 5); and (3) ad hoc trade union coalitions with activist groups, inclusive class-based coalitions that attempted to pursue broad policy goals to extend unemployment insurance benefits for all workers (Chapter 6).

**Autonomous Trade Union Action**

The first forms of trade union action in response to unemployment that are analyzed herein are independent trade union responses during normal and crisis periods. Four different unions operating in distinct sectors of the economy were examined: (1) a service sector union, the United Auto Workers Local 259; (2) a manufacturing union, the Amalgamated Clothing and Textile Workers Union; (3) a government union, the Hospital and Health Care Workers Local 420; and (4) a construction union, the International Brotherhood of Electrical Workers Local 3. Key trade union leaders or officials responsible for their unemployed were interviewed to determine their policies on unemployment in both stable and crisis periods, union leaders' justifications for these policies, their attitudes about the significance of unemployment to their unions and the labor movement, and views on political action as a response to unemployment. Examinations of published literature and unpublished archival documents, as well as minutes of meetings specific to each union and industry will supplement these interviews.

A series of interviews were conducted with local observers of trade unions and their leaders in New York. Some of these sources have had ongoing relationships with unions, and may have had information on some of the motivations of trade union leaders and officials. Therefore, it is expected that, in some cases, they have been more candid in accounting for the actions of specific leaders than the leaders themselves. The author deliberately sought out analysts with an interest in both trade unions and their organizations and the issue of unemployment. These individuals include Harry Kelber, former director, Trade Union Leadership Institute (and a current critic of the AFL-CIO); Herman Benson, founder of the Association for Union Democracy (AUD), an organization that promotes union democracy; Susan Jennick, former executive director of AUD; and Jonathan Bloom, executive director, Workers Defense League, an organization that has links to trade unions and works independently on unemployment and civil rights issues.

The interviews of trade union leaders and officials, activist leaders, and labor analysts will reveal the attitudes of trade union and activist leaders toward the problems of unemployment and the independent and collective actions they have taken in response to it, and justifications for their actions and the limits of these actions. One of the main objectives in these interviews is to detect trade union official and activist sentiment toward the unemployed to ascertain whether these groups see the unemployed as a benefit or hindrance to their organizations.

## Established Union Coalitions

The primary organization for joint action in the trade union movement is the New York City Central Labor Council, the local affiliate of the AFL-CIO. The CLC has pursued a variety of strategies in response to unemployment. Each of these are documented as articulated in organizational periodicals and archives, interviews with Howard Van Jones (the coordinator of the CLC's unemployment policy), various meetings (in which the author participated or had records of minutes) on the dilemma posed by unemployed to unions in New York City. Joe McDermott, the executive director of the Consortium for Worker Education, a trade union retraining and education institute in New York was also interviewed. In addition, labor officials integral to the organization of the "Jobs Now" building trades labor coalition, an organization that received substantial support from the Central Labor Council were interviewed. These officials include Peter J. Brennan, then president of the Building and Construction Trades Council of New York and former U.S. Secretary of Labor in the Nixon administration; Neil Madonna, vice president of Building Material, Local 282 of the International Brotherhood of Teamsters (currently under Federal Trusteeship); and Vincent McElroen, an influential business agent of the International Brotherhood of Electrical Workers, Local 3.

## Ad Hoc Union and Activist Coalitions

The best known ad hoc community labor coalition to directly consider strategies to respond to the problem of unemployment was the New York Labor Campaign on Unemployment, an organization formed by left-leaning trade union officials at the urging of several activist organizations. Participant observation and interview methods were used to obtain data on this organization. The author was directly involved in the formation of the organization by participating in the coalition's general meetings and steering committee meetings. Also interviewed were key trade union officials and activist leaders involved in the coalition to discern their views on why the effort succeeded or failed. The most important of these officials are Jim Butler, president of Local 420 of American Federation of State County and Municipal Employees Union; Nick Unger, political director of ACTWU; William Henning, vice president of Communications Workers Local 1180; Miriam Thompson, former education director of UAW Local 259; Jim Guyette, former organizing director American Federation of State, County and Municipal Employees DC 1707; John Glasel, president American Federation of Musicians Local 802; Bill Pike, former vice president of American Lithographers Union Local 1; Joel LeFebvre, secretary treasurer (president) of Teamsters Local 840, a union representing clerical, maintenance, and other semi-skilled and unskilled workers; and Bill Hamilton, an active member of the now defunct Amalgamated Transit Union Local 1202, a small union that represented Greyhound Bus Company employees. The primary activist leaders include Keith Brooks, currently director of the New York Unemployed Committee, and Ray Rogers, director of Corporate Campaign. Other interviews included other active members of the New York Unemployed Committee: Donald Moe, an unemployed carpenter who was active in his union; and Curtis Fergus, an enthusiastic volunteer, who both played valuable roles in building and directing outreach efforts to jobless workers at unemployment centers and in their communities in Brooklyn. Additional interviews were held with leaders of other ad hoc coalitions, including Lynn Bell, the chairperson of the Community/Labor Campaign to Save Taystee Jobs; James Haughton, executive director, and Gil Banks, assistant director, of Harlem Fight Back, an activist minority coalition in the construction industry; and Wing Lam, executive director of the Chinese Staff and Workers Association.

# Interviews

Gil Banks, assistant director, Harlem Fight Back

Lynn Bell, chairperson, Community/Labor Campaign to Save Taystee Jobs

Herman Benson, founder, Association for Union Democracy

Jonathan Bloom, executive director, Workers Defense League

Peter J. Brennan, former president, Building and Construction Trades Council of New York, and former U.S. Secretary of Labor

Keith Brooks, founder and director, New York Unemployed Committee

Jim Butler, President Local 420 of District Council 37, American Federation of State County and Municipal Employees Union

Bill Cunningham, lobbyist, and assistant director of political affairs, AFL-CIO

John Dodds, director, Philadelphia Unemployment Project

Curtis Fergus, security guard, member, New York Unemployed Committee

John Glasel, former president, American Federation of Musicians Local 802

Victor Gotbaum, former executive director, District Council 37 of the American Federation of State County and Municipal
Employees Union

Jim Guyette, former organizing director, District Council 1707 of the American Federation of State County and Municipal Employees Union and former president P9, United Food and Commercial Workers Union, Austin, Minnesota

Bill Hamilton, former active union member, Amalgamated Transit Union Local 1202

William Henning, vice president, Communication Workers Local 1180

James Haughton, executive director, Harlem Fight Back

Susan Jennick, former executive director, Association for Union Democracy

Harry Kelber, former director, Trade Union Leadership Institute

Wing Lam, executive director, Chinese Staff and Workers Association

Joel LeFebvre, secretary treasurer, International Brotherhood of Teamsters Local 840

Joe McDermott, executive director, Consortium for Worker Education

Vincent McElroen, business agent, International Brotherhood of Electrical Workers, Local 3.

Neil Madonna, vice president, Building Material Local 282, International Brotherhood of Teamsters

Sam Meyers, president, United Auto Workers Local 259

Donald Moe, carpenter, member, New York Unemployed Committee

Ed Ott, political consultant, Communication Workers of America Local 1180

Marcella Perry, jobs referral director, United Auto Workers, Local 259

Bill Pike, former vice president, American Lithographers Union Local 1

Alan Ring, unemployment claims administrator, Dean Street and Fourth Avenue Unemployment Claims Office, Brooklyn, New York

Judy Roberson, second vice president, United Auto Workers, Local 259

Martin Roberson, mechanic, member, New York Unemployed Committee

Ray Rogers, executive director, Corporate Campaign

Evelyn Seinfeld, research director, District Council 37, American Federation of State County and Municipal Employees Union

Joan Shephard, union activist, The Newspaper Guild, Local 3

Bobby Shlosko, director, Local 259 Unemployed Project

Miriam Thompson, former education director, United Auto Workers Local 259

Nick Unger, political director, Amalgamated Clothing and Textile Workers Union

Howard Van Jones, Coordinator, Central Labor Council Employment and Training Program

United Auto Workers Local 259 Unemployed Committee, various interviews with anonymous unemployed former members.

# Roster of Unions Participating in New York Labor Campaign on Unemployment

**UNION PARTICIPANTS**

Actors Equity Association
Amalgamated Clothing and Textile Workers Union
Amalgamated Transit Union, Local 1202
American Federation of Musicians, Local 802
American Federation of State, County & Municipal Employees
    District Council 37
American Federation of State, County & Municipal Employees
    District Council 1707
American Federation of Television and Radio Artists 7075
American Lithographers Union, Local 1
Communication Workers of America, Local 1150
Communication Workers of America, Local 1180
Communication Workers of America, Local 1183
Council of Motion Picture and TV Unions
Hotel, Restaurant & Club Employees and Bartenders Union, Local 6
International Association of Theater and Stage Employees
    Local 644
    Local 674
Mailhandlers Local 300
New York Hotel & Motel Trades Council
Public Employees Federation of New York State

Retail, Wholesale, Department Store Union, District Council of United Food and Commercial Workers Union
Screen Actors Guild
The Newspaper Guild, Local 3
United Auto Workers, Local 259

## NON-UNION PARTICIPANTS IN NEW YORK LABOR CAMPAIGN

Association for Union Democracy
Corporate Campaign
Long Island Progressive Coalition
New Initiatives on Full Employment
New York Unemployed Committee (5 members)
Northstar Fund
People's New World Order

# Local 259 Survey of Unemployed Members

1. Are You Unemployed?
   Yes:             32
   No:               8

2. Do You Want to Join Our Unemployed Support Group?
   Yes:             15
   No:              25

## JOB TRAINING

1. Do you think you need new skills for advancement?
   Yes:             26
   No:              14

2. Retraining for a new career?
   Yes:             25
   No:              15

3. Job search skills?
   Yes:             22
   No:              18

4. Resume writing?
   Yes:             18
   No:              22

5. Interview skills?
   Yes:             19

No:                  21

## COUNSELING AND REFERRALS

1. Family counseling?
    Yes:              1
    No:              39

2. Drug and/or alcohol?
    Yes:              0
    No:              40

3. Health insurance information?
    Yes:             14
    No:              26

## INFORMATION AND HELP

1. Assistance in applying for unemployment &/or extensions?
    Yes:             12
    No:              28

2 Public assistance?
    Yes:             11
    No:              29

3. Utility, food, Medicare, housing?
    Yes:             17
    No:              23

4. Tax information?
    Yes:              7
    No:              33

# Key Unions Participating in The New York Labor Campaign on Unemployment

*ACTWU New York Joint Board.* The union represents men's clothing and textile workers in New York City (see chapter 3). Many members are women, immigrant, and minority workers. ACTWU is a leader among progressive trade unions that form independent coalitions in New York. Approval by ACTWU political director, Nick Unger, is required prior to participation in an outside coalition.

ACTWU was a key organizer of labor- and community-based campaigns in the early 1990s in New York City, including Jobs with Justice Health Care Campaign; New York City Labor and Environment Network; opposition to the North American Free Trade Act; the Labor Coalition to Rebuild New York; and the New York Labor Campaign on Unemployment. Although some issue campaigns that ACTWU joins do not have the official endorsement of the AFL-CIO, Nick Unger often claims that the union's ultimate objective is to persuade the local and national labor movement to subscribe to and support more progressive goals as part of an effort of building a broad base of support. ACTWU's most important campaigns during the 1980s and early 1990s focused on efforts to prevent undocumented immigrants working at subminimum wages in illegal sweatshops from competing against unionized textile shops.

*American Federation of Musicians Local 802.* Since the mid-1980s, following election of John Glasel as union president, Local 802 has been an active member of progressive labor-coalitions devoted to jobs creation, unemployment insurance, health care, and international solidarity with workers in South Africa and Latin America. The AFL-CIO and its state and local constituent organizations often spurn these coalitions.

Local 802 represents professional musicians in New York City and Long Island. Due to the seasonal nature of the music industry, most are unemployed at least part of the year, and even in ordinary circumstances many must rely on unemployment benefits to make ends meet. The recent recession made these benefits doubly important. The union estimates that 70 percent of its approximately 14,000 members experienced bouts of joblessness in 1990. As a consequence of widespread unemployment in the union, Local 802 has supported various political efforts to extend jobless benefits. While Local 802 represents professional musicians, most members do not depend on the union for work, and, as a consequence, usually do not hold the union responsible for unemployment.[3]

Two Local 802 organizers (Keith Brooks and myself) founded the New York Unemployed Committee, an activist organization that directly mobilized jobless workers at unemployment offices in the region (see New York Unemployed Committee above). And Glasel called the first two meetings of the New York Labor Campaign on Unemployment in the winter and spring of 1991 at the urging of progressive union officials, NYUC organizers, and in response to concern about rising joblessness in the union.

*United Auto Workers Local 259.* Under the stewardship of Sam Meyers, president of the union, Local 259 has supported coalitions advancing progressive social goals (see chapter 3). From the mid 1980s to the early 1990s, the union was influential in coalitions promoting job retention and creation, health care, and international labor solidarity. Before that, the union had been a leader in the civil rights movement.

Miriam Thompson, former education director of Local 259, was a leading organizer for left-leaning unions around many of these campaigns. She actively supported the New York Unemployed Committee in organizing the unemployed and initiated efforts by local unions to form a broader community-labor coalition on jobs and unemployment. In 1992, Thompson left the union to become executive director of the Center for Constitutional Rights.[4]

Local 259's interest in rising unemployment increased in the early 1990s as layoffs in the union's industrial facilities and auto repair shops accelerated rapidly, jeopardizing the survival of the organization as an autonomous entity. From 1989 to 1994 the union lost more than half of its 4,500 members as a result of mass layoffs and shop closures.

*Communications Workers of America Local 1180.* Under the leadership of Arthur Cheliotis, union president, and William Henning, vice president, Local 1180 has become a prominent player in broad-based issue coalitions. The union is a central actor in most progressive coalitions, including promotion of job retention and creation, health care, and international labor solidarity. Unlike other public sector unions, Local 1180 has joined forces in coalitions with other unions representing private sector workers.

Local 1180 represents about 10,000 administrative government workers, in welfare offices and other agencies in New York City. The union was not itself harmed by layoffs, due to high turnover and the large volume of work in city welfare offices.[5] Although Local 1180 members were not directly at risk in the recession of the early 1990s, union leaders were actively defending and advocating expanding public and private-sector jobs. The union initiated the Labor Coalition to Rebuild New York in 1991 to save public sector jobs and create industrial and construction jobs. Local 802 was among the few unions to forcefully resist proposals by New York City's Mayor Guiliani to lay off municipal workers in 1994 and 1995.

*Amalgamated Lithographers Union Local 1* Although ATU Local 1 is not ordinarily considered a member of New York City's more progressive unions, a crisis of unemployment in the union gave it reason to join the coalition. In the 1960s, Amalgamated Lithographers Local 1 was a thriving union representing some 11,000 skilled workers who were employed in printing facilities throughout the New York and New Jersey. Since then, technological innovation and plant relocations to other regions, and the emergence of nonunion facilities has severely reduced the demand for skilled lithographers and devastated the union. By September 1994, union membership had declined to 1,202 active members (10 percent of its membership in the 1990s) and 3,451 retirees. The union also had about 500 active unemployed members who retained their affiliation after they were laid off. The result was an increasingly insupportable burden on the union's active members, who continued to support services to non-active members and retirees. According to Bill Pike, who became vice president of Local 1 in 1990, rising unemployment in the late 1980s and early 1990s jeopardized contributions to the union's health insurance fund, pension fund, and supplemental unemployment insurance fund, creating a budget crisis and impairing the union's ability to provide benefits to workers. Pike told me that from 1989 to 1993 Local 1 experienced a rate of unemployment ranging from 20 percent to 25 percent, straining union resources, which provided laid off members $100 a week for 52 weeks, a generous health insurance plan, and a generous pension plan. Pike said that the union's supplemental unemployment insurance was used as a means to keep skilled craftsmen in the industry:

> So if you are going to carry them unemployment wise, if you are getting $300 from the state, $100 from the union, and your medical benefits will carry—that's equivalent to $500 a week. A guy won't get rich off of that, but he'll feel whole until a job comes up.[6]

In 1992, Pike had to cut unemployment benefits to 26 weeks, restrict access to health insurance, and cut the monthly pension benefits from $1,400 a month to $700 a month. He attributes his subsequent loss in a re-election bid for union executive vice president to these cuts.[7] It is understandable, then, that, in 1991 and 1992, when the union was considering the cuts, Pike was active in the effort to extend federal unemployment benefits to jobless workers beyond 26 weeks. He was referred by U.S. Representative Downey to the New York Unemployed Committee, which was then forming the New York Labor Campaign on Unemployment.[8]

*AFSCME District Council 1707.* This union represents low-income home health care and child care workers employed by private service providers under contract to New York City agencies. The union also represents workers employed in philanthropic, social work, community agencies, and civil rights and civil liberties groups in New York City. By the late 1970s, the union's membership expanded to fourteen thousand.[9] In the early 1990s, District Council 1707 participated in ad hoc coalitions formed by progressive unions to pursue job creation, health coverage, and extension of unemployment benefits.

Union president Robert McEnroe was one of six union presidents to sign a letter inviting local unions to the second general meeting of the New York Labor Campaign on Unemployment in May 1991. Jim Guyette, formerly organizing director of the union, was instrumental in bringing the coalition together and took an active role both on the coalition steering committee and in the effort to extend unemployment benefits in the early 1990s. Guyette's motivation for participating in the coalition was to show his personal support for the effort to extend benefits and to demonstrate its importance to other unions. As he put it:

> There was and remains a great desperation among the unemployed. ... In many instances labor unions don't even understand the connection between a secure system of social protections, including unemployment insurance, and their own power. We have sort of lost this vision as a social organization to make change that helps all working people. And it is reflected in society and the decline of the trade union movement.[10]

Guyette is former president of Local P-9, United Food and Commercial Workers Union, and served during an unauthorized strike against Hormel Foods in Austin, Minnesota (see Corporate Campaign below). He took part in deliberations leading to formation of the Labor Campaign and served as an informal consultant to members of the New York Unemployed Committee.[11]

*AFSCME District Council 37.* The district council represents about 80,000 government workers employed in public hospitals and agencies in New York City. Many DC 37 members are unskilled or semi-skilled workers and face layoffs when declines in the economy reduce government revenues. While the union should have a profound interest in increasing protections for its members, it did not send a high level official to Campaign meetings or participate in the steering committee. Although the leadership of DC 37 did not actively participate in the coalition, its Local 420 affiliate independently joined some protests and demonstrations organized by the New York Unemployed Committee, the Community/Labor Coalition to Save Taystee Jobs and other grass-roots organizations.

District Council 37 tends to join coalitions that concern public sector workers directly. The union was a major organizer of the

Coalition to Save New York, protesting plans by the city for budget cuts that would result in layoffs of its members in 1990. The Coalition was made up mostly of unions representing state and city workers threatened by budget cuts.[12] On April 30, 1990, Save New York organized a rally of rank-and-file union members in downtown Manhattan calling for taxation of wealthy individuals and corporations to balance the budget.

*Amalgamated Transit Union, Local 1202.* Local 1202 was the New York representative of Greyhound Bus Line workers, affiliated with the Amalgamated Transit Union. The union weathered a bruising strike against Greyhound beginning in 1983, which decimated membership. Following the 1983-1985 strike, Greyhound employees were forced to take a 25 percent cut in pay. From 1985 to 1994, national membership declined from 12,000 to 13,000 workers to 4,000 workers and local membership declined from 800 members to 500 members.[13] On March 1, 1990, both local and national unions began another unsuccessful three year strike against Greyhound that ended in May 1993 and culminated in the disbanding of the local union. In March 1992, union president Harold Menlowitz disappeared, leaving the union in complete disarray.[14] The bus company hired often underqualified drivers and mechanics to replace union members who were on strike and broke the union. All the Greyhound Locals were disbanded by the Amalgamated Transit Union prior to the settlement of the strike and unified under National Local 1700, based in Chicago, Illinois.

ATU Local 1202 participated in the deliberations of the New York Labor Campaign on Unemployment. In February 1991, Menlowitz expressed interest in taking part in the labor coalition and support for the drive to extend unemployment benefits.[15] Bruce Hamilton, an active union member since 1971, was the union's representative at Labor Campaign meetings.[16] Hamilton told me that the extension of unemployment benefit had a positive effect in helping members survive during the strike, though ultimately it could not compensate for the fact that Greyhound was able to replace its workers. The union's six month strike benefit of $50 a week was exhausted by December 1990. Union members were eligible for unemployment insurance after the first two months of the strike, and so by the end of 1990, striking workers were in a great need for unemployment benefits.

*Hotel and Motel Trades Council.* The union represents primarily unskilled workers who are employed in large New York hotels. Many of Local 6 members are unskilled and semi-skilled low wage workers, including cooks, waitresses, porters, custodial and maintenance personnel who benefit from the union's ability to negotiate wages collectively and to safeguard job security. Under the leadership of union president Vito J. Pitta, the Hotel and Motel Trades Council initiated several boycotts against non-union hoteliers that opened in New York City during the late 1980s and early 1990s. The union leadership is aware of the vulnerable position of its workers to growing competition from unorganized and unemployed workers entering the work force. To increase wages in the industry, the union supports increased availability of unemployment insurance benefits and higher minimum wages. Although the Hotel and Motel Trades Council endorsed the formation of the Campaign and was the largest union contributor to the organizing efforts of the NYUC, it did not actively participate in either effort.

## NOTES

1. This method, according to Eckstein (1975), extends empirical knowledge of a subject where theoretical explanations already exist.

2. A growing body of recent political science literature on trade unions emphasizes the value of examining individual unions (Golden and Pontusson 1991; Marks 1989), rather than national labor movements.

3. Local 802 represents professional musicians through collective bargaining agreements that are negotiated with employers (orchestras, Broadway producers, club date bands, etc.) where union members work.

4. Thompson resigned as executive director of the Center for Constitutional Rights in 1994 after serving for two years and was replaced by Ron Daniels. She later became a consultant to UAW Local 259 president Sam Meyers.

5. Interview, William Henning, vice president, Communication Workers of America, Local 1180, February 16, 1994. The union lost about 100 positions during the early 1990s New York City recession.

6. Interview, Bill Pike, former vice president, Amalgamated Lithographers of America, Local 1, October 14, 1994.

7. Interview, Bill Pike, member, Amalgamated Lithographers Local 1, October 14, 1994.

8. Congressman Downey was a Democratic congressman from Long Island and chair of the Subcommittee on Human Resources of the Committee on Ways and Means, U.S. House of Representatives who introduced H.R. 1367 and other bills that proposed to increase federal supplemental unemployment compensation. Downey was defeated in his 1992 bid for reelection.

9. See Al Nash, "Local 1707, CSAE: Facets of A Union in the Non-Profit Field," in *Labor History*, Volume 20, Number 2, Spring 1979, for an early examination of the union's organizational changes during its expansion in the late 1950s and early 1960s.

10. Interview, Jim Guyette, organizing director, County and State Employees of America, September 28, 1994.

11. Interview, Jim Guyette, September 28, 1994. While unemployment benefit extensions would have helped DC 1707's members, working at low wages and frequently vulnerable to job loss, Guyette contends that his support for the unemployment effort in the early 1990s derives from his own personal experience on unemployment in the 1980s and his unwavering commitment to defending the lot of workers in America. "I've been unemployed—therein lies a big difference between my thinking and others in the labor movement," said Guyette. "I did this not because we were organizing poor people at the time, it was out of a commitment in general. Because I was unemployed and I know the concerns of people trying to provide for their families—the disarray and disrepair.

12. Participation in the Coalition to Save New York included DC 37 and its affiliate unions; United Federation of Teachers; New York State Public Employee Federation; Teamsters Local 237; CWA Local 1180; New York State Nurses Association; and Professional Staff Congress Local 2334. The coalition also included ACTWU, Local 802, the Newspaper Guild, and other private sector unions that opposed budget cuts due to the impact it would have on services.

13. Interview, Bruce Hamilton, union activist, Amalgamated Transit Union, October 18, 1994.

14. According to Bruce Hamilton, an active union member in Local 1202, Menlowitz was discovered to have been committed to a mental institution.

15. Interview, Harold Menlowitz, former president Local 1202, March 1992.

16. Hamilton believes that the strike effort against Greyhound Bus Lines ultimately failed because his union failed to mobilize its members: "I believe that we should have undertaken a campaign to shut down the Port

Authority. Unions are totally afraid to use their power." Interview, October 18, 1994.

.

# References

Allen, Christopher. Book Review of Gary Marks and Peter Swensson. *American Political Science Review*, Vol. 84, June 1990, pp. 694-96.

*AFL-CIO News*. July 29, 1991 and October 14, 1991.

Amalgamated Clothing and Textile Workers Union. *Report of the General Executive Board*. Sixth Constitutional Convention, Las Vegas, Nevada: June 7-10, 1993.

Anekwe, Simon. "Union to Protest Plans to Close City Hospitals." *Amsterdam News*. April 21, 1990.

Aronowitz, Stanley. *False Promises: The Shaping of American Working Class Consciousness*. New York: McGraw-Hill, 1973.

Arrighi, Giovanni. "Marxist Century—American Century: The Making and Remaking of the World Labor Movement," in Amin, Samir, Giovanni Arrighi, Andre Gunder Frank, Immanuel Wallerstein, (Eds.). *Transforming the Revolution: Social Movements and the World System*. New York: Monthly Review Press, 1991.

Bailey, Thomas and Waldinger, Roger, in Mollenkopf, John and Manuel Castells (Eds.). *Dual City: Restructuring New York*, New York: The Sage Foundation, 1993.

Bellush Jewel and Bernard Bellush. *Union Power & New York: Victor Gotbaum and District Council 37*, New York: Praeger Publishers, 1984.

Benson, Herman. Democratic Rights for Union Members: *A Guide to Internal Union Democracy*. New York: Association for Union Democracy, 1979.

Bernstein, Irving. *Turbulent Years*. Boston: Houghton Mifflin, 1969.

Bigart Homer. War Foes Here Attacked by Construction Workers." *New York Times*. May 9, 1970.

Bigart, Homer. "Huge City Hall Rally Backs Nixon's Indochina Policies." *New York Times*. May 21, 1970.

Block, Fred. "The Myth of Reindustrialization." *Socialist Review.* 73 January-February, 1984, pp. 59-74.

Block, Fred. "Postindustrial Development and the Obsolescence of Economic Categories." *Politics and Society.* 14, 1985, 77-99.

Bluestone, Barry and Bennett Harrison. *The Deindustrialization of America: Plant Closings, Community Abandonment, and the Dismantling of Basic Industry.* New York: Basic Books, 1982.

Brecher, Charles and Raymond D. Horton. *Power Failure: New York City Politics & Policy Since 1960.* New York: Oxford University Press, 1993.

Brecher, Jeremy and Tim Costello. "The New Hard Times," *Z Magazine.* January 1992, pp. 83-88.

Brecher, Jeremy and Tim Costello. *Building Bridges: The Emerging Grassroots Coalition of Labor and Community.* New York: Monthly Review Press, 1990.

Brody, David. *In Labor's Cause.* New York: Oxford University Press, 1993.

Brody, David. "Breakdown of Labor's Social Contract," in *Dissent.* Volume 39, Winter 1992, pp. 32-41.

Brooks, Keith. "Organizing the Unemployed—Baltimore." *Labor Research Review,* Vol. I, No. 3, Summer 1983, pp. 23-37.

Brooks, Keith and Kwazi Nkrumah, "Unemployed Committee Wins Benefits Extension for Jobless Maryland Workers," *Labor Notes,* Number 45, October 26, 1982, pp. 1-14.

Brooks, Keith and Manny Ness. "Employer Benefits." *The Nation.* Volume 253, July 1991, p. 41.

Brooks, Keith and Manny Ness. "Activists Kick off Campaign to Organize the Unemployed. *Labor Notes.* February 1991, p. 7.

Brooks, Keith and Manny Ness. "Jobless-Insurance Cuts: Out of Work? Out of Luck," in *The Nation.* Volume 253, December 24, 1990, pp. 800-802.

Brown, Clayola. Vice-President, ACTWU, *Our Members Need Unemployment Insurance Reform Now!.* Testimony. Hearings of the Subcommittee on Social Security and Family Policy, Senate Finance Committee. New York City, June 24, 1991.

*Bylaws of Local Union Number 3,* International Brotherhood of Electrical Workers. New York: IBEW, February 14, 1985.

Burawoy, Michael. *Manufacturing Consent: Changes in the Labor Process Under Monopoly Capitalism.* Chicago: University of Chicago Press 1979.

Burtless, Gary (ed.) *A Future of Lousy Jobs? The Changing Structure of U.S. Wages.* Washington, D.C.: The Brookings Institution, 1990.

Coletti, Louis J. "Is the 'Jobs Now' Rally Working?" *Building Congress Update,* Spring 1992.

Dao, James. "Pataki Proposes broad Reductions in State Spending," *The New York Times*. February 2, 1995.

Davis, Mike. *Prisoners of the American Dream*. London: Verso, 1986

DeLeon, Dennis. *Building Barrier: Discrimination in New York City's Construction Trades*. New York: New York Commission on Human Rights, December 1993.

Delgado, Hector L. *New Immigrants, Old Unions: Organizing Undocumented Workers in Los Angeles*. Philadelphia: Temple University Press, 1993.

District Council 37. *22 Years: Local 420 Hospital Division of District Council 37: We Want Our Jobs Not Welfare*. New York: DC 37 American Federation of State County and Municipal Employees, 1975.

Dowd, Maureen. "Bush Chides Protesters on 'Excesses.'" *New York Times*, Saturday, August 17, 1991.

Drennan, Matthew P., "Local Economy and Local Revenues," in Brecher, Charles, and Raymond D. Horton, eds., *Setting Municipal Priorities*, New York: New York University Press, 1987.

Dubofsky, Melvyn. *When Workers Organize: New York in the Progressive Era*. Amherst, Massachusetts: University of Massachusetts Press, 1968.

duRivage, Virginia L. ed., *New Policies for the Part-Time and Contingent Workforce*. Armonk, NY: M.E. Sharpe/Economic Policy Institute, 1992.

Eckstein, Harry. "Case Study and Theory in Political Science," in Greenstein, Fred I. and Nelson W. Polsby, eds., *Handbook of Political Science, Volume 7, Strategies of Inquiry*.
Reading, Massachusetts: Addison-Wesley Publishing Company, 1975, pp. 79-137.

Ehrenhalt, Samuel. U.S. Department of Labor. Bureau of Labor Statistics. 1986, 1990, 1991, 1992, 1993.

*Electrical Union World* New York: Local 3, International Brotherhood of Electrical Workers, December 19, 1991, January 28, 1992, February 27, 1992.

English, Merle. "Drive for Better Jobless Benefits." *New York Newsday*. December 11, 1990.

Erlich, Mark. "Who Will Build the Future." *Labor Research Review*. Number 12, Volume VII(2), Fall 1988, pp. 1-19.

Fantasia, Rick. *Cultures of Solidarity: Consciousness, Action, and Contemporary American Workers*. Berkeley, Ca.: University of California Press, 1989.

Finkel Gerald. *History and Organization of the Joint Industry Board of the Electrical Industry: 50 Years of Labor-Management Relations 1943-1993*. Flushing, NY: Joint Industry Board of the Electrical Industry, 1993.

Fitch, Robert. *The Assassination of New York*. London: Verso Books, 1993.

Folsom, Franklin. *Impatient Armies of the Poor: The Story of Collective Action of the Unemployed 1808-1942*. Niwot, Colorado: University Press of Colorado, 1991.

Foner, Philip S. *The History of the Labor Movement in the United States*. Volume 2, *From the Founding of the A.F. of L. to the Emergence of American Imperialism*. 2nd ed. New York: International Publishers, 1975.

Foner, Philip S. *Organized Labor & The Black Worker, 1619-1973*. New York: International Publishers, 1976.

Foner, Philip S. *The History of the Labor Movement in the United States*. Volume 4. *The Industrial Workers of the World, 1905-1917*. New York: International Publishers, 1965.

Foner, Philip S. *U.S. Labor and the Vietnam War*. New York: International Publishers, 1989.

Forrester, Keith and Kevin Ward. Trade Union Services for the Unemployed: The Unemployed Workers' Centres. *British Journal of Industrial Relations*. Volume 28, Number 3, November 1990, pp. 387-395.

Forrester, K, Ward K, Simon B. *TUC Centres for the Unemployed*. Leeds, U.K.: University of Leeds, July 1988.

Freeman, Richard B. and James L. Medoff. *What Do Unions Do?* New York: Basic Books, 1984.

Friedman, Samuel R., "Worker Opposition Movements," *Research in Social Movements, Conflict and Change*. Vol. 8, 1985, pp. 133-170.

Galenson, Walter. *Rival Unionism in the United States*. New York: American Council on Public Affairs, 1940.

Garraty, John A. *Unemployment in History: Economics, Thought and Public Policy*. New York: Harper & Row, 1978.

Ginsberg, Helen. *Full Employment and Public Policy: The United States and Sweden*. Lexington, Massachusetts: Lexington Books, 1983.

Golden, Miriam. "The Politics of Job Loss." *American Journal of Political Science*. Vol. 36, No.2, May 1992, pp. 408-430.

Goldfield, Michael. *The Decline of Organized Labor in The United States*. Chicago: University of Chicago Press, 1988.

Goldfield, Michael. "Worker Insurgency, Radical Organization, and New Deal Labor Legislation," in *American Political Science Review*. Volume 83: 1989, pp. 1257-1282.

Gourevitch, Peter, Andrew Martin, George Ross, Christopher Allen, Stephen Bornstein, Andrei Markovits. *Unions and Economic Crisis: Britain, West Germany and Sweden*. London: George Allen & Unwin, 1984.

Governor's Advisory Committee for Black Affairs. *Improving the Labor Market Status of Black New Yorkers: Policy and Program Recommendations*. Albany, New York: State of New York, November, 1988.

Grasmuck, Sherri. "Immigration, Ethnic Stratification, and Native Working Class Discipline." *International Migration Review*. Volume 18, Number 3, Fall 1984, pp. 692-713.

*Guild Strike News*. New York: Newspaper Guild Local 3, February 27, 1991.

Harrison, Bennett and Barry Bluestone. *The Great U-Turn: Corporate Restructuring and the Polarizing of America*. New York: Basic Books, 1988.

Hathaway, Dale A. *The Politics of Deindustrialization: An Explanation of Worker Quiescence Based on Responses to the Decimation of Pittsburgh's Steel Industry in the 1990's*. Ph.D. Dissertation. Cornell University, 1990.

Haughton, James. *Coalition for Massive Jobs Through Housing: Proposal for a Mass Mobilization of the Building Trades and Non-White Community for a Massive Jobs Through Housing Program to Revitalize the Economy and Put New York City to Work*. New York: Fight Back, 1992.

Henneberger, Melinda. "Lessons from Health and Hospitals' Unions." *New York Times*. September 26, 1994.

Hudson, Edward. "Building Trades Set Rally Today." *New York Times*. May 20, 1970.

Huxley, Christopher, David Kettler, and James Struthers. "Is Canada's Experience Especially Instructive?" in Lipset, Seymour Martin (ed.) *Unions in Transition: Entering the Second Century*. San Francisco: Institute for Contemporary Studies, 1986.

International Union, United Automobile, Aerospace and Agricultural Implement Workers of America, UAW. *Proceedings of Thirtieth Constitutional Convention*. San Diego, California: June 14-18, 1992.

Kaufman, Michael T. "Labor Day Approaches for Harvard." *New York Times*. September 3, 1994.

Kadetsky, Elizabeth. "Minority Hard Hats: Muscling in on Construction Jobs." *The Nation*. Volume 255, July 13, 1992, pp. 45-48.

Kelber, Harry. *How Unions Can Increase their Political Power and Why They Must Do it Now*. New York: Union Leadership Training Institute, 1991.

Keyssar, Alexander. "History and the Problem of Unemployment." *Socialist Review*. Volume 19, Number 4, 1989, pp. 15-32.

Kimeldorf, Howard. *Reds or Rackets? The Making of Radical and Conservative Unions on the Waterfront.* Berkeley, California: University of California Press, 1988.

Kornbluh, Joyce L. *Rebel Voices: An IWW Anthology.* Ann Arbor: University of Michigan Press, 1963.

Krugman, Paul. *The Age of Diminished Expectations: U.S. Economic Policy in the 1990s.* Cambridge, Massachusetts: MIT Press, 1992.

*Labor Educator.* "Has the AFL-CIO Abandoned the Unemployed?" Volume 3, Number 1, 1994, pp. 1-4.

*Labor Educator.* "Verbal Support for the Unemployed But No Campaign on Issue of Jobs". Volume 3, Number 4, 1994, pp. 1-3.

Lafer, Gordon. "Minority Unemployment, Labor Market Segmentation, and the Failure of Job-Training Policy in New York City." *Urban Affairs Quarterly.* Volume 28, No. 2, December 1992, pp. 206-235.

Lafer, Gordon. "Politics of Job Training: Urban Poverty and the False Promise of JTPA. *Politics and Society.* Volume 22, September 1994, pp. 349-388.

Lange, Peter and Marino Regini. *State, Market and Social Regulation: New Perspectives on Italy.* Cambridge: Cambridge University Press, 1989.

Leab, Daniel J. "'United We Eat': The Creation and Organization of the Unemployed Councils in 1930. *Labor History.* Number 8, Fall 1967, pp. 300-315.

Lenin, V.I. *"Left Wing" Communism—An Infantile Disorder.* (originally published June 12, 1920) in *V.I. Lenin: Selected Works.* New York: International Publishers, 1976.

Leroy, Greg, Dan Swinney, Elaine Charpentier. *Early Warning Manual Against Plant Closings, Chicago: Midwest Center for Labor Research.* Working Papers, 2 (undated).

Levitan, Sar A. and Isaac Shapiro. *Working But Poor: America's Contradiction.* Baltimore: Johns Hopkins University Press, 1987.

Lipset, Seymour Martin, Martin Trow, and James Coleman, *Union Democracy: The Internal Politics of the International Typographical Union.* Garden City, NY: Anchor Books, 1956.

Luxemburg, Rosa. "The Mass Strike, the Political Party and Trade Unions," in Waters, Mary-Alice (ed.) *Rosa Luxemburg Speaks.* New York: Pathfinder Press, 1970.

Lynd, Staughton. *American Labor Radicalism: Testimonies and Interpretations.* New York: John Wiley & Sons, 1973.

Maier, Mark H. *City Unions: Managing Discontent in New York City.* New Brunswick, N.J.: Rutgers University Press, 1987.

Mandel, Ernest. *Power and Money: A Marxist Theory of Bureaucracy.*
London, Verso, 1992.

Marks, Gary. "Variables in Union Political Activity in the United States,
Britain and Germany from the Nineteenth Century. *Comparative Politics.*
October 1989, pp. 83-104.

Marks, Gary. *Unions in Politics: Britain, Germany, and the United States in
the Nineteenth and Early Twentieth Centuries.* Princeton: Princeton
University Press, 1989.

Massa, Robert. "The Age of AIDS: Where Was George?" *Village Voice.*
September 17, 1991, p. 20.

Marx, Karl. *The General Council of the First International, 1864-1866.* in
Larson, Simeon and Bruce Nissen (eds.) Theories of the Labor
Movement. Detroit: Wayne State University Press, 1987.

Michels, Robert. *Political Parties.* New York: The Free Press, 1962.

Miliband, Ralph. *Divided Societies: Class Struggle in Contemporary
Capitalism.* Oxford: Oxford University Press, 1991.

Mills, C. Wright. *The New Men of Power: America's Labor Leaders.* New
York: Augustus M. Kelley Publishers, 1971.

Mollenkopf John and Manuel Castells, eds., *Dual City: Restructuring New
York.* New York: Russell Sage Foundation, 1991.

Moody, Kim. *An Injury to All: The Decline of American Unionism.* London:
Verso, 1988.

Moody, Kim. *Workers in a Lean World: Unions in the International Economy.*
London: Verso, 1988.

Nash, Al. "Local 1707, CSAE: Facets of a Union in the Non-Profit Field."
*Labor History.* Volume 20, Number 2, Spring, 1979, pp. 256-277.

Nash, Margo. *Local 259: United Automobile Workers of America.* New York:
UAW Local 259, 1983.

Nelson, Bruce. *Workers on the Waterfront: Seamen, Longshoremen, and
Unionism in the 1930s.* Urbana, Illinois: University of Illinois Press,
1988.

Ness, Immanuel. "Review of Union Power and New York." *Labor Studies
Journal.* Winter 1987, pp. 303-304.

Ness, Manny and Keith Brooks. "Organizing the Unemployed." *Social Policy.*
Volume 21, Number 4, Spring 1991, pp. 2-4.

New York City Central Labor Council. *Labor News.* January 1992.

New York City Commission on Human Rights. *Building Barriers:
Discrimination in New York City's Construction Trades.* New York,
1993.

New York Building Congress and the Council of Business & Labor for the Economic Development of New York. *Building Congress Update.* Special 1992.

New York State Department of Economic Development. *New York State 1991-92 County Profiles*, (Albany, N.Y.: Bureau of Economic and Demographic Information, 1993).

Offe, Claus. "Competitive Party Democracy and the Keynesian Welfare State: Factors of Stability and Disorganization," in Ferguson, Thomas and Joel Rogers (ed.) *The Political Economy: Readings in the Politics and Economics of American Public Policy.* Armonk, N.Y.: M.E. Sharpe Inc., 1984.

Oppenheimer, Irene. *The Organization of the Unemployed, 1930-1940.* (Unpublished MA Essay), Columbia University, 1940, 36. Referred to by Rosenzweig, 1979.

Phillips, A.W. "The Relation between Unemployment and the Rate of Money Wage Rates in the United Kingdom, 1861-1957." *Economica* Number 25, 1958. pp. 283-99.

Pianin, Eric. "Bush Remark on Jobless Bill Irks Democrats." *The Washington Post.* September 26, 1991.

Piven, Frances Fox and Richard Cloward. *Poor People's Movements.* New York: Vintage, 1979.

Piven, Frances Fox and Richard Cloward. *The New Class War: Reagan's Attack on the Welfare State and its Consequences.* New York: Pantheon, Books, 1982.

Pontusson, Jonas. "Introduction: Organizational and Political-Economic Perspectives on Union Politics," in Golden, Miriam and Jonas Pontusson (eds.). *Bargaining for Change: Union Politics in North America and Europe.* Ithaca, NY: Cornell University Press, 1992.

Purdum, Todd S. "Dinkins Says He Is Considering Laying Off 15,000 City Workers." *New York Times.* October 5, 1990.

Purdum, Todd S. "Dinkins Links a Loss of Jobs to Pay Raises." *New York Times.* October 27, 1990.

Ragin, Charles. *The Comparative Method. Moving Beyond Qualitative and Quantitative Strategies.* Berkeley, University of California Press, 1987.

Rees, Albert. *The Economics of Trade Unions.* Third Edition. Chicago: University of Chicago Press, 1989.

Reich, Robert. *The Work of Nations.* New York: Vintage, 1991.

Report of the General Executive Board. Amalgamated Clothing and Textile Workers Union, AFL-CIO, CLC. Sixth Constitutional Convention, Las Vegas, Nevada, June 7-10, 1993.

Rosenberg, Terry J. *Poverty in New York City, 1993: An Update*. New York: Community Service Society of New York, 1994.

Rosenzweig, Roy. "Organizing the Unemployed: The Early Years of the Great Depression, 1929-1933." *Radical America* Volume 10, Number 4, July-August, 1976, pp. 37-60.

Rosenzweig, Roy. "Radicals and the Jobless: The Musteites and the Unemployed Leagues, 1932-1936." *Labor History* Number 16, Winter 1975, pp. 52-77.

Rosenzweig, Roy. "'Socialism in Our Time': the Socialist Party and the Unemployed, 1932-1936." *Labor History* Number 20, Fall 1979, pp. 485-510.

Sabel, Charles. *Work and Politics: The Division of Labor in Industry*. Cambridge: Cambridge University Press, 1987.

Sabel, Charles and Michael Piore. *The Second Industrial Divide*. New York: Basic Books, 1984.

Sassen, Saskia, "The Informal Economy," Mollenkopf, John and Manuel Castells, eds., *Dual City: Restructuring New York*. New York: Russell Sage Foundation, 1991.

Schleicher, Bill. "Severance Pay Agreement." *Public Employee Press*. April 8, 1994, p. 3.

Schlozman, Kay Lehman and Sidney Verba. *Injury to Insult: Unemployment, Class, and Political Response*. Cambridge: Harvard University Press, 1979.

Scott, Gale. "Hospital Unions Plan to Sue Over Layoffs, *New York Newsday*. October 27, 1994.

Semple Jr. Robert B. "Nixon Meets Heads of 2 City Unions; Hails War Support." *New York Times*. May 27, 1970.

Shostak, Arthur B. *Robust Unionism: Innovations in the Labor Movement*. Ithaca, NY: ILR Press, 1991.

Silver, Mark L. *Under Construction: Work and Alienation in the Building Trades*. Albany, N.Y.: State University of New York Press, 1986.

Sims, Calvin. "Idle, Angry Hard Hats Tell off City Hall: Protesters, Many Unemployed, Want More Public Works Projects." *The New York Times*. December 20, 1991.

Sloane, Leonard. "The Two Big Apparel Unions to Outline a Merger Today." *The New York Times*, February 20, 1995.

Stafford, Walter. *Closed Labor Markets: Underrepresentation of Blacks, Hispanics and Women in New York City's Core Industries and Jobs*. New York: Community Service Society of New York, 1985.

Stafford, Walter. *Employment Segregation in New York City Municipal Agencies.* New York: Community Service Society of New York, 1989.

Stevens, B. "Labor Unions, Employee Benefits, and the Privatization of the American Welfare State." *Journal of Policy History,* Volume 2, Number 3 (1990), pp. 233-260.

Strauss, George and Daniel G. Gallagher, and Jack Fiorito. *The State of the Unions.* Madison, Wisconsin: Industrial Relations Research Association, 1991.

Svensson, Sven. "General Strike Threat," *Sweden Report.* No. 1, 1993, p. 1.

Therborn, Goran. *Why Some Peoples Are More Unemployed Than Others.* London: Verso, 1986.

Touraine, Alain. "Unionism as a Social Movement," in Lipset, Seymour Martin, (ed.) *Unions in Transition: Entering the Second Century.* San Francisco: Institute for Contemporary Studies, 1986.

Troy, Leo and Sheflin, Neil. *U.S. Union Sourcebook: Membership, Finances, Structure, Directory.* West Orange, N.J.: IRDIS, 1985.

Trumka, Richard. "On Becoming A Movement: Rethinking Labor's Strategy," in *Dissent.* Winter 1992.

Uchitelle, Louis. "Job Extinction Evolving Into a Fact of Life in U.S." *The New York Times.* March 22, 1994.

Uchitelle, Louis. "Labor Federation Expresses its Vulnerability in Hostile Times. *The New York Times,* February 26, 1995.

U.S. Department of Labor. Bureau of Labor Statistics. 1986, 1990, 1991, 1992, 1993.

U.S. Department of Labor, Bureau of Labor Statistics. *Employment and Earnings, States and Areas.* Washington, D.C., 1993.

U.S. Department of Labor, Bureau of Labor Statistics. *Geographic Profile of Employment and Unemployment, 1992.* Bulletin 2428, July 1993.

U.S. Department of Labor, Bureau of Labor Statistics. *Occupational Compensation Survey: Pay Only, New York, New York Metropolitan Area, May 1994.* Bulletin 3075-16, November 1994.

U.S. Department of Labor, Bureau of Labor Statistics. Middle Atlantic Regional Office, Unpublished Data. 1994.

Van Arsdale, Thomas. *Testimony.* New York City Commission on Civil Rights, Local 3, and April 26, 1990.

Verba, Sidney and Gary Oren. *Equality in America: A View from the Top.* Cambridge: Harvard University Press, 1985.

Vroman, Wayne. "The Aggregate Performance of Unemployment Insurance, 1980-1985," in Hansen, W. Lee and James F. Byers, (Eds.)

*Unemployment Insurance: The Second Half-Century*. Madison: University of Wisconsin Press, 1990.

Waldinger, Roger and Thomas Bailey. "The Continuing Significance of Race: Racial Conflict and Racial Discrimination in Construction," *Politics & Society*, Number 19, Number 3, September 1991, pp. 291-323.

Wallerstein, Michael. Unemployment, Collective Bargaining, and the Demand for Protection. *American Journal of Political Science*. Volume 31, Number 4, November 1987, pp. 729-752.

Wallerstein, Michael. Union Organization in Advanced Industrial Democracies. *American Political Science Review*. Volume 83, Number 2, June 1989, pp. 481-501.

Winpisinger, William, Fred Block, Wilson Riles, Jr., Jim Harding, Barbara Ehrenreich. "Growth and Employment," in *Socialist Review*. Numbers 75/76. May-August 1984, pp. 9-29.

Wright, Chapin. "Unemployed Overwhelm Brooklyn Claims Office," *New York Newsday*, December 31, 1991.

Yellowitz, Irwin. "The Origins of Unemployment Reform in the United States," in *Labor History*, 1968, pp. 338-360.

Young, Joyce. "Jobless Eye Maine." *Daily News*. August 18, 1991.

Young, Joyce. "To Be Heard, Jobless Employ a March." *Daily News*. December 31, 1991.

# Index